Keane

Keane

The Autobiography

ROY KEANE

with Eamon Dunphy

MICHAEL JOSEPH
an imprint of
PENGUIN BOOKS

MICHAEL JOSEPH

Published by the Penguin Group

Penguin Books Ltd, 80 Strand, London WC2R 0RL, England
Penguin Putnam Inc., 375 Hudson Street, New York, New York 10014, USA
Penguin Books Australia Ltd, 250 Camberwell Road, Camberwell, Victoria 3124, Australia
Penguin Books Canada Ltd, 10 Alcorn Avenue, Toronto, Ontario, Canada M4V 3B2
Penguin Books India (P) Ltd, 11 Community Centre,
Panchsheel Park, New Delhi – 110 017, India
Penguin Books (NZ) Ltd, Cnr Rosedale and Airborne Roads,
Albany, Auckland, New Zealand
Penguin Books (South Africa) (Pty) Ltd, 24 Sturdee Avenue,
Rosebank 2196, South Africa

Penguin Books Ltd, Registered Offices: 80 Strand, London WC2R 0RL, England

www.penguin.com

First published 2002
10

INSET PICTURE CREDITS

23, 27, 49, 66 Action Images; 25, 47, 54, 55, 56, 58, 62, 65, 67, 68, 69, 70 Getty Images; 48 Action
Images/ Darren Walsh; 52, 76 Justin Downing/© Sporting Pictures; 53 Peter Bennett/© Sporting
Pictures; 57 Action Images/John Sibley; 59 Crispin Thurston/© Sporting Pictures; 63 Robin Hume/©
Sporting Pictures; 73, 74 Inpho/Andrew Paton; 75 RTE Archive. Every effort has been made to trace
copyright holders and we apologize in advance for any unintentional omission.
We would be pleased to insert the appropriate acknowledgement in any subsequent edition.

Set in 13/16 pt Monotype Bembo
Typeset by Rowland Phototypesetting Ltd,
Bury St Edmunds, Suffolk
Printed in Great Britain by Clays Ltd, St Ives plc

A CIP catalogue record for this book is available from the British Library

ISBN 0-718-14554-2

Stephen M. Marshall.
October 2002

For Theresa

Acknowledgements

I would like to express my appreciation to those who have helped me tell my story. Rowland White at Penguin has been a discerning, rigorous editor. David Watson has devoted himself to editing the copy and checking the facts. Elementary. His professionalism and quiet diligence were inspirational. Eamon Dunphy, Jane and Rosie Gogan and Emma Calvert, who transcribed the tapes. All worked hard in Dublin. My thanks also to John English of *Rothmans Football Yearbook*. I am grateful to all of you. And of course for so much, so generously given, to Michael Kennedy. Pity he's an Arsenal fan.

Prologue

Theresa had told me on the phone that I was Disgraced World Cup Star Roy Keane. Sent home from the World Cup finals. I was standing in the airport in Saipan. The journalists and photographers were hovering. I was saying nothing. I felt calm. Sometimes you wonder about a decision, even little things like getting a haircut, or buying a pair of shoes. Is it cut too short? Are they the right colour? But I was sure about my 'disgrace'. There was no disgrace in telling the truth. It was hassle, though, which I suppose is why people keep quiet. I'd kept quiet for a long time. Well, relatively speaking.

I knew the press in London would be waiting. That would be tomorrow. Calm on one level, I was burning on another. I'd prepared for the World Cup. All through the qualifying games I'd grafted hard to reach the finals. Almost thirty-one, I knew this would probably be my last shot at a World Cup. I knew the Irish set-up was less than perfect, everybody knew that. But even by Irish standards the past week had been beyond belief. Beneath the calm front I was really angry and hurt.

Angry about the unprofessionalism in the Irish camp, the absence of real ambition, the going-through-the-motions approach to a tournament that ought to be the goal of every footballer. We were Irish, we did it our way. That was the boast. The world loved us, we told ourselves. Weren't we the cabaret act, there to get the party going, before leaving when the tournament got serious? Then back home for another party to celebrate the one good result we usually got. Watch the final stages on the telly. Great. Was that why we battled through our group, knocked out Holland, finished unbeaten, second to the Portuguese? Not for me. I was a Manchester United player. We only partied when we won.

'Roy, can we have a word?' I blanked the reporter as I moved along the line towards the check-in counter. Other passengers were looking at me, wondering who I was. A fugitive? On the run from the law? As I bent down to get my passport out of my suitcase I noticed an 'exit' sign behind me. The snapper moved in. She had her picture. Keane Exit.

I was hurt. For Theresa, for my family in Cork. I'd spent 30,000 euros to give my brothers Denis, Johnson and Pat and my cousin John Lynch their dream trip to the World Cup finals. They wouldn't go now. I'd spoiled it for them. And my mam and dad. I phoned them. They were trapped in the house watching Sky Television, listening to the radio, reading in the newspapers about their disgraced son. I could handle it. It was torture for them.

On the plane at last. Thank God for Manchester United. I'd called Ann Wiley at the club. She'd booked my flight. To throw the press pack off the scent Ann had booked me through Guam rather than Tokyo. Guam, Hong Kong, London, Manchester. Theresa, my children Shannon, Caragh, Aidan and Leah. And Triggs my dog. And peace.

On the flight I watched some DVDs: *Fawlty Towers*. Good old Basil. *He* could manage Ireland.

In Guam you got off the plane, got your passport stamped and got back on. There was a problem. The flight was delayed. I'd probably miss my connection in Hong Kong. We waited for two or three hours. An English guy working in Hong Kong came over. He would see I wasn't feeling the best. Roy, would you like a cup of tea? At times when you're disgraced, when you feel that awful violation that accompanies media exposure, a small gesture means a lot. I accepted the Englishman's offer with gratitude.

Now I knew I'd miss my connection in Hong Kong. We were advised that it was impossible to get a hotel room in Hong Kong on a Friday night. So I was looking at a night in the airport. Fuck it, it could be worse. Maybe I'll give it a blast in Hong Kong, have a mad night on the tear! No. I want to be in good shape when I get home.

When we arrived in Hong Kong there was somebody from British Airways waiting for me. Ann Wiley had discovered our flight was late and booked me on a later flight to London. First class. A bed. I was ready for sleep. I'll never forget British Airways. They were brilliant, just brilliant all the way. I couldn't sleep. My head was racing. I watched a video, Denzel Washington in *Training Day*. Not very good. The two air hostesses were really kind. We support you 100 per cent, they said. They were making breakfast. I went to the galley to chat to them. I wondered what I'd face in London.

When I got off the plane BA had a buggy waiting to take me to the other terminal for my Manchester flight. As I was getting in the buggy with my luggage, a baggage handler passed by. I was waiting for a smart remark, probably an Arsenal or Spurs fan, I thought. 'Well done, Keano,' he smiled. 'Chin up.' A small thing, this cheered me up enormously. Fair play to him. He'd no doubt be giving me stick next season!

They sneaked me through to the British Midland departure lounge. Michael Kennedy, my agent, walked in. He said he'd come to Manchester with me. No, there's no need, I insisted. He said there's bad stuff on the internet. About my private life.

What?

My wife Theresa had been getting phone calls from some woman. I rang home. Don't worry, Theresa said, just come home.

Michael said there was a lot of interest in the press. I'd have to make a statement. I told him I just wanted to get home.

United had a car waiting at Manchester airport. I was home in five minutes. The house was under siege. Reporters, television trailers with their satellite dishes. I thought, hello, is Bill Clinton visiting?

Theresa explained that she hadn't been able to get out of the house.

'The dog hasn't been out for a couple of days.'

I waited an hour, played with the kids, then got Triggs. I had nothing to be ashamed of. My life was going to be as normal as it could be.

'Come on, girl, we're going for a walk.'

I

I was born on 10 August 1971, the fourth of five children, at 88 Ballinderry Park, in Mayfield, a northern suburb of Cork city. Later, my mum and dad, my older brothers, Johnson and Denis, myself and my sister Hilary (my younger brother, Pat, came along later) moved to Lotamore Park, also in Mayfield. I was named Roy Maurice, the second name being after my dad, who is better known as Mossie. My mother Marie (née Lynch) came from a well-known sporting family.

Though my father worked at one stage for the local Sunbeam Wolsey knitwear company, it had gone into liquidation by the time I was growing up. After that, at a time when work was hard to come by, my dad, like many another man, took work wherever he could find it, including jobs at Guinness and Pfizer's, two major employers in Cork. These were the 1970s and 1980s when one world recession seemed to follow another, creating very difficult times for the Irish economy. And Cork city suffered more than most.

Growing up, I was aware that money was always scarce, for example, we never had a car. Yet to be honest I was never really short of anything. My mother, Marie, and my father were warm, loving parents. My older brothers and my sister looked out for me. Maybe being the youngest (until Pat came along) I was spoilt.

I went to the local primary school, St John's. I didn't shine in the classroom. I was quiet, happy not to be noticed. For me and my friends it was sport rather than education that really mattered in our lives. Life began when the bell rang to signal the end of the school day.

Cork's sporting traditions are strong and varied. In our house soccer was the game. Others preferred the Gaelic games of hurling and football. Sport was sometimes a source of bitter divisions. Gaelic games were identified as being truly Irish in a way that other sports such as soccer and rugby could never be. Foreign games, especially those associated with Britain, were frowned upon by the more passionate Gaels. Of course, Jack Charlton would later change all that. Still, sadly, it is a fact that until a year before I was born any Gaelic hurler or footballer caught attending a soccer or rugby match was automatically banned for life.

Ours was a staunch soccer family. My father was a useful player with Crofton and North End, two local junior clubs. On my mother's side of the family her dad and two uncles all won FAI junior medals. Two of her brothers, Mick and Pat Lynch, played for Rockmount, one of the oldest and most renowned junior clubs in Cork. So my brothers and I were bred to play. Indeed, one of the enduring jokes we share in the family is the one about what great footballers my dad and Uncle so-and-so were. My brothers and I would laugh because it seemed that every player was 'great' back then.

Like most Cork people I am inordinately proud of my roots. When asked about their origins Cork people invariably reply with a mischievous grin, 'Irish by birth: Cork by the grace of God.'

Laughter is something I'll always associate with my own home and my city. Laughter through good times and bad. Laughter at conceit or pretence. And laughter at any poor fool not blessed by being born in the Rebel County. A superiority complex is the mark of a sound Corkman. And the women are worse.

After school our lives centred round the local community. Trips to the city, which was five miles away, were a rare treat. Every St Stephen's Day (Boxing Day) we'd go into town to see the latest picture, followed by a visit to Burgerland. Sport was our drug of choice. Before finally choosing soccer I had a go at hurling and boxing. My hurling career was brief (unlike Denis Irwin, who was a very accomplished hurler, considered good enough to make the Cork county team if he'd stuck at it). Cork's senior hurling team had won the All-Ireland many times with men like Jack Lynch and Christy Ring regarded as folk heroes by the people, held in as much esteem as Stanley Matthews and Tom Finney were in England. My involvement with the game was ended by a nasty accident. In what could be termed a clash of the ash, the boss (base) of my hurley broke and a splinter shot into the back of my leg, causing a wound that took the best part of six months to heal.

I boxed at Brian Dillon's Boxing Club at Dillon's Cross. I only had four bouts, in the Irish Novice League, though I won them all. This was because I was only nine when I joined up and the regulations didn't permit me to box officially until I was twelve. So, I ended up training for three years – I suppose you could describe it as sparring – without actually getting involved in a proper bout. When my chance eventually came, I must have been the fittest boxer in creation. And the hungriest. But I also had a problem, being an established player with Rockmount by that stage. My boxing coach gave me an ultimatum to pick soccer or boxing. So the boxing was ditched.

But boxing had helped me develop as a sportsman. Skipping and sparring made me more agile. I also acquired a certain confidence when confronted by physical aggression. I was still very small for my age and the techniques and disciplines learned in the boxing ring provided me with a psychological edge: I could look after myself even though I was small and shy.

When forced to choose between boxing and soccer there was never any doubt what the answer would be. Nor was there ever any doubt that I would opt for Rockmount AFC instead of my local club in Mayfield, where all my school-friends played. The fact that Denis and Johnson played for Rockmount was one good reason. The real clincher though was an even more important fact: Rockmount was a very successful club. I joined when I was eight going on nine, even then my desire to win was strong. Because of its renown Rockmount attracted the best young footballers from all over the Cork suburbs, places like the Glen, Knockmahenny and Blackpool. For me it meant a seven-mile journey there and back, but it wasn't a bother. My mother was always good for the bus fare. And if I needed a pair of football boots she would miraculously provide them. Maybe not the best brand on the market, but more than adequate for me.

I loved my first games of properly organized football. Pulling on a jersey, wearing real football boots. Playing on pitches that were marked with (rough) white lines, goalposts and nets. This was the real thing. I even loved the referees for settling the disputes that sometimes caused our street games in Mayfield to end in chaos and recrimination. Joining Rockmount was a huge leap forward in my young life. At last I was a footballer.

As a nine-year-old I played for the under-11 team. I was giving away quite a lot in height and weight but nothing in terms of attitude. I played to my strengths. I could run, I could pass the ball accurately, I could tackle. Indeed, after the marathon games we were accustomed to on Mayfield's all-weather pitch, the thirty-five minutes each half of the under-11 league was a doddle.

Everyone in Mayfield followed an English club; Spurs was mine. Why? Because most of my pals followed bloody Manchester United, Liverpool or Arsenal who won the double the year I was born. Glenn Hoddle was my favourite player. One of my happiest childhood days was spent watching Spurs beat Man. City in a replay to win the centenary Cup final. Ricardo Villa's winning goal after a mazy thirty-yard dribble that took him past defender after defender was a sensational climax to a thrilling game.

Although I would love to have emulated dazzling players like Ricky Villa or Glenn Hoddle, my game was different. I was a worker rather than a dazzler. I grafted for goals, grafted to win the ball back when we lost it and generally put myself about. I listened to our coaches, Timmy Murphy and Gene O'Sullivan, particularly when they referred to attitude. Their credo was simple yet true: take the field with the wrong attitude and no matter how much ability you possess, you'll lose. I believed them. I still do.

At the end of my first season at Rockmount I was voted Player of the Year. I was incredibly proud that I had upheld the Keane family tradition at the club where my brothers and uncles had played.

Looking back, I now understand that this relatively modest experience was to shape my whole life. What would have become of me without Rockmount . . . without football . . . without the all-weather pitch in Mayfield where I learned to play the game before I joined my first real football club? What if my family had not been steeped in soccer . . . had not encouraged me to play? What would my life have been without men like Timmy Murphy and Gene O'Sullivan, and later John Delea . . . without Rockmount AFC? I owe them all a debt I can never fully repay. Which is why loyalty to family and friends remains a cornerstone of my life.

Football now became my life to the exclusion of almost everything else, education in particular. Some weekends I'd play an under-10 game on Saturday morning, play for the under-11s in the afternoon and the under-12s on Sunday.

Some of the best schoolboy footballers in Cork were being scouted by Timmy and Gene. In my second season with the club we won the under-11 league and cup double. By then Rockmount AFC had signed Paul McCarthy, Alan O'Sullivan, Damien Martin and Len Downey (all of whom went on to represent Ireland at various levels). They formed the nucleus of our team, which completed the league and cup double for six straight years. Incredibly, for schoolboy soccer in Cork was massively competitive, we remained unbeaten for five seasons.

When I was twelve, I entered Mayfield Community School. My brother Johnson had established a Keane profile at the school. As a consequence I was behind the eight ball from day one.

First class teacher: 'Name?'

Me: 'Keane. Roy Keane.'

Teacher: 'Are you Johnson's brother?'

'Yes.'

'Oh! Right.' His rather grim expression didn't really require elaboration. I was a marked man, one to watch out for.

In fact, I steered clear of trouble. I also steered clear of application. To observe that in 1983 the Irish economy was a basket case of high unemployment, high interest rates and rising inflation is not to pardon my lack of interest in learning.

For I didn't know those economic statistics. What I do recall is the palpable sense of pessimism and apathy among the people Mayfield Community School purported to serve. This I understood, if not through reasoning, then instinctively. Generally I stayed out of trouble in the bottom half of the class.

I did get into a spot of embarrassing trouble one day when me and a friend, Anthony Kenneally, were caught reading a couple of so-called 'dirty books'. The books were confiscated. The embarrassment came a few days later when we were summoned to the headmaster's office to reclaim our reading material. 'Ah,' he exclaimed, 'the two perverts are here for their dirty books.' Briefly shamed – and named – we returned to our customary obscurity at the back of the classroom.

My indifference to education would not be without consequence. At fifteen I had to sit my Intermediate Certificate exam. If I failed, school was over, my only prospect a dead-end job or the dole. If I passed my Inter Cert, a feat I still vaguely thought was possible, then I could proceed to take my Leaving Cert, which was the accepted route to a good job and the security and relative prosperity that went with it. Again it is worth recording that with the Irish economy heading for the rocks, Inter Certs, even Leaving Certs, were not the guarantee of good work they had been just a few years before. This does not excuse my neglect of education or even explain it. Nevertheless, it was a fact of life of which we were all aware.

My obsession with football offered no prospect of job security either yet, curiously, I had more faith in my ability to become a professional footballer than I had in my capacity to cope with the Inter Cert. I can't really explain where that belief in myself came from. There were few signs of encouragement. If anything the signs pointed the other way.

Most of our young players nurtured dreams of a career in

the professional game in England. To achieve that goal success in Cork was not enough. The first step on the road to England was selection for the Irish under-15 international team, a prize that to us seemed reserved for stars on the Dublin schoolboy scene. Rockmount's success could not be ignored. Myself, Alan, Len, Paul and Damien were all selected for trials for local and national under-14 representative sides. Sadly, I was the one who never made the final cut. The word was that I was too small. Some also questioned my temperament. The irony was that I had the 'temperament' because I was so small. When the ball was there to be won I didn't hold back. Being small, I made a point of establishing my ball-winning ability as early as possible in every game. A lot of those big guys didn't like it when the studs were flying. And although I was small, my studs were as big as anyone else's.

I got a reputation which pleased me. He doesn't take no shit. Once established, the reputation helped. It helped a lot. There were still guys who fancied their chances, but fewer and fewer as time passed.

Of course, in Mayfield this was also true. Some considered me a traitor for joining Rockmount. Our success didn't help in that regard. Some real spice was added to our Mayfield matches, in which there was often an us and them vibe. I was them. The rest were us! Sometimes things got out of hand. This was a hard school, my real education, and the lessons learned about sporting warfare would serve me well.

I did fail my Inter Cert exam. It hurt. Even though it wasn't entirely unexpected, I felt I'd let myself and my parents down. Maybe it wasn't the end of the world but it certainly placed a question mark against my future. Time, energy and imagination I should have spent on lessons and homework had instead been invested in endless hours of football. This is not an option I recommend. Football isn't on the school curriculum for a very good reason: very few can make a living from the professional game. Today kids are smarter, or should be. An education and a career in football are not mutually exclusive options.

The reason the under-15 year was critical for schoolboy footballers was that if you were picked for the Irish team you were in the shop window for English club scouts. This was a make-or-break season. Making the Irish team was a much more important matter than passing the Inter Cert. The previous season I'd played for the Cork under-14 side that won the national inter-county trophy. Our successful Rockmount team provided the majority of the players for the Cork squad. So the prospect of a schoolboy international cap seemed realistic. If you got your cap you stood a very good chance of getting a trial with an English club.

The trials for the international team were held in Dublin. You weren't formally informed if you'd been selected for the trials. Your club received a letter in due course. But the newspapers were the first to know. One evening after school I came home to find my dad smiling with a copy of our local paper, the *Evening Echo*, in his hand. 'You're in, boy, you're in the trials in Dublin.'

Your heart does leap! Well something happens, and it feels bloody marvellous. I was going to Dublin. So too were my Rockmount mates, Alan, Paul, Damien and Len.

We headed off to Dublin by train. The only lingering doubt we shared concerned the perceived pro-Dublin bias for which the international selection committee was notorious, at least in Cork.

I played really well in the trial game. When I was substituted with about fifteen minutes to go, I thought it was because the selectors had seen enough to be persuaded. Back in Cork I waited anxiously for news of the final trial. When it came, again thanks to the *Evening Echo*, it was bad. A. O'Sullivan, P. McCarthy, L. Downey and D. Martin were all listed to return to Dublin. The name R. Keane was not there however many times I looked, and believe me, I double-checked. I was devastated. This was the worst disappointment of my life. The door to my dream slammed shut in my face.

Alan, Paul, Len and Damien had been selected for the international squad. Word came back from the Cork selector that 'Roy was just too small'. As a result of their international appearances, Alan, who was a left winger, and Paul, who was a centre-forward, joined English clubs, Alan going to Luton Town, Paul to Brighton.

Back in Mayfield, I joined a special course set up for guys like me who'd failed to achieve the educational standard required for the Leaving Cert. The one-year course was designed to equip us for some kind of semi-skilled employment. However, in mid-1980s Ireland the economic crisis was the cause of much national gloom. Employment of any kind was at a premium. In those circumstances the motivation to train for jobs that didn't exist was weak to non-existent. Which is why our special course for educational laggards shut down after six months due to insufficient numbers.

My mother was worried, watching the world apparently closing in around me. For a while I lost my characteristic defiance. I suffered another blow when Paul McCarthy got in touch to tell me that he'd arranged a trial for me with Brighton. Everything was arranged. I would get the train to Dublin, catch a flight to London, then another train to Brighton. The night before I was due to leave, Paul called to say the trial was off. Having checked out Paul's recommendation, Brighton backed away from the idea. They'd heard I was too small to make a pro.

Gutted, I slipped into a kind of half-life, drifting aimlessly through long, dull days. I got out of bed at one o'clock for the day's first treat: the latest episode of *Neighbours*, which was screened at 1.30. After that, I'd walk my dog Ben, a black mongrel who had replaced Lucky, another mongrel so called because he was a stray who we figured was lucky to find R. Keane. I loved my dogs, really adored them (and still do to this day). Unlike people, dogs don't talk shite. They won't betray you or otherwise let you down. What you give you get back, and more. Ben, like Lucky and the other dogs I've had, was warm and loyal. And funny too. They each have a character that's distinct to them. For me the most magical of all their traits is that your dog won't know or care if you're the captain of Manchester United or an unemployed, uneducated sixteen-year-old wannabe pro footballer. Walking Ben was the best part of my day. I still loved my football and trained and played with the same enthusiasm, despite sensing that an important opportunity had passed, maybe the last I'd get.

I never drew the dole for the simple reason that you had to be eighteen to qualify. Money was a problem. My mother and father didn't have much yet they never really saw me short. Denis and Johnson would also 'sub' me from time to time. I took the odd labouring job when one could be found. The easiest of these was in Galvin's off-licence in Blackpool. According to a story I read somewhere, I took this job to build my muscles by lugging barrels of beer from the stockroom to the shop. The truth is I took the job for the money – £3.50 an hour – and spent most of my time stealing Galvin's chocolate to stuff my face. It was just before Christmas, the money was handy. I lasted three weeks.

The worst job I got was for some cowboy contractor who

hired a group of us to strip acid off metal plates. To do this we were given a blow torch but no protective clothing! It was dangerous work but paid money in hand, fifty quid a week. I stuck it for three months. Then in the spring I went potato picking, cycling about fifteen miles there and back. This was a killer, back-breaking work, the legacy being a bad back that still bothers me today.

Perhaps noticing my despair about my football prospects, Timmy Murphy, Gene O'Sullivan and John Delea, who was now coaching our Rockmount team, encouraged me to write away for trials with English clubs. I did, and the letters of reply tell their own bleak story:

'I'm afraid that we have no vacancies at the present time, but would like to thank you for your interest, and would like to wish you every success in the future.' (Derby County)

'I thank you for your recent letter, but regret that we are not able to help at all. At the present time we have our full quota of playing staff and will not hold any trial games in the near future.' (Sheffield Wednesday)

'Unfortunately, I am unable to meet your request for an opportunity with Aston Villa, as we are adequately staffed with players in your position.' (Aston Villa)

'I very much regret to advise you that since having to recently review our youth structure, I am only able to offer trials to boys under the age of 15 at the beginning of the season. I am sorry to disappoint you but would like to say that we do, along with most other clubs, have a large number of scouts watching games of all ages, and if you are good enough to become a professional footballer, you do have every chance of being "spotted".' (Chelsea)

'As I am sure you will appreciate, we receive literally hundreds of similar letters each week . . . As it is usual to favour letters from players who have representative honours, or ones who are highly recommended by someone close to football, I regret that we are unable to offer you a trial.' (Nottingham Forest)

Looking back, I understand what it was — apart from size — that the keen-eyed scouts didn't see. Brilliance. I was an all-rounder, I thought of myself as a team player. I could score goals, but I wasn't prolific. Although I could dominate midfield, I didn't go on mazy runs, beating man after man, or carving defences apart with forty-yard passes. I read the game, intercepted passes, cut off opposing players' options, passed the ball simply myself. I worked box to box, unceasingly, defending as well as I attacked. For every stunning goal I scored, and there were a few, there were a hundred little things, offensive and defensive, that went unnoticed. I worked for every second of a game with complete determination and absolute concentration. The determination was obvious, my trademark. The concentration was invisible. To catch even the most tutored eye brilliance was required.

Although I was unaware of it, help was at hand from a most unlikely source: the government. In an initiative that was one part well-meaning, three parts cynical, Charlie Haughey's government introduced the FÁS training programme. Unemployment was bad for the jobless, much worse for these politicians charged with providing work. Hectored by all and sundry for their failure to provide employment, the government introduced the FÁS scheme. The idea was to train you for work, skilled or semi-skilled. Youth unemployment being a particular national scandal, the jobless young were urged to sign up for FÁS. This meant they came off the unemployment register and the government could claim credit for dealing with the job crisis.

In 1989 the Irish government, in conjunction with the Football Association of Ireland, set up the inaugural FÁS football course for elite young footballers. Each of the twenty-four National League clubs (twelve in each of two divisions) could send their most promising young player on this course. I read about this and saw an opening. So did my mate Len Downey, who was just about to sign for Cork City, our local National League club. Len was a typical shrewd Cork lad. But R. Keane was streetwise too. City had also approached me, I'd even signed a bloody form committing to the club. I knew they could only send one player to Dublin and the FÁS course. So when Len told me that City were sending him on the FÁS course, I was gutted.

Thank God Eddie O'Rourke got in touch with me that very day. Eddie was a carpenter and youth team coach for Cobh Ramblers, a Second Division National League club, ten miles east of Cork. He'd known me through the years, seen me in many battles against Springfield, the Cobh schoolboy club who were Rockmount's fiercest rivals, invariably finishing runners-up to our double-winning teams.

'Would you join Cobh Ramblers?' Eddie asked.

'I've just signed for City,' I replied.

'When?'

'Yesterday!'

'Hang on. I'll make a call to the FAI to see if they've registered you.'

Had I known how much would be decided by the phone call, I would have died.

Cork City hadn't bothered to send the form I'd signed. But they were a First Division club, so I told Eddie I would only sign for Ramblers if they gave me the allotted place on the FÁS football course. He agreed. The deal was done, the form rushed express post to Dublin.

Cobh was once known as Queenstown and, among other things, is famous as the last port of call for the liner *Titanic* before it made its ill-fated voyage across the Atlantic in 1912. True, the Ramblers were a Second Division club, but the real prize was a place on the FÁS course. This would allow me to test myself against the best players of my age in the country and perhaps help me reach a new target I'd set for myself: an Irish under-18 cap. For the next eight months I would train like a full-time pro – harder as it turned out – and be paid £30 a week plus travel expenses, an extra £40 plus bonuses (£10 for a win, £5 for a draw) if I made Cobh's first team, which I did within weeks.

The FÁS course was based in Palmerstown on the west side of Dublin city. Leaving home was a wrench, even though I wasn't going to the moon. I was still extremely shy with strangers, so the presence of Len Downey made me feel a lot more secure than might otherwise have been the case.

In terms of travelling and training the FÁS regime was brutal. After playing for our clubs on Sunday, Len and me caught the first Dublin train from Cork on Monday morning. We trained each day from ten till twelve in the morning, and two till four in the afternoon. The work, more intense and structured than anything I'd experienced, consisted of routines aimed at improving every aspect of our game. We began with our warm-up and stretches in the morning. Then ball work to improve our touch and control, followed by a session in which we split up into four groups of six to play three-against-three games with small five-a-side goals which were exactly like the scratch games we'd played on the all-weather in

Mayfield. But the standard was higher, with no prisoners taken. We were, at least I felt I was, playing for our lives.

Maurice Price was one of the course directors. He was also a member of Jack Charlton's back-room staff with the Irish international team which had qualified for the European Championship finals in Germany the year before, returning to Ireland as national heroes having beaten England 1-0 in Stuttgart. It would be an understatement to say I wanted to impress a coach so close to the centre of our footballing universe.

Afternoons, except for two devoted to our further education, which I ignored, allowed us more ball work and sessions devoted to shooting practice and specialized instruction on defensive, midfield and forward play. We occasionally worked with weights and there was also plenty of stamina training.

The highlights of the course were the games against various Irish underage teams who played practice matches against us as part of their preparation for their international matches. These were torrid affairs: we FÁS lads had a point to prove; that we were good enough to match our opponents, many of whom were playing for top English clubs.

The schedule was gruelling, especially for us country lads, who were either training, travelling or playing for our clubs seven days a week. Time off in the evenings caused me some heartache. Lodging with a family in Leixlip close to the Amenities Centre in Palmerstown where we trained, I was quite lonely. I missed my family, Ben and my small but comfortable world in Mayfield. Most nights I'd get a bus down to Lucan, where Len was in 'digs'. Watching telly was all we were good for. Especially during the first couple of months when full-time training and club commitments really took their toll on us. On Thursday nights we allowed ourselves a few beers before heading home on Friday afternoon.

I was happy. I relished the hard work of training. The travelling up and down from Cork to Dublin was a pain. But I had a few pounds in my pocket, earned by playing football. I was a professional player even if I was at the bottom of what looked like a very steep hill. Again, it is worth pointing out unemployment and its attendant indignities was still very much a feature of Irish working-class life. Among my own in Mayfield, indeed in our family, immediate and extended, a decent job was highly prized. As I was now in Ramblers first team, I was able to tuck around £50 a week in my back pocket.

The National League Second Division was a tough school for a seventeen-year-old. Most of the players were battle-hardened semi-pros who, in terms of ability and nous, were much better than anything I'd experienced. Respect was hard earned, from opponents and your own team-mates. Any exhibitionist flourishes on the ball were promptly punished. Any fannying around and they'd put you in the stand. The opposition took no prisoners either!

Six months into my FÁS course, in the spring of 1990, I was, I felt, a very improved player. My aim from the start had been to become the best footballer on the training scheme. Training every day with twenty-three of the best young footballers in the country, one thing was obvious: ability was not enough. To succeed you needed strength of body, and strength of mind.

Our physical training took care of itself if you put in the work which I did. The mind was a different, more challenging proposition. On cold winter mornings, on a muddy surface, with a cutting east wind lashing across the Amenities Centre, not everyone was up for it. There's no atmosphere on the training ground unless you create it yourself. You don't win any prizes on Monday morning, except the most important one: self-satisfaction. There's no glory here. Yet I knew that if I could push myself through the mental barriers that others baulked at, it would be an important victory. When the day's work was done, I would feel the warm glow of pure satisfaction that lies on the other side of those mental barriers you push through.

In those not-so-distant days when I'd lounged in bed until lunchtime, rising only for my daily episode of *Neighbours*, I'd experienced the alternative to hard graft. I'd nearly slipped under. I was never going to flirt with idleness again.

While Cobh Ramblers first team stalled in mid-table, the youth team managed by Eddie O'Rourke made dramatic progress in the National Under-18 Cup. I was still eligible for this competition and it was while playing for the under-18 side that I was truly able to gauge the progress I'd made. I'd grown in height and strength. I was no longer the little guy. In the course of a few short months I'd grown from boy to man. Mentally I'd always had an edge; now I had the muscle to back it up. Kamikaze Man was transformed into a footballer who understood the ebb and flow of a contest. In control of my emotions, I could exert control over the rhythm of the game. Slow it down, step it up, whatever was required. I was no Glenn Hoddle, in fact he was no longer my most admired player. Although still a Spurs fan, my favourite player and role model now was Manchester United's Bryan Robson. His tackling, goalscoring and box-to-box presence for Manchester United and England were proof that you could be a great player without doing tricks. Robson wasn't brilliant. But he was awesome.

My principal aim for the season was a place in the Irish under-18 team. And essential to that ambition was a good cup run with the Ramblers youth team. When we were drawn against Belvedere Boys, a top Dublin club, it was bad news. The good news was that we were drawn to play at home. The 1-1 result was disappointing, despite the fact that I scored our equalizing goal.

On the day of the replay, 18 February 1990, everything went wrong from the start. The bus was late picking us up in Cobh. The traffic was heavy. Most of the journey was spent looking anxiously at clocks and watches. Would we make it by kick-off time? We got to Fairview Park, an open, windswept public park, with only minutes to spare. We were knackered, beaten before we began. Belvedere hammered us 4-0. It was a fucking cock-up, Micky fucking Mouse, typical Cork, leaving the big boys from Dublin with a handy task which they accomplished in typically arrogant style. If I played like a demented man that day it was because I was one.

Belvedere were big-time and there was a large crowd in Fairview Park to watch them. I played for myself. Even when I knew the game was lost I kept going. I'd show those Dublin bastards that I could fucking play. Some days you can feel an appreciative vibe off even a hostile crowd. You can earn respect, however grudging. So the gut-aching feeling of failure, the same old story for us in Dublin, became just another pain barrier to push through. I was like a man possessed – by that strange compound of anger, frustration and personal pride. That compound can turn games; even the most hopeless situation can be retrieved. But not on this day in Fairview.

Afterwards we went across the road to a pub for a glass of orange and a sandwich. John O'Rourke, the Ramblers vice-chairman, came and sat beside me: 'Roy, there was a scout from Nottingham Forest over there. He said they'd like you to go over for a trial.'

My heart didn't leap. Where's the scout? was my immediate reaction. If he was that impressed why wasn't he here himself? The Brighton experience was still very much in my mind.

'He said they'll be in touch,' John continued. He was merely conveying a message. Until I heard it from the real McCoy, I wasn't going to get excited.

A few weeks elapsed before I got a phone call from Cobh asking me if I would meet the Forest scout, Noel McCabe, in the Aisling Hotel, a modest little place just across the bridge from Heuston Station, where the Cork train arrives in Dublin. I like Noel as soon as we start chatting. He's straight with me. He's offering me a trial, not a contract which isn't in his gift. 'But you're a Forest-type player, son. You can pass the ball simply, work the two boxes, and score goals. You'll be all right with Brian Clough,' Noel assures me. He strikes me as a genuine man.

Now the excitement I suppressed in the pub in Fairview is bubbling to the surface. I somehow sense that this is it. My chance has finally come. I'm ready. I swore after the Brighton fiasco that I'd only believe the English dream when the ticket was in my hand. But I have no doubt Noel McCabe will deliver on his word. I am about to encounter another disappointment. I get the ticket in my hand. But when I arrive in Nottingham there is no trial match. Every day I'm there I anticipate the match. Every day I go through a training session with youth team coach Archie Gemmill. Where's Brian Clough . . . Liam O'Kane . . . Ronnie Fenton?

'Is this it?'

'Yep!'

After a week I'm given a ticket home, one-way. 'We'll be in touch,' they tell me.

'How'd it go?' they ask me back in Cobh.

'It didn't,' I explain.

Noel McCabe is contacted. He makes a call to Forest. There's been a cock-up. I'll be going back in April.

When I returned to Nottingham I trained for a couple of days with the reserves. I was told I'd be playing for Forest against Tranmere Rovers in a Midland League game. Liam O'Kane and Forest's chief scout Alan Hill would be there. This was make or break. Again!

The ground at Tranmere was empty. I didn't care. I'd learned the trick of creating atmosphere in my head. From Mayfield's all-weather pitch, to Palmerstown's training ground, in all the dingy, clapped-out excuses for stadiums in the National League, I'd discovered the knack of generating your own passion. Against Tranmere on a dreary late-spring afternoon much of what I'd learned, which had seemed of no importance at the time, kicked in. I played well, passed, ran, tackled, won balls in the air that I had no right to get. They took me off after seventy minutes. I'd been there before. Yet somehow this time I could tell the vibes were good.

Next day Brian Clough tells me he's going to try and sign me. Arrangements are made for negotiations with Cobh Ramblers. My fear is that they'll want too much. I thought I was worth about £5,000.

John O'Rourke and vice-president John Meade lead the Cobh Ramblers delegation to strike a deal with Forest. The club has enlisted the assistance of former Chelsea and England player John Hollins, who's familiar with such deals. Hollins picked us up in his Range Rover at Heathrow.

At Nottingham Ronnie Fenton presided over the negotiation. As the bargaining for my services began, I struggled to appear calm. The Cobh lads were talking big money. Things weren't going well until Brian Clough entered the boardroom.

He wore an old green sweater and had his golden retriever with him. As I played with the dog the rest talked money. Clough ordered Ronnie Fenton to give 'the gentlemen from Ireland' a drink.

'Is he any good?' Clough asked Fenton, pointing at me.

'He can play a bit, boss,' Fenton replied.

They were now talking real money. £20,000 up front, another £10,000 after ten first team games, and a further £10,000 when I'd played twenty games for Forest. Another £7,000 would go to Cobh when I'd won five Irish caps.

'You've got a deal, Mr Clough,' I heard John O'Rourke say.

'This money's not going in your own pockets, is it?' Clough barked.

'Mr Clough, we've had to take a day off work to come over here. It's costing us money,' John O'Rourke replied.

'OK, Ronnie, give 'em the money.' Turning to our delegation, he added, 'You can call me Brian. Now let's have a drink.' Turning to me – and the dog – he snapped, 'Except for you, you call me Mr Clough.' They broke the mould when they created this guy, I thought to myself.

Forest gave me a three-year contract at £250 a week, of which £50 would be for rent on the house I would be sharing with two other players. I also received a signing-on fee of £1,500 a year, which amounted to £4,500. To be perfectly honest, I would have signed for a fraction of those terms. As it was, I felt like I'd won the Pools.

Mr Clough told me to report for pre-season training in July. Feeling like a millionaire, I returned to Cork. Over the next few weeks I drank and ate much more than I should have. With my brothers and a couple of close friends, Derek Buckley and John Ricken, I hit the town running to celebrate the Great Escape.

When the time came to return to Nottingham, my feeling of exhilaration was laced with sadness. This was the chance of my life, yet leaving home was hard. We were a close, loving family who'd stuck by each other through thick and thin. Now for me, my mother and father, Denis, Johnson, Pat and Hilary there was a poignant sense of something ending.

2

I paid for my celebration when I reported back to Forest for the pre-season training. The first week was hell. We didn't see a ball for the first few days. We ran, working first on stamina, then on fitness, with interval training where the emphasis was on quick recovery. Fortunately, the house I was sharing with Gary Bowyer and Raymond Byrne was beside the City Ground (I could see the pitch from my bedroom window) so I just about made it home just about each evening. Pros dread pre-season, even the fittest feel the pain for the first few days.

I'd always taken my general fitness and stamina for granted. I now knew the difference between the pro and semi-pro games. I could also see that I wasn't alone. After the first few days the balls came out. I had survived the worst of the physical torture. Now I began to enjoy myself.

Taking stock of my surroundings, I tried to figure out the exact nature of the challenge I faced if I was going to make it here. Forest had won the Littlewoods (League) Cup the week before I joined. The first team was full of outstanding players. Stuart Pearce, Des Walker and Steve Hodge were current England internationals. Nigel Clough was on the brink of representative honours at that level. Pearce was obviously a strong character. He'd just returned from the World Cup finals where he'd missed a crucial penalty in the semi-final shoot-out. That hadn't diminished his authority at the City Ground, which was evident to my curious eye.

Among the reserves I was training with Steve Stone, Ian Woan and Scot Gemmill, Archie's son, stood out as very good players. Philip Starbuck was another outstanding young player who'd made a couple of first team appearances.

We didn't see much of Brian Clough. Liam O'Kane took the first team training, Archie Gemmill looked after us. Even though he wasn't visible all the time, Clough's presence was felt. His golden retriever, Dell, would often bound into view, signalling Clough's arrival on the training ground. Suddenly everyone stepped up a couple of gears. Except me. I was going flat out anyway.

I loved the work, if you could call it that, the five-a-sides, the practice matches, even the fitness training. I knew it was doing me good. I felt stronger every day as I grew accustomed to the pace of the professional game.

Considering where I'd come from, this to me was heaven: the uncertainty, the perpetual feeling of drift, the rumours of scouts supposed to be interested, trials that never materialized, the odd jobs, one step away from the dole, the virtual seven-day week I'd endured combining the FÁS course with playing for Ramblers, lying in bed waiting for *Neighbours* (fantasizing about Kylie!), worrying where the next 'fiver' would come from. Compared to my recent existence this was fabulous. In those first few weeks of proper full-time training I felt a buzz every morning. I celebrated my nineteenth birthday on 10 August feeling for the first time really that I had a real life.

In the reserve team dressing room my youthful joy was not the norm. I was surprised, shocked even, by the attitude some players displayed. They moaned about everything. Some because they weren't included in the first team photo shoot, which they deemed a bad omen for the coming season. Perhaps it was, but fuck it, you could do something about it! Then Archie Gemmill was a wanker. Brian Clough was lazy. We were working too hard. The season hadn't even started and these guys were whingeing. Looking for excuses to fail. I didn't say much, but I took it all in and vowed never to become a whinger. If only these guys knew how many kids outside would give their right arm to be sitting there on a beautiful summer's day being paid good money to be a footballer.

On reflection, I view my late arrival in the pro game as a blessing. At nineteen I was giving the others a four-year start. Or so it seemed. In fact, the reverse was true. While I'd been out in the real world learning to cope with failure, desperate for a chance to be part of this, the whingers and moaners, most of them pros since they were fifteen, had existed in a fantasy world. For them being a pro with Forest was a ticket to the big time. A place in the first team and happiness ever after would automatically follow. That was their entitlement, they believed. Now life wasn't delivering on its promise. For a hungry young working-class Irishman from Mayfield, life had never made any promises. I didn't feel anybody owed me – in fact, I felt exactly the opposite.

While the first team squad left for their pre-season tour in Italy I headed off with the under-21s for a pre-season tournament in Holland. Sporting Lisbon, Barcelona, PSV Eindhoven and Haarlem, the host club, were our opponents. We easily beat Sporting Lisbon 2-0 in our opening game. I was comfortable; the Portuguese were good touch players but they didn't relish the physical element of the game.

Next, we hammered PSV 5-1 and I scored my first professional goal. Haarlem beat us 2-0 in the next game – being the hosts, they didn't feel obliged to comply with the under-21 rule, fielding instead their first team. We'd qualified for the semi-final, anyway, where we faced Barcelona. They took an early lead. That made it a test of character, which Barcelona failed. As soon as we upped the tempo they started ducking and diving. The diving drove me crazy. Some of the Barcelona players were cheating bastards, looking for fouls for nothing, basically looking for an easy way out. Even though they were ahead they were hoisting the white flag. You can feel it, smell the scent of blood. We passed and tackled them to death, contested every loose ball, winning comfortably, 3-1, in the end.

In the final we played Haarlem again. It was a tight game, Phil Starbuck equalizing from a penalty for a 1-1 draw, which meant a penalty shoot-out. Everyone had the recent World Cup finals at the back of their minds as we faced up to this ordeal. England had gone out after a shoot-out at the semi-final stage, and West Germany had gone on to win the trophy. We weren't playing for similar stakes, although it didn't feel like that when my turn came to take the deciding kick. I never doubted that I'd pass my first big test as a Forest player. Anyway I did.

I was comfortable playing alongside good players such as Steve Stone, Ian Woan, Phil Starbuck and Scot Gemmill. The game at this level was actually easier for me, because I didn't feel I had to cover every blade of grass. Surrounded by better players, I could concentrate more on my own contribution, working box to box, getting on to the end of chances in our opponents' penalty area.

My first target for the season was a regular place in Forest's reserve side. The tournament in Haarlem was therefore encouraging. Back home, the reserves' first pre-season game was against Sutton-in-Ashfield, a non-league side. I was selected to sit on the bench. Which was a bit disappointing, because

Brian Clough was there and I was anxious to impress him. He arrived in the dressing room at half-time and asked Archie Gemmill to come outside.

I only later learned about their conversation.

Clough: 'I want you to have a look at the Irishman. Get your son Scot [who was playing in midfield] off.'

Archie: 'I'll put him on in the second half.'

Shortly after the second half began I saw Clough climbing over the touchline wall: 'Archie,' he barked, 'get the Irishman on.' Nothing happened for another fifteen minutes. I kept my head down. With twenty minutes to go, Archie took Scot off and put me on. I was in, on sufferance, I felt, but I gave it a lash for the time remaining.

A few days later, the reserves travelled to play another local non-league side, Arnold Town. Some of our pros felt that this stuff was beneath them. This was not The Dream they were born to live. You could feel the resentment in the dressing room before the game. This time I was starting and up for it big time. And I knew the territory. Arnold Town were like Cobh Ramblers, a mixture of part-time pros with great attitude but little ability – and guys with loads of ability but questionable temperament. For all of them, particularly the good footballers with dodgy attitude, a game against Nottingham Forest was a special occasion. They'd fucking show us they could play (they would all be wearing Forest shirts if fate hadn't screwed them somewhere along the line).

I knew that feeling. Only a few months before, I'd played for Ramblers when West Bromwich Albion had been the visitors. For WBA this was a stroll in the park in what they regarded as a hick town. For us it was the World Cup final. We steamed into them, urged on by our local fans, for whom this was far from a 'friendly' match.

Arnold Town got stuck into Forest in a big way. We were 3-1 down and facing humiliation in the blink of an eye. Their little ground was packed with about a thousand people, who started jeering and taking the piss. I was mortified, raging at our own players, trying to shock them into some response. This was where the bloody whingeing and moaning of the reserve team dressing room led to. Call yourselves professionals, and you let Arnold Town take the piss out of you. They're playing and starting to strut like fucking Real Madrid.

A few of the real pros now got the message. We started tackling and working. I scored to make it 3-2. Now we'll find out whether these guys are Real Madrid or Arnold fucking Town. I scored again. That shut the crowd up. And got us out of there with a degree of self-respect.

My first few weeks as a professional player with Forest confirmed what I suppose I'd always known: the world was full of bluffers, con-men and whingers; in this particular case guys who were content to wear the badge of professionalism without meeting the standards required to justify that status. And they were having a go at Archie Gemmill, who'd played for Scotland and won Championship medals and the European Cup. And at the manager who'd won two Championships – for two small clubs, Forest and Derby – and two European Cups. Was this a joke or what?

I was no paragon of virtue, as time would prove. But very early in the game I understood the difference between calling yourself a pro and earning the right to be respected by people like Gemmill, Clough and Stuart Pearce. Theirs was the standard I set for myself and I knew I had a very long way to go.

But not as far as I thought. A dramatic few days lay ahead. On Saturday, Forest opened the First Division season with a

1–1 home draw against QPR. Nigel Jemson got the goal from the penalty spot. I was an intrigued spectator. The atmosphere was great, the pitch a lovely carpet. This was football in the First Division as I'd always imagined it. The result was disappointing for Forest, who were still a force at the highest level, if not the force of previous seasons.

After the game I was disappointed to learn that my perform-ance at Arnold Town had not secured me a place in the reserves against Rotherham on Monday night. I'd be a sub. Again. I got on for the last ten minutes, no time to make an impact. Afterwards, I joined the rest of the reserves for a night on the town. Several pints later I slumped into bed. It was close to 2 a.m.

Next morning, I showed up for training. The first team were playing that night at Anfield. As soon as I arrived at the City Ground, nursing a slight hangover from the night before, Ronnie Fenton approached me and Phil Starbuck in the dressing room. 'You two are going to Anfield,' he said. 'Oh, and bring your boots,' he added.

Hello!

Well, I thought, Phil had played a couple of first team games, he was a gifted lad, so bringing him made sense. I was obviously going for the experience, to carry the bags and help the kit man. Stuart Pearce, Steve Hodge and Terry Wilson were, it turned out, injured.

The first team squad had travelled overnight, so Phil and I took a ride in Ronnie Fenton's car. On the way to Liverpool we diverted to Derby to pick up the manager. Brian Clough lived in a big pad. I was dispatched to ring the doorbell.

'Irishman, how are you doing?'

'Fine, Boss.'

He's putting out the milk bottles, his wife is standing

upstairs. He reaches back inside the door and produces a three-quarters-full bottle of milk.

'Here, Irishman, get that down you.'

Jesus! I hate milk.

'I don't like milk, Boss.'

'Get it down you.'

Shut up, Roy . . . and get it down you!

'Thanks, Boss.' And down she goes.

Meanwhile, Mr and Mrs Clough begin to exchange heated words. She obviously has more 'bottle' than me.

'Come on, Irishman, we're off.'

'Bye, Mrs Clough, nice to meet you.'

When we arrive at the hotel where the first team are staying, we go in for the pre-match meal. I stick close to Phil, who's really the only player in this room I know. I feel a bit surplus to requirements.

Anfield seems vast. An hour before kick-off the atmosphere is humming. The Liverpool side were the aristocrats of the English game. Ian Rush, Peter Beardsley, John Barnes, Ray Houghton and Ronnie Whelan. Well, they were all internationals, and the sum was even greater than the parts. It was the kind of stage Brian Clough loved. Where other teams were beaten before they even saw the famous 'This Is Anfield' sign in the tunnel leading to the pitch, Clough relished the challenge of taking on the Anfield legend, and that transmitted itself to his players.

To make myself useful, I began to help the kit man lay out the gear.

'Irishman, what are you doing?'

'Helping?' I replied.

'Well get hold of a number 7 shirt. You're playing.'

'Excuse me?'

'You're playing.'

I was shocked.

Fortunately, there was no time to think too much about the circumstances of my debut in the First Division. Against the best side in Britain. At Anfield. In the space of forty-five minutes there is enough to do. Like introducing myself to Forest's established first-teamers, none of whom knew who the hell 'Irishman' was!

During the warm-up on the pitch I'm still answering the question 'What's your name again, son?'

'Roy,' I tell them.

They were great. The collective message was: 'Good luck, son.'

Strangely enough, I was calm leaving the dressing room. Clough had been daring and clever. He wasn't afraid to back his judgement, and the way things had happened, he'd placed no pressure on me.

Although Liverpool beat us comfortably on the night 2-0, with Rush and Beardsley scoring the goals, I felt I did OK. I remember tracking back alongside Steve McMahon and doing a double-take: is this really happening, then thinking: yes, and it's fine, I'm comfortable enough.

The big Anfield crowd were knowledgeable, a pleasure to play in front of. The things I did well drew appreciative responses from an audience that for all its partisanship is never shy when it comes to acknowledging good football, whoever's playing it. I also discovered the limits of patriotism at Anfield that night. Dubliner Ronnie Whelan welcomed his young Mayfield compatriot Roy Whatshisname to the big time with a bruising over-the-top tackle. I also 'got involved' with Ray Houghton in a bonecrushingly unsentimental Irish encounter.

For one of the few times in my career I was pleased to leave the field after a defeat. We'd given it our best shot. And if the guys didn't know my name at the start of the match, I felt they knew it now.

When I phoned my dad after the game to tell him I'd played against Liverpool he was as shocked as I'd been a couple of hours before.

'How did it go, son?' he asked.

I replied, 'OK.'

And that was an accurate expression of how I felt. I had proved nothing, except that I could handle a one-off appearance at the highest level. Nothing had been expected of me. Next time I would have a reputation to defend and the pressure of expectation. Now that I'd had a taste, my aim was to secure a regular first team place.

When I met Brian Clough in the dressing room at the City Ground the following morning, he asked me my name. 'Roy,' I replied. Then he took off his shoes, which were muddy, as he'd been walking his dog, Dell, round the pitch. 'Give those a clean for me, will you, Roy?' I was delighted to oblige. I knew what he was doing and why. But there was never any danger that I would get carried away.

I kept my place in the side for the away game at Coventry the following Saturday. We got a draw, which could have been a win if I'd converted a good chance late in the game. The following week I made my home debut against Southampton. My mum and dad and a couple of my uncles travelled over for the game. While a friend of mine picked my family up from East Midlands Airport, I went off to watch the youth team play their morning match. Archie Gemmill went crazy when he saw me standing on the touchline.

'What are you doing here?' he asked. 'You've got a big game this afternoon. Go home and get your rest.'

At nineteen rest is not that easy to come by on the morning of your home debut. Especially with your family coming all the way from Cork for a special occasion.

The City Ground and Forest fans will always have a special place in my heart. Players often say that they don't notice the crowd and it is true that the more experienced you become, the less you are affected by crowds, whether they are on your side or not. But whether it's shutting up a home crowd or responding to the passions of your own supporters the fans – particularly the knowledgeable, committed fans – are an integral part of the drama.

My first game at the City Ground ended ten minutes from the end when Brian Clough substituted me. We were 3-1 ahead. I'd made the first goal and played well. In all the circumstances, especially with my family present, it was a dream debut. As I left the field the crowd gave me a standing ovation. I was pleased, relieved, embarrassed. I was in the dressing room heading for the bath when Archie Gemmill came in and said that the boss wanted me to go back out to the dug-out. Surprised, I followed Archie outside. I was even more surprised when Brian Clough embraced me and planted a kiss on my cheek, to the delight and amusement of the crowd.

This was an astonishing climax to a great day. The presence of my parents and brothers – and Noel McCabe, who'd made the journey over to witness my first home game – reminded me how dramatically my life had changed in the six months since Cobh Ramblers' 4-0 thrashing in Fairview Park.

I would later have my differences with Brian Clough – none of them very serious – and would hear all the stories of 'bungs' and 'booze', but I've never forgotten what he did for me – and how he did it. He was his own man, prepared to be daring, at odds with the conventional wisdom of any given day. On the day of the Southampton game, Clough was particularly courteous to my family. For all his success Clough could be touchingly human, which is not too frequently the case with living legends.

Over the next few months the transformation of my life was complete. Week in week out I was playing against clubs and players I'd been watching on *Match of the Day* the previous season. In October, we played Spurs at the City Ground. My first encounter with the club I'd followed. And with Paul Gascoigne, whose tears in the previous summer's World Cup finals had made him a national icon, and drawn the English people into an emotional engagement with football that would lead to the creation of the Premiership and the loadsamoney Sky Television contract. Football was fashionable, a soap opera with real tears – Gazza's – in which everyone had a hero and a favourite club.

Stuart Pearce and Des Walker, Gazza's England team-mates, warned me before the game that he would try to wind me up. This he duly did, the thrust of his 'verbals' being that I was an Irish wanker who couldn't fucking play. A lot of the talk was lost on me. I couldn't understand his thick Geordie accent. He was actually very funny. Alas, for such a superbly gifted player to spend so much energy trying to get me going seemed a waste. Spurs won the game with a goal in the closing minutes.

Later that month I was picked for the Irish under-21 team against Turkey in Dublin. I was pleased. Obviously it was an honour to play for my country, but to be honest, my primary concern at that time was my future at Forest.

Unfortunately, the Irish set-up, training, preparation and coaching seemed a bit of a joke. Jack Charlton was God in Ireland. Maurice Setters, his right-hand man, was in charge of the under-21 side. Apart from a few clichés about 'having a go' and 'putting 'em under pressure', Setters had very little to say. The set-up didn't impress me. I smelt bullshit.

Life was intoxicating at this point. Although I maintained a quiet demeanour, and tried very hard not to get carried away, every day was a buzz, as I experienced each new situation for the first time. Recognition around Nottingham, for example, was a mixed blessing. People were generally nice but privacy, a bit of space, had always been essential to me and that was largely denied to a 'rising young Forest star'.

I loved Nottingham. It was very similar to Cork in many ways, both being provincial cities. Reaction to my Irishness amused me. Bord Failte, the Irish Tourist Board, marketed my native country as a land of green fields and mountains, full of happy Guinness-drinking folk who loved to fish. When I explained to new acquaintances that I neither drank Guinness nor fished, they were surprised. I came from urban Ireland, the part that doesn't feature in tourist brochures. Therefore, Nottingham was in more respects like home.

Still I occasionally yearned for Mayfield and my family. Sensitive to this, Brian Clough was very accommodating to my regular requests for a few days' home leave. I'd go to him after a game on Saturday, usually after a good result, and his response was invariably, 'Off you go, son, see you on Thursday.'

If I have conveyed an impression of myself as a model pro at this time, that is not quite the complete story. In truth, I abused Clough's generosity, developing a routine for these home visits which varies very significantly from the textbook How To Fulfil Your Promise And Make It To The Top Of The Professional Game.

Buoyed by my success, I'd head off to Cork on Saturday

night with a few quid in my pocket, and a profound sense of well-being in my heart. I was in celebration mode. Training for next week's fixture was not on the agenda. I wouldn't even bother to bring any training gear home with me.

My itinerary was roughly as follows. Leave Nottingham after Saturday's game. Arrive in Cork for 'last orders' at The Templeacre. Meet Denis, Johnson and perhaps my dad and a couple of other friends, John Ricken and Derek Buckley. Head into town for a bite to eat, and maybe a few more drinks in a club. There was the news from home to catch up on. And, of course, I had my own stories to tell about my new life as a 'rising star'.

What was Brian Clough really like? Was Gazza as daft as he looked? The questions were harmless enough, the gossip eagerly consumed. Ireland's successful Italia '90, where Jack Charlton's squad had reached the quarter-finals, drove the country football crazy. Charlton was a national hero, soccer newly respectable where once, not long before, it had been the despised 'foreign game'.

After a good lie-in on Sunday, the celebrations would continue, again starting at The Templeacre and ending in a city disco. Between pints of lager and kebabs we reminisced about the good old days and plotted new after-midnight adventures. On Monday, Tuesday and Wednesday we'd be out following the same routine. After the hard slog of full-time training I felt entitled to a blow-out. So when I flew back to Nottingham, I felt no pangs of guilt.

The one thing that did bother me was that I hadn't scored a goal for Forest. In fact, it was December before I scored my first League goal against Sheffield United at Bramall Lane. Unfortunately, we lost the game. My next goal against Wimbledon proved to be the winner.

Shortly afterwards, Brian Clough calls me into his office. The terms of my contract meant that I was entitled to a club car. 'Irishman, take these,' he said, tossing me a set of car keys across his desk. 'Look after it.'

The car was a Ford Orion, brand new. I was thrilled. This was another symbol of progress, proof that the last six months hadn't been a dream. And I did look after my car like a baby. Every Sunday I washed it. Frequently, I went for a drive with no particular destination in mind, just to get a buzz from my new 'wheels'.

The FA Cup-tie against Crystal Palace gave me my first taste of a competition that was still of immense importance to footballers in 1991. Reaching a Wembley cup final was an aspiration cherished by every pro, and every fan of every club in England. For Brian Clough the FA Cup was particularly special: it was the one major trophy he'd never won.

We were drawn away to Crystal Palace. We battled for a 0-0 draw. In the replay at the City Ground we were 2-1 up when I underhit a back pass to keeper Mark Crossley with disastrous consequences. Mark managed to hook the ball clear but only to John Salako, who chipped him from fifty yards. 2-2. Fuck.

When I walked into the dressing room after the game, Clough punched me straight in the face. 'Don't pass the ball back to the goalkeeper,' he screamed as I lay on the floor, him standing over me. I was hurt and shocked, too shocked to do anything but nod my head in agreement. My honeymoon with Clough and professional football was over. Dressing rooms can be hard, unforgiving places. Being knocked down by Clough was part of my learning curve. Knowing the pressure he was under, I didn't hold this incident against him. He never said sorry, but the following week I was given a few days off to go home to Cork.

After a second replay against Palace, which we won 3-0, Forest were drawn away to Newcastle in the fourth round. Newcastle was never an easy place to visit. They came out with all guns blazing. We were two down within quarter of an hour.

There are people who call themselves professionals, but in Stuart Pearce we had a player who really gave meaning to the word. Pearce was a leader, a real pro, as he proved in the Newcastle cup-tie. He led by example. His defiance was infectious. When other heads were beginning to drop, Pearce would spot it and urge those players on. Some needed a bollocking, others a pat on the back.

At St James's Park we fought desperately to get back in the game. Although playing left back Pearce was the driving force. At times like this 'Psycho' could seem like a man possessed. His tackling was sharp. He intimidated all but the bravest forwards. On the ball his wonderful left foot was by turns subtle and deadly.

Against Newcastle that day his was the decisive contribution. His goal got us back in the tie. Nigel Clough scored the equalizer with two minutes to go. It was for performances like that that Brian Clough loved Stuart Pearce. He was an amazing warrior, relishing every moment of our fightback, relishing too, I noticed, his reputation as a man it didn't pay to mess with. Most opponents 'bottled' it when Pearce was on their case. That cup-tie taught me an important lesson. Willpower and desire mattered. Indeed, the mental strength to out-battle the opposition was more important than mere technical ability.

We easily beat Newcastle 3-0 in the replay. Once again we were drawn away from home, this time at Southampton.

Shortly after the Newcastle game I was selected to travel

abroad with the Irish squad. This trip clashed with Forest's Zenith Data Systems Cup-tie away to Barnsley. It was clear that Brian Clough wanted me to travel to Barnsley. Forest were my bread and butter, so I informed the Football Association of Ireland that I wasn't available. I received a phone call from Maurice Price, my old coach from the FÁS course. He told me that I had to travel. I explained my commitment to Forest.

'Well, Roy, Big Jack has told me that if you pull out of this trip you'll never play for Ireland again,' Price replied.

Stunned for the moment, I made a quick calculation. It didn't take more than thirty seconds to work out what to do. 'If that's the way it is, Maurice, so be it,' I responded as politely as I could. I owed everything I had to Brian Clough and Forest. I was proud to be Irish, but Forest paid my wages. It was to them that I owed my allegiance. I was disappointed that Charlton would seek to bully a player like this.

We drew our fifth round FA Cup-tie at Southampton and Nigel Jemson scored a hat trick to give us a comfortable victory in the replay. Reaching Wembley now began to seem a real possibility, even though we were again drawn away, this time to Norwich.

On the way to Carrow Road, our coach broke down. We had to walk the last three miles to the ground, Brian Clough leading the way, much to the amusement of the Norwich fans. With both sides only two games away from Wembley, the Norwich game was tense and tight. Again, Stuart Pearce was the inspiration in what was mostly a backs-to-the-wall battle. Again, his was the most important presence.

A 0-0 draw would have suited us. In the end a replay wasn't necessary as I scored a late winner. Another battle won, another victory for attitude, as epitomized by Pearce, our leader.

Feeling pleased with myself, I asked Brian Clough for a few days' home leave. This was granted: 'See you on Friday,' was Clough's curt reply.

Twenty-four hours later I was sitting in The Templeacre with Denis, Johnson, John Ricken and Derek Buckley. They'd read about my run-in with Big Jack. Was I crazy to turn down a chance to play for Ireland? I explained my priorities . . . also that my experience of Maurice Setters had been less than inspiring.

A few pints of Heineken later, we set off for Cork city. Sidetrax Disco was our destination. I was happy. Coming home having earned my few days of rock 'n' roll was sweet, the best of all possible worlds.

The only cloud on my horizon was recognition and the hassle that increasingly came with it. Around Mayfield and The Templeacre there was no problem. The city was different. Since I'd made the first team at Forest, a simple night out in the city had become a bit of an ordeal. I was very shy and the feeling of being watched really made me uncomfortable. The same was true in Nottingham, but it was easier to accept there. On nights out in England I was usually with other Forest players and there was some safety in numbers. Cork was my home town. I was leading an ordinary life, or trying to. Slowly I was discovering that if you had a public profile, leading an ordinary life was difficult, if not impossible. I didn't feel that I was flash, yet clearly certain people resented the fact that I had a few bob in my pocket and was enjoying myself.

Of course, on reflection I must admit that when I hit the city after a session at The Templeacre with Denis, Johnson, Derek and John, all of us well oiled, we weren't exactly unobtrusive. In 1991, things were still hard for a significant number of Irish people. The curse of joblessness still hung over Cork, although you'd never have guessed it as the city centre hummed on Thursday, Friday and Saturday nights. Come to think of it, Sundays were pretty lively as well, with people celebrating (or lamenting) the performance of Cork's renowned Gaelic footballers or hurlers. Looking back, I can see how our gang with 'your man Roy Keane' in the middle might have seemed provocative to some. Most people were fine, their attitude being 'fair play to you boy'. Others seemed to take a different view. I might be queuing for fish and chips or a kebab (my favourite) when I'd hear someone asking 'Who does he think he is?' A small thing, but incidents like that reminded me that fame came with a price tag.

On the night after the Norwich game we arrived in Sidetrax Disco in flying form. We'd graduated to double Bacardi and Cokes and it was my turn to get the drinks in. As I made my way back to our table from the bar, hands full of drink, a guy appeared out of nowhere and smacked me in the face. The drink crashed on the floor and the next thing I know I'm fighting two guys. It was quite dark, so my mates didn't realize at first that it was me in the middle of what was now an ugly scene. Luckily one of them recognized my shirt: 'That's Roy.' The two guys who'd attacked me got a right hammering and were thrown out. The whole episode had a dream-like quality to it, like something out of a movie. My shirt was ripped to pieces with blood all over it. The attack was totally unprovoked, although I had a hard time convincing people who subsequently heard that 'Roy Keane had been involved in a brawl'. Fortunately, news of the incident didn't reach the newspapers. This time. We finished our drinks and went off for something to eat as if nothing had happened. When I got home, my mam and dad were still up. Seeing the state of me, all they were capable of saying was: 'Good night, was it?' I laughed and went to bed.

I was hurt and embarrassed. Not for the last time I vowed to stay out of the city at night. But of course, the following night there'd be more drink and when we were steamed up again there was nothing for it except another trip to town. Sure I knew there might be further hassle, but I didn't like the idea of people dictating how I should live my life. I was from Cork. I was enjoying myself, doing nothing wrong.

If only life – my new life – were that simple.

3

Our FA Cup semi-final against West Ham at Villa Park turned out to be the easiest game of our cup run. After the opening fifteen minutes when they had a go – and hit the post – West Ham didn't have the bottle for it. Their cause wasn't helped when their centre-half Tony Gale was sent off after twenty-five minutes. But by then we'd started winning the little battles all over the pitch, inspired yet again by Stuart Pearce.

Cup semi-finals are traditionally tense. The prospect of reaching the final usually causes teams to be cautious. Fear of failure is palpable, nobody wants to make the mistake that ends the dream. The combination of Brian Clough's cunning and 'Psycho's' determination ensured that we took the field in the right frame of mind. Clough's message was simple, and reassuring: 'It's just another game, play your football, you'll win.' He never harped on about the fact that the FA Cup was the only major trophy he'd never won, although this was the angle the media focused on. Nor did he remind us of another ominous statistic that the press made much of, that Forest had won only two of the eleven FA Cup semi-finals they'd played in.

Looking around the dressing room, I felt no fear. Stuart Pearce, Des Walker and Steve Hodge were all England internationals. Gary Charles, myself, Nigel Jemson and Gary Crosby, being young and much less experienced, responded to the mood of the senior pros, Pearce in particular. And there was something else that struck me. Far from being afraid,

Pearce, Des Walker and Brian Clough were actually looking forward to the game. 'Come on, let's go, enjoy it, these big games are what all the hard work is for,' was the message.

I left the dressing room for the biggest game of my career feeling good. That was what I'd always wanted.

West Ham were a Second Division side, a useful one, odds-on to gain promotion. Gary Crosby, myself, Stuart Pearce and Gary Charles were the scorers in an easy 4-0 win. Spurs beat Arsenal in the other semi-final. Brian Clough would get another shot at the FA Cup. Twelve months after my first meeting with Noel McCabe, I was heading for Wembley.

Two weeks before the Cup final I did my ankle ligament in a League game at White Hart Lane. This was a serious blow. I was desperate to play against Spurs at Wembley. Yet I knew that Forest wouldn't play me unless I could prove my fitness. I was selected for a reserve match on the Monday night, to establish if I was fit. I got through that game with my ankle strapped up. Just about.

On the Thursday Brian Clough defied conventional wisdom by naming his Cup final eleven two days before the game. I was in at the expense of England international Steve Hodge.

We travelled to London on Thursday. When we arrived at the hotel, Ron Fenton announced that Steve and I would be sharing a room. I wasn't sure what Brian Clough's psychological ploy was meant to achieve. I'd never roomed with Steve before, and in the circumstances both of us felt distinctly uneasy. This arrangement led to a fraught couple of days. Like me, Steve was not much of a talker. On this occasion neither of us felt inclined to mention the thing uppermost in our minds: his omission, my amazing leap from the FÁS scheme to a Wembley Cup final.

The other big issue for all the Forest players was Cup final tickets. Our ticket allocation of twenty was guaranteed to cause everyone grief. Friends, family, relatives, anyone who'd ever done you a favour (or had ever done a favour for any of your friends, family, or relatives) all wanted a Cup final ticket. It was life or death, a considerable burden on players facing an important football match.

My ankle was still troubling me. The atmosphere in the bedroom was tense. But I can honestly say that in the forty-eight hours leading up to the Cup final I fretted more about tickets than anything else. Between family, friends and acquaintances I had requests for forty-five tickets. Even then I was bound to make enemies. Unbelievably, my abiding memory of my first major football occasion concerns the scramble for precious tickets. Everyone was coming from Cork. What should have been a wonderful landmark in my life became a bloody nightmare. I was desperate not to snub anyone. My family were in a similar situation. (The ticket problem would persist, indeed become, perhaps, the biggest single source of anxiety, a recurring feature of my life, when I moved to Manchester United.)

Feeling that I didn't want to let anyone down, and desperate also to demonstrate that despite moving up in the world I hadn't changed, I begged and scrounged every ticket I could lay my hands on. Two hours before the game the ticket crisis was still the major preoccupation. Denis and Johnson still had no tickets. The Keanes being Keanes, everyone else had been fixed up. I'd arranged to meet Denis and Johnson outside the dressing rooms an hour before the game. Maybe I'd cop a couple of spare tickets at the last minute. In the end, I got my hands on one spare ticket. But one was not enough. I had £900 in cash in my pocket (four weeks' wages!). Fuck it, I thought, I'll give it to the lads and they can buy two off the ticket touts. I gave my brothers the money, and prayed they'd find a tout. The traditional demand for Cup final tickets had been compounded by the fact that Spurs were a London club.

Forty-five minutes before kick-off, I finally started preparing for the game. As I began to change, suddenly two more tickets appeared. Alas, it was too late. Now, after all the hassle, we had two spare tickets!

The ticket crisis had taken its roll. As we began the walk down the Wembley tunnel led by Brian Clough, I was weary. All the nervous energy dissipated in the previous eight hours had left me drained and virtually legless. My ankle wasn't the best either.

The media had prepared a script for the Spurs/Forest Cup final. According to the commentators, Wembley was an appropriate stage for Paul Gascoigne to prove that he was a player worthy of the adoration that England had bestowed upon him ever since his tearful exit from the World Cup twelve months before. Would this be Gazza's finest hour? The other issue – according to the media – concerned Brian Clough. Could he cap a wonderful career in management by capturing the one major trophy that had eluded him?

Walking out on to this 'great stage', it was difficult to concentrate. The crowd was noisy, yet curiously remote. Brian Clough was marching jauntily ahead of us, holding Terry Venables by the hand. I was wondering if Denis and Johnson had got their tickets. (Somewhere in the back of my mind there was a nagging concern about friends and acquaintances I hadn't fixed up. Unbelievable, but true.)

Prince Charles shook my hand.

Gazza looked crazy.

Two minutes into the game, Gascoigne took out Gary

Parker with a kung-fu kick that caught Gary on his chest. We looked at the ref. Nothing. His eyes were glazed. So were Gascoigne's. It was clear he was out of control. Manic. Crazy. Ten minutes later, Gascoigne was on a stretcher. Gary Charles had released the ball long before Gascoigne went so far over the top it was untrue. In the process he'd injured himself. As it turned out, the self-inflicted damage to his cruciate ligament would also damage Gazza's career – he was never the same player again. Incredibly, the referee didn't book him for the challenge on Charles.

As always, Stuart Pearce was superb. As Gazza headed for the tunnel, Pearce struck a beautiful free-kick into the back of the net.

We were still a goal up at half-time. I was struggling with my ankle but wouldn't admit that I was far from fit enough to get away with another forty-five minutes. The second half was a disaster. Mark Crossley had saved a Gary Lineker penalty in the first half. But Spurs kept coming at us. An equalizer was inevitable. It came, and the game went to extra-time.

Despite my ankle I put myself about, but I contributed very little. The pitch pulled on my legs, the crowd remained a remote blur, a background noise, lacking the intimacy of a normal Saturday afternoon. When Des Walker scored an own goal to win the Cup for Spurs, it seemed an appropriate end to a bloody awful day. Tickets, ankle, Gazza, rooming with the guy I was keeping out of the side! Afterwards, in the dressing room, I felt empty.

I learned two lessons from Cup final day. The first reinforced a belief I'd always held: that football is first and foremost a team game. The way Spurs coach Terry Venables reorganized his side when Gazza was carried off was very impressive. Had Gazza stayed on, we might have been able to shut him out of the contest, leaving Spurs no alternative threat. As it was, they'd reshuffled the pack, producing a result by virtue of the fact that Spurs whole were greater than the sum of their parts. The other thing I learned was how destructive off-field distractions can be, in my case the hunt for tickets. It would take me a long time to put into practice the lessons learned in this context. One other thought occurred to me: the media hype of Cup final week can suck you in, causing you to lose sight of the fact that the Cup final is just another game of football. The real loser on this occasion was Paul Gascoigne, who suffered for his attempt to live up to the outrageous burden the media placed on his fragile shoulders.

I now know that, although Forest lost that Wembley Cup final, the experience was good for me. The season had in many respects been a dream come true. Failure at Wembley brought me down to earth. I woke up from my year-long dream and understood that professional soccer was a brutal business. I also understood that I had a long way to go.

Immediately after the Cup final I was selected to play my first full international game for Ireland, a friendly against Chile at Lansdowne Road. This was my first encounter with Jack Charlton – 'Big Jack' – whose achievements with the Irish team had made him a national hero. I was pleased to be selected, but it wasn't a particularly memorable occasion. Ireland hadn't lost a game at Lansdowne Road for five years. The Chileans almost ruined that record. Only a David Kelly equalizer ten minutes from the end allowed us to get out with a draw. My own contribution was unexceptional. Friendly internationals are a contradiction in terms, presenting a problem in my mind. You're expected to perform and get a result, yet it doesn't really matter.

Charlton's approach to football was profoundly at odds with

the game we played at Forest. Passing the ball was not a priority. What he demanded was a kind of football by numbers, the emphasis being on inconveniencing the opposition rather than being creative ourselves. The idea was to fire long balls in behind the opposing defence, then hunt them down, with the intention of trapping them in their own half of the field, where we hoped we'd force them to make mistakes. This fairly primitive approach, executed by some outstanding players, had seen Ireland qualify for two major championship finals: Euro '88 and Italia '90. 'Put 'em under pressure' was Jack's football conviction. And 'Make no mistakes, don't fanny around in your own half of the field' was the message.

Not knowing exactly what was expected of me, apart from the effort I was happy to provide, I kept my head down and did my best to work out if there was any more to Charlton's magic formula than there appeared to be on first acquaintance. Time would prove that there wasn't.

I spent the summer in Cork. After all I'd experienced, it was wonderful to go home to my family and friends. For six weeks I indulged myself as never before. With Denis, Johnson, Derek and John I drank, danced and ate (kebabs) almost every night. Occasional bouts of night-time, drink-relaxed hassle apart, this was a glorious summer. My Cup final appearance and the international debut for 'Big Jack' had unfortunately raised my profile. The 'Who does he think he is?' question surfaced from time to time, as did my temper.

I still found it hard – impossible really – to come to terms with the fact that fame denied me the private existence I felt entitled to. So I was belligerent and stood my ground when trouble loomed, especially late at night. The more I reacted, the faster I acquired a reputation as a hothead.

The truth is, I wasn't prepared to conform with the stereotype of an international footballer, playing for one of the top English clubs. I resisted. I was desperate to prove to my friends, indeed to myself, that success hadn't changed me. I was still Roy, up for a few drinks, a dance, no different from any other nineteen-year-old from Mayfield. Now I understood that success changed other people's perception of you. Certain things are expected of well-known people, and mostly we are happy to oblige. The deal is roughly this: you're polite; you smile and nod your head like a zombie; you play the modest hero and treat every fool you meet like a long-lost friend; and you never get angry; you become kind of superhuman, immune to alcohol and all other temptations.

At nineteen I'm afraid I wasn't ready for the role of well-known person. On the contrary, I resolved to challenge what I regarded as an assault on my natural inclinations. I wouldn't play the fame game. So I kept breaking my vow to steer clear of Cork city – or anywhere else I wanted to go – to enjoy myself. I would conform to the demands of my professional football career, but I wouldn't forsake my family and friends and become a well-known zombie. Hence the seeds of much trouble were sown. Not for the last time people asked, 'What's bugging Roy?'

After six weeks of partying I returned to Nottingham a stone overweight. As always, pre-season training was murder. But the weight came off pretty quickly. After a successful first season Brian Clough gave me a new contract for £700 a week plus a £15,000 signing-on fee.

In October I played my first competitive game for Ireland against Poland, in a game we had to win to qualify for the 1992 European Championship finals. Having led 3-1, we conceded two late goals to allow the Poles a point they probably deserved. Playing for Ireland was a strange experience.

I'd watched Jack Charlton's teams in Euro '88 and Italia '90 as a fan, so I knew the style was pretty basic, and difficult to come to terms with for someone coming from my Forest background, where we played a passing game. Ireland had some very good footballers – Denis Irwin, David O'Leary, Paul McGrath, Andy Townsend, Ray Houghton and Kevin Sheedy among them. Yet playing football in any systematic way, in the pass-and-move style we adopted at Forest, for example, or Denis Irwin was accustomed to at Man. United, was frowned upon by Charlton.

My job was to close down the opposition and if possible win the ball. Having gained possession, passing to an Irish colleague seemed the obvious next move. But that was not what Charlton wanted. His fear of Ireland giving the ball away – especially in our own half of the field – caused real inhibitions for me and most of the other players, who were forced to adapt our own games to the Charlton Method. 'Don't give the fucking ball away,' Charlton would shout in the dressing room if by chance you had lost possession trying to start a move in your own half of the pitch or in midfield. 'Hit the front men' was his slogan. Tony Cascarino, Niall Quinn and John Aldridge were our forward players. Their instructions were (a) to win the long balls knocked up to them, (b) to try and get in behind their markers for long balls played into space behind defenders. In situation (a) myself and Andy Townsend were to push forward to try and win balls knocked down or flicked on by Cas or Niall. In situation (b) the whole side pushed forward with the intention of trapping our opponents in their own territory. Situation (b) didn't really suit Cas and Niall, neither of whom was very mobile. John Aldridge was better suited to making runs in behind defenders. 'Knock it into space down the gulleys,' Charlton urged.

An additional eccentricity in the Irish set-up was the presence of Paul McGrath as the holding player in midfield. Paul was an outstanding footballing centre-half, still playing for Man. United. At this time, Paul's role was to win the ball while close marking the opposition's play-maker.

Although we conceded three goals against Poland in Poznań, Charlton's tactics proved very effective against European teams who were used to playing the ball out from the back in a fairly leisurely way and found this impossible to accomplish against an Irish side which put them under fierce pressure in their own half of the field. We scrapped for every ball, turning every game into a ninety-minute war of attrition. This was football Wimbledon/Watford style, and it had proved very effective in the international arena of that era.

There was, however, a contradiction at the heart of Charlton's footballing beliefs. On the one hand he urged us not to give the ball away, on the other he insisted that we play the kind of long-ball game that ensured that for much of any ninety-minute battle we didn't actually have possession. The idea was to force our opponents to make mistakes. By pressing forward to put them under pressure we would deny them the opportunity to impose their rhythm on the game. Attempting to be creative ourselves wasn't really an option for Charlton's Ireland. He didn't encourage variations to his game plan. The risk of incurring his rage by attempting something original was ever present. It was clear that he didn't trust even the best of Ireland's players to play the game as they did in their clubs. For trying to do so, outstanding players like Liam Brady and Ronnie Whelan had run foul of Charlton and seen their international careers terminated.

The kind of football Charlton demanded we play took some getting used to. Home and away the Irish supporters were brilliant. We'd never achieved much as a footballing nation, so results rather than style was all they required. And to be fair to Charlton, we got our share of good results against countries with far greater football resources than Ireland.

In other respects playing for Ireland was very disappointing. Preparation, training, medical facilities and travel arrangements were all far below the level of the English First Division. There was more than a touch of Carry On To The World Cup Finals about the atmosphere in the camp. To describe the Football Association of Ireland as amateur would be an insult to amateurs. Given the resources available to them, the set-up at Rockmount AFC seemed far more professional.

Faced with off-the-field cock-ups most of the players laughed (crying was the only alternative), as when for example we'd turn up at Lansdowne Road for a major international and find ourselves playing on a sub-standard pitch. This was frequently the case. Jack Charlton never seemed particularly upset by the state of the playing surface at Lansdowne Road. On the contrary, he seemed to believe that it would upset the opposition more than us. The bog-like pitch would suit our style of play. The fact that we possessed good footballers more than capable of matching the visiting European sides did not seem to be a belief Charlton shared.

Ireland's perception of Big Jack as a tactical genius, the man who'd transformed our fortunes in the international game by turning sows' ears – the players – into silk purses, didn't square with the footballing reality I experienced. I found it impossible to relate to him as a man or a coach. As for Maurice Setters, I was never sure what his role was. He did, however, keep Big Jack supplied with chewing-gum.

My second season as a Forest first team player featured two visits to Wembley for the Zenith Data Systems Cup final and

1. Meeting Father Christmas with my sister Hilary and brother Johnson. I'm in the centre – not happy!

2. Another year and the mood's improved. With Father Christmas again, with (from left to right) my sister Hilary and brothers Pat and Johnson.

3. On the day I was confirmed.

4. The day of my first Communion. With my father, Hilary, Pat and a neighbour.

5. On the same day with my godfather Pat Lynch.

6. In the ring aged ten, with boxing coach Tom Kelleher.

7. Referee Billy Lingane raises my hand after I've won. In my first year of boxing I won all my fights.

8. The St John's school running team. I'm on the far right in the front row.

9. In 1984, aged twelve, receiving the Val O'Connor Tournament trophy with Rockmount.

10. With the Rockmount team. I'm in the middle of the back row, pleased to have scored a hat trick to win the final.

11. Receiving another trophy as Rockmount captain.

12. In 1985, aged fourteen. With my father on the left and my uncle, Michael Lynch, on the right and some cousins in front. I'd just won man of the match at Rockmount.

13. With the Rockmount team. I'm second from the right at the front.

14. In 1986, with the Cork team in the All-Ireland Cup. I'm in the front row holding the ball – the captain and smallest member of the team.

15. With Rockmount team-mates (from left to right) Len Downey, Paul McCarthy, Damien Martin and Alan Sullivan after winning the All-Ireland Cup playing for Cork.

16. Receiving the Cup.

17. With Cork selector Gerard Delaney (left) and Irish trainer Liam O'Brien.

18. Receiving my Ireland under-16 cap in the 1987/88 season.

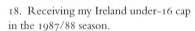

19. Aged seventeen, winning Player of the Year at Rockmount 1988/89.

20. Irish Under-21s v. England. With Paul McCarthy, now playing for Wycombe Wanderers.

21. My debut for Nottingham Forest in September 1990.

22. Scoring my first goal for Forest a couple of weeks later against Burnley.

23. Playing Chelsea later the same season.

24. With Forest manager Brian Clough in March 1992. He's receiving the Manager of the Month award.

the Rumbelows (League) Cup final. Brian Clough had signed Teddy Sheringham from Millwall, adding a touch of class and penetration to the side.

In the Zenith Data Systems Cup final we beat Southampton 3–2 at Wembley. This wasn't a competition the big clubs paid much attention to. But for us it was a welcome distraction from League football and I was delighted to win my first medal in the English game.

The Rumbelows Cup was more significant in the pre-Premiership era. I scored the winning goal in extra-time in the semi-final against Spurs at White Hart Lane. I felt stronger and fitter with every game during my second season as a pro. I now had a reputation, which meant that the opposition paid more attention to me. I was learning all the time. How to lose my marker, how to pace the game, how to time my runs into the opposition's penalty area; most of all, perhaps, I learned that in every game you had to win the individual battle with the opponent in your own area of the pitch.

I was fortunate to be in a good side, supported by a great manager. Stuart Pearce, Des Walker, Nigel Clough and Teddy Sheringham were top-class players, providing a good balance between class and competitiveness to our play. Although it was clear that we were always going to struggle to compete with the top clubs – Liverpool, Arsenal, Manchester United and Leeds – for the Championship, we could match any of them on a good day. But over a full League season Forest couldn't match the big clubs for strength in depth.

We finished eighth in the First Division and lost to Man. United in the Rumbelows Cup final. Once again, Wembley was an anti-climax. We made the game a battle, but United edged a 1–0 victory.

Even though we'd reached Wembley twice and finished

respectably in the League, a feeling persisted around the City Ground that Forest had underachieved. The formation of the Premier League had been announced. A television contract with Sky Television was in the process of being signed. The deal promised fabulous amounts of money to the top clubs, who'd broken away from the rest of the Football League.

Under Brian Clough's leadership Forest had won a Championship and two European Cups. This incredible achievement had been gained without splashing out big transfer fees for top players. Really, this was a miracle of the loaves and fishes applied to football. It was against this glorious past that everything our team achieved was being measured. The anxiety about how Forest would fare in the new elite Premier League was compounded for Forest fans by the prevailing sense that Brian Clough was no longer the man of legend capable of delivering the game's major prizes to a club that couldn't really afford to sign the kind of players you would need to be competitive in the new era that was dawning.

Opinions about Clough were mixed in the dressing room: some players were afraid of him; others disliked him; few grumbled that we didn't see enough of the manager. My own view of Clough was coloured by the fact which remained foremost in my mind: he'd given me my chance, and I owed everything I now had to him. How many managers would risk their reputation by throwing a nineteen-year-old into the first team, at Anfield, a kid with no professional experience? More than that, his generous response to my requests for trips home to Cork had helped me through the difficult early days at Forest. Sure, he had his own way of doing things, but it worked for Forest. And for me.

Observing the mood in the Forest dressing room, I was beginning to understand even more clearly than before that too many pros felt the world owed them a living. Turn up for training in the morning, have a laugh, and a moan, for a couple of hours, before going back to the comfort of their homes, out shopping, or straight to the golf club. After good results they wallowed in the glory. When the results went the wrong way, they blamed someone else. This pissed me off. I'm certain my late arrival in the game was a decisive influence in my own attitude. To Brian Clough, to everything, really. I was hungrier than most, though not hungrier than Stuart Pearce. The more I saw of Pearce, the more impressed I was by his unswerving professionalism. Players moaned about him too. 'Fuck off, Pearcie,' they'd whine when he demanded more – in training or a match. They whispered that he was a 'tight bastard' with money (he was!). But so what? We were paid to do the business and Stuart Pearce led by example. He never demanded anything of anyone that he wasn't prepared to do himself.

His relationship with Clough was one of mutual respect and trust. Between them, and Liam O'Kane, they would decide how hard we needed to train – and when. After one Saturday game Clough decided to order us in for training on the Monday.

'But Boss, me and Liz are going to London for a few days,' Pearce pleaded.

'OK, see you all on Tuesday,' Clough replied.

Ultimately I respected Clough for his knowledge of the game. He may have been a remote figure day to day on the training ground, but on match days his presence, and his eye for detail, made the difference. If you weren't doing your stuff, Clough would spot it. A seemingly innocuous mistake that resulted in a goal conceded three or four minutes later, a tackle missed, or a failure to make the right run, or pass, would be correctly identified as the cause of the goal. It was no use pointing the finger at someone else – which is second nature to most players. He knew, you knew he knew.

Every football match consists of a thousand little things which, added together, amount to the final score. The manager who can't spot the details in the forensic manner that Clough could is simply bluffing. The game is full of bluffers, banging on about 'rolling your sleeves up', 'having the right attitude' and taking 'some pride in the shirt you're wearing'. A manager or coach who trades in those clichéd generalizations – and there are many of them – is missing the point. Brian Clough dealt in detail, facts, specific incidents, and invariably he got it right. Playing for him was demanding. I loved it because no less than anyone else my instinctive reaction was 'Not me, Boss'. Brian Clough and Stuart Pearce helped me shed that habit. I lived and learned in that hard school.

Clough was exceptional in many other ways. One day, when he was absent from the training ground, weights were produced and we were set to work on a mini Charles Atlas course. After half an hour, Dell, the manager's dog, scampered into view, followed by his master, dressed as usual in a sheepskin coat, a green tracksuit top and wellies. 'What the fuck are these?' Clough asked Liam O'Kane, pointing at the weights. Before Liam could explain, Clough ordered, 'Get them out of here . . . and get the balls out.' That was his strength. And I suppose his weakness, for the game was changing as we prepared to enter the Premier League era. Sadly, like Margaret Thatcher, the lady he despised, Brian Clough was not for turning.

Where other older pros took issue with the manager's unorthodox ways, I was on the whole prepared to go along. One day, after a game at Middlesbrough, where he'd been a player, he insisted that we sit on the coach signing autographs for a couple of hours. The north-east was his part of the world, and this was his grand gesture. Several hundred fans were lined up outside the coach and, marshalled by Clough, they entered the bus at the front, got their autograph before exiting through the back door. With wives and families to get home to, the senior players were going crazy as darkness descended and the prospect of a seriously delayed arrival home in Nottingham loomed. I just kept signing. It was better than signing on the dole.

That is not to suggest that I wasn't looking forward to my Saturday night out in Nottingham. When the business was done I loved my nights on the town. 'Work hard, play hard' was very much my motto. If Stuart Pearce was my role model in football matters, Des Walker was the Man for night-time adventures. Des was an outstanding player. He was also a world-class playboy. He owned the cars, wore the clothes and pulled the girls. He liked a drink and he was great company after dark.

I was still very shy. But Des took me and many of the young Forest players under his wing on his tours of Nottingham's fleshpots. While he held court, surrounded by, to my innocent Irish eye, astonishing-looking girls, buying drinks for all and sundry, we were happy to play quiet supporting roles. Young, single and Forest players, we couldn't go wrong.

Around this time I spotted a beautiful girl in a club in town. Her name was Theresa Doyle. I showed out but she blanked me. She was in a steady relationship and didn't seem at all impressed by Roy Keane, the great footballer. In fact, I think my reputation was a downer for all kinds of reasons. From time to time we ran into each other around Nottingham. I knew some of her friends who told me Theresa was a dentist's assistant. Eventually after her relationship broke up she relented and we went out together. I was in love. We became great friends. Theresa, though born in Nottingham, was of Irish descent. Her parents were from County Dublin – Bray and Lusk.

Unfortunately, the late-night problems I encountered in Cork also occasionally surfaced in Nottingham. Confronted by the house hard man, usually a messer who posed the question 'Who do you think you are?', I was never inclined to back away from trouble.

The 1991–92 season ended with the Irish squad at a post-season friendly international tournament in the United States. This seemed a meaningless exercise, part competitive, part piss-up, in desperately humid conditions. In this sporting limbo – were we here to play, or to play around? – I felt distinctly uneasy. 'Big Jack' was in his element, loving every minute of celebrity, as Irish emigrants clamoured for a piece of the man who'd saved the nation's football team. I wondered what the hell I was doing here, knackered after a hard season, surrounded by the by now familiar chaos of the Irish international camp. We lost our first game in the tournament 3-1 to the USA; from there it was a downfall all the way.

For some of the Blazers of the Football Association of Ireland this was the life. 'The trip of a lifetime', I heard one Blazer gleefully tell another. I felt the football was merely an excuse to justify this 'trip of a lifetime'. The lads were dog tired at the end of an English season. Nobody seemed to give a damn.

On the morning we were due to fly home, Steve Staunton and I went out for a drink. It was our turn to party now – in fact we were merely carrying on from the night before. Merry and giddy, we forgot about the time. We were late arriving back at the team hotel. The rest of the party were sitting in the coach outside. Steve and I raced to our rooms to pack our bags.

As we boarded the coach, 'Big Jack' started ranting and roaring: 'Where the fuckin' 'ell have you been? You've kept us all waiting, you two.'

'Why didn't you go without us?' I shot back. 'I didn't ask you to wait.' In the silence that followed I looked him straight in the eye. He neither frightened nor impressed me. He was a bully, who didn't like it when the boot was on the other foot. He backed off. I took my seat at the back of the bus.

'You're right out of order, you.' Looking up, I saw Mick McCarthy, 'Captain Fantastic' himself, glaring down at me.

'Go and fuck yourself,' I told him.

4

We made a great start to our Premier League campaign, beating Liverpool 1-0 in the first game to be televised by Sky Television. Teddy Sheringham scored. Then we began a nightmare run of six matches, all of which we lost. Except for Teddy Sheringham, who left to join Spurs in September, this was the same side that finished eighth the previous season – and reached two Wembley cup finals.

We were bottom of the Premier League in October. We had conceded twenty-two goals in the first ten games. This was a major crisis for Forest. It was generally believed that no club could survive as a major player in the game if it dropped out of the Premier League. The gap between the rich, who benefited from television money, and the poor, those outside the golden circle, would grow. So Nottingham Forest was fighting for its life.

In all of this my own situation was complicated. Newspapers began to speculate about big clubs wanting to buy me. Blackburn, Arsenal, Aston Villa and Liverpool were all mentioned. According to the press, these clubs were willing to break the English transfer record to sign me. Although publicly I affected to ignore these stories, privately I knew that this was a decisive period in my life.

If Forest were relegated – and, as was also being suggested, Brian Clough retired – where would that leave me? I was still on a contract worth £700 a week, much less than many other Forest players. The contract had eighteen months to run. I'd

just paid £100,000 for a nice house in the village of Scarrington. This was slightly more than I could afford. I was
overdrawn at the bank, a situation Brian Clough somehow
found out about. He suggested that I talk to Ron Fenton
about a new contract. Ron dealt with contracts and transfer
talks, Clough only getting involved at the last minute.

Around this time a friend of Kenny Dalglish's contacted me
to inform me that the Blackburn manager wanted to meet
me. Alan Shearer had just rejected a move to Man. United –
from Southampton – to join Blackburn, whose drive for the
Premier League title was being funded by Jack Walker. An
arrangement was made to meet Dalglish and Blackburn coach
Ray Harford at David O'Leary's house in Hertfordshire. They
asked about my contractual situation at Forest. When I told
them I had been offered a new contract, they urged me not
to sign. And if I did sign, to make sure I inserted a clause that
would allow me to leave Forest if they were relegated. It was
made clear to me that Blackburn would be willing to pay a
new British transfer fee record of £3.5m to close the deal.

I knew 'tapping' players in this way was against the rules,
but par for the course in the game. My hand was considerably
strengthened in my talks with Ron Fenton. I wasn't entirely
comfortable with the duplicity involved in these discussions.
But knowing that there was an alternative to going down with
Forest enabled me to negotiate from a position of strength.

While Ron and I talked, media speculation intensified.
Brian Clough went public to accuse me of being 'a greedy
child'. Newspapers claimed that I was demanding £1m over
three years to commit myself to Forest. That figure was
roughly correct. Through his intermediary Kenny Dalglish
had intimated that my wages at Blackburn would be £250,000
a year with a £500,000 signing-on fee.

Privately, Brian Clough and I got on fine, even as he lashed me in the papers. 'Keane is like a kid who wakes up on Christmas morning and finds an apple, an orange and a box of Smarties in his stocking. He wants more,' Clough told the local newspaper. 'He is a highly talented young man. Everything has come quickly for him and he is loved by everybody in football, particularly those at Forest. Keane is the hottest property in the game right now, but he is not going to bankrupt this club. We have made him an offer. He has his own ideas but he is ours for eighteen months and talks are on ice for now. I don't want to know about silly clauses, talking about what he'll do if we get relegated. I want him to sign a straight, no-nonsense contract that is within our budget.'

All the speculation started to take its toll on my performances. I scored a couple of goals when we beat Leeds 4-1 at Elland Road in December, a rare good result that gave us some hope of surviving the drop. But a few weeks later, I was substituted against Man. United at Old Trafford, a game I was anxious – too anxious – to do well in.

Scoring goals was our biggest problem. Also undermining us was a growing feeling that Brian Clough had lost the confidence of the Forest board. A special shareholders' meeting was convened for the first time in twenty years. Brian Clough was the only item on the agenda. The bad vibes from all of this fed into the dressing room. I was aware that a few of the players were muttering about my own situation, suggesting that it would help our survival effort if I signed my new contract to boost morale!

Stuart Pearce, whose loyalty and authority were unquestioned, came to my rescue after training one morning. He went round the room, stopping at each player, to ask the question, 'Are you happy with your contract?' One by one the players answered, 'Yes.' 'Right,' Pearce barked, 'if you're happy, leave Roy alone. He's entitled to fight for the best deal he can get.' I was very grateful for the intervention.

Away from the public gaze my negotiations with Ron Fenton continued. He didn't disagree with my argument that I'd only cost Forest £47,000 and that the club could now sell me for over £3m. He also conceded that I was one of the lowest-paid players in the first team on £700 per week. There were two sticking points: the escape clause if Forest were relegated, and my demand for a £125,000 signing-on fee.

By this stage a number of agents had contacted me, offering to act on my behalf. Although I was tempted by one or two of them, my general impression was that agents regarded footballers as pawns in their own games and would always ultimately serve their own ends – and those of their manager friends – rather than your interests.

In the middle of yet another bout of negotiating Brian Clough strode into Ron Fenton's office. He inquired how things were going. Ron outlined his sticking points. Without a second's hesitation Clough made his call. 'Ron, give Roy what he wants.' Half an hour later, the contract was drawn up. With the get-out clause in place, I was delighted to sign a three-and-a-half-year contract, although in my bones I felt that I would probably never see it out. Even if we avoided relegation, the air of foreboding around the City Ground was such that it seemed unlikely that Forest could, or would, prosper in the new money-driven Premier League. The power of money, as exemplified by Jack Walker, who bankrolled Blackburn, was such that Nottingham Forest could not compete.

Although my form had dipped as a result of the very public row about my contract negotiations, I never lost sight of the thing that mattered most: performing on Saturday afternoons. I didn't resent Brian Clough's public criticism of me. He was under pressure himself and had his own job to do. I never forgot what he'd done for me, nor, it seemed to me, did the Forest fans ever forget the glorious times they'd enjoyed thanks to him. There were players in his own dressing room – and some club directors – who were on Clough's case. I was determined to repay the debt I owed him by doing everything I could on the pitch to ensure Forest's Premier League survival. I didn't see any conflict fighting for Forest and acquiring the best deal I could get from the club for the services I provided. Services may seem a strange word to use in this context, but if I'd understood one thing in my first three years as a professional player, it was that football was a business, at times a very cruel business.

To add to our woes, Stuart Pearce was injured. It looked like he'd be out of the side for a couple of months. Without his presence – not to mention his talent – the team was critically diminished. In the circumstances we found ourselves in, Pearce was irreplaceable. To try and plug the gap Clough selected me to play centre-half on a number of occasions. Our biggest problem, though, was scoring goals. Teddy Sheringham's departure had deprived us of a vital offensive ingredient. Teddy scored and created goals. He was allowed to leave for commercial reasons. There was a price to pay for keeping Forest's bankers happy. That was the bottom line.

Brian Clough was not immune to the pressures of the relegation dog-fight, although he worked hard trying to project a devil-may-care attitude. After one home game, I went to see him to seek permission for a few days' home leave. It was around 5.30 on a dark winter afternoon. His secretary took me up to the manager's office. Graham Taylor was sitting in the corridor outside what appeared to be an empty office. There was no light on. His secretary opened the door and beckoned me in. As I made to take a seat to await Clough's arrival – I assumed he was in the boardroom – a voice whispered from the corner: 'Roy, Roy, over here.' And there was one of the game's great managers sitting in a corner of the room.

'Is Taylor still out there?' he asked.

'Yes, Boss,' I replied. Raising a finger to his lips he urged me to be quiet.

'He wants to see me about Nigel [Clough], but I don't want to talk to him. Ron's told him I've gone home,' Clough whispered.

The scene was comical in one way, sad in another. Taylor was the England manager, a job Clough had coveted. Nigel was a contender for a place in the England side. I gathered that, after another disappointing Saturday afternoon, Clough couldn't be bothered with the kind of after-match shite talk football managers are obliged to engage in.

'Can I have a few days off, Boss?' I whispered.

'Of course you can. But leave by the other door, I'm staying in here until that fucker's gone.'

As I left Brian Clough cowering in his own office, I reflected on the toll football could take on one of its most combative characters.

My life away from football was a bit more relaxed now that I'd moved to Scarrington. I was less tempted by Nottingham nightlife, although I still enjoyed my Saturday-night outings with Des Walker. If avoiding temptations was the principal reason for living away from the city, the plan worked. Up to a point.

Shortly after settling into my new home, I discovered that

former Forest player and English international Ian Storey-Moore was the landlord of the village inn. So that became a regular haunt, trouble-free because the local people got to know me and treated me like a normal person rather than a football star.

The absence of normality was a depressing and persistent problem, worse now as my profile grew in the wake of transfer rumours and my new deal with Forest. The arrival of Sky Television and the Premier League had inflated more than salaries. After Gazza's tears at Italia '90 football was fashionable. More attention was focused on the game and, of course, on those of us who played it.

Except in the company of friends I remained on the quiet side. I disliked that goldfish-bowl existence intensely. Glad-handing, back-slapping and good fellowship was not my scene. It was false. There was an irony here. Bonhomie being an Irish characteristic, people expected me to be hail-fellow-well-met. When I failed to conform to the stereotype, trouble often ensued.

Shortly after I signed my new contract, Brian Clough sent us to Jersey for a few days' rest and recreation. The Jersey branch of the Irish Supporters' Club had asked me to bring a signed international shirt, which they wanted to auction. I brought the shirt with me and made an appointment to meet a guy who was to pick it up in our hotel. He never showed.

The plan for the trip was to do some light training in the morning and relax for the rest of the day. Some of the lads headed for the golf course; others, including Des Walker and me, headed for a bar. On the second day, Des and I enjoyed a long afternoon session before heading back to the hotel for dinner. In the hotel we met Liam O'Kane, the first team coach, Archie Gemmill and Alan Hill, Forest's chief scout. In the far corner of the lounge a large group were celebrating. They turned out to be a ladies hockey team and their husbands.

A lady approached. 'Are you Roy Keane?' she inquired.

'Yes.'

'Would you like to contribute to our charity auction?' she went on. 'We're auctioning off famous people's underwear, signed by them.'

'I'm sorry,' I replied, 'but I've got a signed Irish international shirt upstairs, I'll get that for you.'

'It's got to be underwear,' she insisted.

'I'm sorry I can't help you, but you can have the Irish shirt,' I suggested.

'An Irish shirt,' she sneered. 'Who wants an Irish shirt?'

Des and the coaching staff were enjoying my discomfort.

Without any warning she then threw her gin and tonic straight into my face. I was stunned and embarrassed. When I recovered my composure, such as it was, for I was 'well-on' myself, the hockey player was making her way back to her company. I picked up my pint of lager, went over to her table and poured the drink over her head. Next thing, her husband and I were on the floor, exchanging blows.

Stuart Pearce took me upstairs to my room. When Brian Clough arrived in Jersey the following morning he ordered me back to Nottingham. He accepted that I had been pro-voked but insisted I shouldn't have retaliated. And he fined me £5,000, a week's wages.

Forest's survival in the Premier League now depended on our last two games. Defeat at home to Sheffield United or away to Ipswich would mean we were down. The fact that my contract allowed me to leave if the club was relegated didn't cause me to lessen my efforts to ensure that Forest survived. On the contrary. Somebody at the club had leaked the news about my escape clause to the press. This led some people to question my commitment to the relegation battle. So I had something to prove in the final two games.

As we prepared for the Sheffield United game, Brian Clough announced that he was resigning at the end of the season. There had been speculation about his future for months, yet I was still shocked and a little dismayed by the news. There was no sign of Clough after he made his resignation statement. At first, nobody paid attention to this, because he would often be out of sight — if not mind — for a day or two. But when Friday came and passed without a visit from the manager, we began to wonder what was up.

When we reported to the City Ground at lunchtime on Saturday, Clough's absence, and the possible reasons for it, caused much comment in the dressing room. At two o'clock there was still no sign of him. When we went out for our warm-up, the tension round the stadium was obvious. For Forest fans no less than players there was much resting on the ninety minutes ahead. Failure to beat Sheffield United could see us out of the Premier League. And that was a bitter pill to swallow for a club that had been champions of Europe not so long ago. We'd finished eighth in the First Division and reached two Wembley finals less than twelve months ago. Now the club — and the players — were fighting to remain in the Premier League elite. The conventional wisdom then — which time has shown to be accurate — was that once out of the Premier League, deprived of the television money on which top clubs now depended, there was probably no way back for a club like Forest.

For players like Des Walker, Stuart Pearce and Nigel Clough, life outside the top division had serious career implications. I felt particularly sorry for Pearce, whose commitment to Forest ran deep. A year previously he'd turned down a move to Manchester United; now he was staring relegation in the face.

Returning to the dressing room twenty minutes before kick-off, we expected to encounter the manager. Even the usually unflappable Stuart Pearce was concerned: 'Where the fuck's the gaffer?' Liam O'Kane didn't have to remind us about what was at stake. As we were walking down the tunnel at five to three, Brian Clough suddenly appeared. He approached from the pitch-end of the tunnel, wearing his sheepskin coat, a pair of wellies, carrying a shovel. And whistling! I think the point he wished to make was that this was just another game. 'Don't worry, lads. I'm not worried.' Bizarre. Pure Clough.

Sadly, on this occasion the trick didn't work. Sheffield United beat us 2-0. Acutely aware of the price of failure, too many of our players froze on the day.

We were, in theory, too good to go down. But somehow the energy and belief that Brian Clough at his best had instilled in his teams had been sucked out of the club. Distracted by things that had no bearing on team affairs, at odds with the Forest board and the shareholders, tired from years of inspiring this relatively small club to punch way above its weight, Brian Clough was now experiencing failure for the first time in his illustrious career. Those in the Forest dressing room who'd muttered about him being 'gone' were now proved right. As always in dressing rooms, the last thing people did was look at themselves and accept responsibility for their own failings.

Within minutes of losing their Premier League status, some of the players were cracking jokes in the showers. I couldn't believe it. Their careers were on the slide and here they were wondering which restaurant to go to tonight! My own reaction was a mixture of guilt and hurt. Subsequently, Frank Clark, who would succeed Brian Clough as Forest manager, stated that 'It's a tribute to Roy Keane's professionalism that he played his heart out to keep Forest in the Premier League.' He was wrong. If it testified to anything, it was to my sense of self-preservation.

And a few weeks later Forest fans voted me Player of the Year, an honour that Stuart Pearce had won for the previous two seasons. I took some consolation from the fact that Forest fans accepted that, despite my contractual arrangements, my commitment to the relegation battle had been genuine.

During a difficult season the most important lesson I learned was that football didn't owe anybody a living. Nobody believed that Brian Clough's side could be relegated. Now even a player as gifted and professional as Stuart Pearce would find himself outside the Premier League. Was football therefore a cruel game? Well, it could be if you dropped your guard, dropped your standards even 5 per cent, started to believe that because you had talent you were 'too good to go down'. There was no shortage of talent in our Forest team. Yet we were gone.

Football wasn't a cruel game. The idea that it was was just a cop-out. Things, good and bad, happened for a reason. In the end, luck evened itself out, therefore you could argue that the League table didn't lie. In that sense football was far from cruel. In fact, it was just, for you generally got what you deserved.

I had no time to dwell on the consequences of relegation, for me or for the club, because Ireland had important World Cup qualifiers to play before the season ended. The qualifying campaign was going well. Spain, Denmark, the European champions, and Northern Ireland were our most serious opponents in a group where Albania, Lithuania and Latvia made up the numbers.

We'd held both Denmark and Spain to 0-0 draws away from home and beaten Northern Ireland 3-0 at Lansdowne Road. USA '94 was now a realistic target, with Denmark and Spain at home and Northern Ireland away being the key qualification games.

The way Jack Charlton approached the game made us difficult to beat away from home. We dug in, scrapped for every ball and pressed our opponents all over the pitch when they had possession. Opponents unfamiliar with the English game didn't relish the constant harassment. Our style didn't change much at Lansdowne Road, where, roared on by a passionate crowd, we played at a pace few visiting sides were comfortable with.

For the more sophisticated European footballers visiting Lansdowne Road, it wasn't just our primitive style that bemused – or terrified – them. Lansdowne Road was a rugby pitch and played like one, particularly when the wear and tear of a rugby season left the pitch bare and rutted. This made the fluent pass-and-move football game favoured by the better sides difficult, if not impossible, to play. It suited Charlton down to the ground. The more difficult it was to control the ball on Lansdowne's poor surface, the more time we had to get our tackles in and regain possession.

The game against Denmark was a fairly typical Lansdowne affair, except that the Danes were made of sterner stuff than some of the more gifted visiting sides. They were up for a battle, although Michael Laudrup, their best footballer, looked distinctly uneasy under the kind of pressure he was subjected to. Fifteen minutes from the end we were a goal down. Then Niall Quinn got on the end of a cross to head an equalizer. It was a scrappy game on a bad pitch, but the point secured kept Ireland's World Cup hopes alive. I contributed little more than effort.

My relationship with Charlton was virtually non-existent. He treated me more or less the same as all the other players. We weren't so much footballers with individual contributions to make as foot soldiers carrying out orders. To describe us as pawns on a chessboard would be unfair – to the game of chess. There was nothing complicated about the style Charlton imposed on his Irish team. If the football he insisted on compared to any board game, draughts, rather than chess, would be the game!

On a personal level Charlton could be OK, when it suited him. He'd allow the lads out for a few drinks when it was appropriate, and he could take a joke against himself when in a certain mood.

The success of the Irish team, which had never reached the final tournament stage of a major championship before he became manager, meant that he was a national hero. And Jack loved that. The extent to which he bought into the glory, and used it to strengthen his own hand in dealing with the media as well as the players, left me cold.

The Charlton myth suggested he was a coaching genius who'd transformed the fortunes of 'the Irish', an expression I felt he frequently used to imply that 'the Irish' were little people who'd learned all we knew about football from him. And Maurice! The view from the dressing room did not support the Charlton myth. The preparation for games was haphazard, the tactics no more sophisticated than those Graham Taylor favoured at Watford and England.

A number of factors combined to make Charlton's achievements look greater than they actually were. For a start, Ireland expected very little. Unlike the English, who demanded not just qualification for major championships but results in the main event itself, 'the Irish' were content just to be there. So Charlton was never subjected to the kind of pressure Bobby Robson or Graham Taylor experienced. This despite the fact that the squad he took over when he got the Irish job was arguably more gifted than its English equivalent. Great players like Paul McGrath, Mark Lawrenson, Liam Brady, David O'Leary and Ronnie Whelan would have been regarded as huge assets in an English squad. Others – Steve Staunton, Ray Houghton, John Aldridge and Frank Stapleton – played for top English clubs. Despite the presence of such talented players in his squad, Charlton adopted a style of play that suited him. It was his crude convictions about football rather than the gifts of his players that determined the way Ireland would play.

To be fair to Charlton, he had achieved some decent results and had taken Ireland to the quarter-finals of Italia '90, which was statistically a historic achievement. But sometimes statistics can lie. An inferior English team reached the semi-finals of that tournament before losing out to the Germans in a penalty shoot-out (Stuart Pearce blasting his penalty over the bar). And the 1990 World Cup final between West Germany and Argentina was the worst final in living memory. It was a sub-standard tournament with no outstanding team and few players of real stature.

Such football considerations made no impact on 'the Irish' or on the Charlton legend. The Irish Taoiseach Charles Haughey flew to Rome for the quarter-final against Italy, and after Ireland's 1–0 defeat accompanied 'Big Jack' on a lap of honour around the Olympic Stadium. Half a million people lined the streets of Dublin to welcome home the hero and his team.

In 1990 I was a fan, of kinds, watching the games on television in The Templeacre. Like many Irish football people I had mixed feelings about Charlton's team. It was nice to see Ireland surviving at Italia '90, but the football was less than inspiring. To the public at large, most of whom wouldn't know a football from an egg-timer, the quality of the football wasn't an issue. Little Ireland was playing against the great nations of the world; just being at Italia '90 was enough. Himself was God. The media, politicians and the public hung on his every word. And when he told 'the Irish' that he loved us, the nation swooned with delight.

It would be wrong to say that Charlton was disliked in the dressing room. Footballers are pragmatists. You play for the manager you have. This is especially true at international level, where for most players being in the team is the main objective. In the Irish dressing room I found a group of good players who were quite willing to play the game Charlton's way, even if the style was not made to measure for their talents. Behind his back, eyebrows were raised and knowing looks exchanged when he set out his tactical stall. We couldn't influence him, so we got on with it. Charlton was so wrapped up in himself that he frequently forgot players' names. That became a joke. On the plus side, he never slagged any of us off in public. He was also sympathetic and protective if anybody stepped out of line, as Paul McGrath discovered on a couple of occasions.

In measuring Jack Charlton the only comparison I could make was with Brian Clough. Where Clough was astute and capable of detailed analysis, Charlton merely blustered, was short on detail, long on generalizations to do with 'putting them under pressure' and 'getting tight' on your man. Unlike Clough, who placed immense trust in the ability of his players, Charlton appeared terrified that players would do their own thing. 'Play it as you see it' was Clough's motto. 'Play it as I see it' was Charlton's.

Maurice Setters used to clap his hands and cry 'Come on now' as we were leaving the dressing room.

After the Denmark game, Ireland had three more World Cup qualifiers – away to Albania, Latvia and Lithuania. However, with the escape clause in my contract now in play, I was more concerned about the next stage of my club career than with my international obligations. I knew Blackburn Rovers wanted to sign me, but would they break the British transfer record to do so?

Did I want to sign for Blackburn? Kenny Dalglish had Jack Walker's money, but Blackburn was a relatively small club. Other clubs such as Arsenal and Liverpool were said to be interested. Would they come in for me? Uncertainty about the future played on my mind. I wasn't sure about my next move, though I knew that if I was bought for the kind of money being talked about, I would be committing myself to a new club for three or four years.

Now that Clough was leaving, I was even more determined to activate the escape clause in my contract. I was still being approached by agents; still I resisted, although I knew I would need some guidance negotiating a deal with Blackburn or any other club who might want to sign me.

David O'Leary was one of the senior players in the Irish squad. David had been a casualty of Charlton's kick-and-rush philosophy, in which classy centre-halves were regarded as a dangerous indulgence. He viewed Charlton much as I did – as a bit of a joke. One evening I asked David who represented him. He told me that all his deals were negotiated by Michael Kennedy, a property lawyer based in London. David would be happy to introduce me to Michael if I wanted.

I also approached the Professional Footballers' Association about representing me in any future deal. Concerned about the growing influence of agents, the PFA had just declared that they were available to assist players in transfer talks.

It wasn't merely the fees they charged that made me hostile to agents. From what I had observed, it was clear that players' footballing fortunes were not agents' prime consideration. The more a player moved around, the more money his agent made. An unsettled player, especially one who was coveted by other clubs, was a potential source of income for his agent. One of the things that unsettled footballers was the transfer rumour mill, which – fed by agents – provided copy for the Sunday newspapers. In this speculative game footballers were pawns, bemused by newspapers seeking stories and agents intent on making money. Determined that nobody was going to manipulate me in this fashion, I settled for the PFA. Michael Kennedy was the other option.

Frank Clark was appointed to succeed Brian Clough. Clark was a former Forest player, regarded as officer material. When I returned from international duty, I went to see Clark. I assured him that, despite the nature of my contract, I'd be fully committed to the club as long as I was there. Clark told me that he understood my position. Without saying as much, he also left the impression that, if any Premier League club was prepared to pay the right fee, Forest wouldn't stand in my way if I wanted to move. We had an understanding. I thought. Now it was up to Blackburn.

Within days of that meeting Frank Clark told the newspapers that he was determined to keep me at Forest. The club was doing everything it could to persuade me to stay and fulfil my ambitions at the City Ground. We were back in the public relations business. According to Clark, he and

I were engaged in 'urgent talks' to secure my future at Forest!

I kept my head down and waited. While I resented Clark's manoeuvring, I accepted that he had a job to do. Playing to the gallery, the Forest fans, through the media was part of the game. He had made no effort to make me stay at Forest, but if he played his cards right the club would end up with £3m plus and some sympathy. There's more to management than picking the team!

Kenny Dalglish moved quickly. After some haggling, a fee of £4m was agreed. I was given permission to talk to Blackburn. Brendan Batson of the PFA accompanied me to the negotiations. I was entitled to a £600,000 payment from Forest according to the terms of my contract with them. The main issue in my discussions with Blackburn was wages.

I'd heard that Alan Shearer was on £500,000 a year, so that's what I demanded. After some bargaining, I accepted their offer of £400,000 a year. A deal was agreed late on Friday afternoon. Dalglish was a huge figure in the game. A great player, he'd also been successful in management with Liverpool. Jack Walker had promised Dalglish an open chequebook to build a Premier League-winning side. Dalglish assured me that if I signed I'd be part of a trophy-winning team. His obvious intelligence and cool persona impressed me.

Terms agreed, I was ready to sign the contract. But when Dalglish phoned Ewood Park, the office staff had left for the weekend. Don't worry, he said, you can sign the forms on Monday. We shook hands.

I went home to Cork for the weekend. On Saturday news of my transfer to Blackburn made the newspapers. The fee set a new British record. Life had changed quite dramatically in the three years since I'd left. Yet, happily, my family and friends remained constant. That nothing changed in this regard was deeply satisfying to me.

With Denis and Johnson I hit the town on Saturday night to celebrate my move. We started at The Templeacre before moving on to the city, where the night ended at Sidetrax. Somewhere along the way we had our kebabs, although I was determined not to put on an extra stone before returning for pre-season training at Blackburn.

On Sunday I woke up with a hangover. I was due back in Blackburn the following day to sign forms. After that I was looking forward to a holiday.

At lunchtime the phone rang. Pat took the call. It was Alex Ferguson. My family were Manchester United daft. 'Roy, it's Alex Ferguson,' Pat shouted. I thought he was winding me up.

He wasn't.

'Roy, it's Alex Ferguson here. Have you signed any forms?'

'No, but I shook hands on the deal, and I'm due to sign the forms tomorrow.'

'Why don't you come to Manchester and have a chat with me before you do anything?'

Wow! Manchester United. The Premier League champions. My mam and dad, Hilary and my brothers are all standing in the hall looking at me. Like they're in shock.

'Yes, but I have agreed the deal,' I tell Ferguson.

'You've signed nothing. Come over for a chat.'

From that moment I was never going to sign for any other club. In my heart of hearts I knew I could never refuse to sign for the world's most famous football club. In my head I knew I had to stay cool. Don't appear too eager, I told myself.

Next morning – after a hectic night on the town – I flew to Manchester. Alex Ferguson met me at the airport. We drove to his home close by. Brian Kidd was there. After a meal and some general chat, Ferguson suggested we have a game of snooker. He was a useful player. I wasn't bad myself. But I thought it prudent to let him win.

I liked him straight away. For a man managing Manchester United, who'd just won the Premier League, he was unaffected, funny and reassuringly human. He was also clearly hungry for more trophies.

'Roy, Manchester United are going to dominate the domestic game with or without you. With you we can win in Europe,' he asserted. It was a persuasive argument. He was pushing at an open door. However, there were a few obstacles to overcome before a deal to join United could be done.

He asked who was representing me. I told him the PFA. He suggested that we wouldn't discuss terms right now. 'Leave that to me,' he urged. We agreed that I would tell Dalglish our deal was off. After that, I would have to sit tight while United dealt with Forest. It wouldn't be easy, Ferguson pointed out, but, he assured me, he would secure what both of us wanted in the end.

I phoned Kenny Dalglish to tell him that I'd changed my mind about joining Blackburn. He went crazy.

'What the fuck do you mean?'

I told him I'd talked to Alex Ferguson.

'We shook hands on a deal. You can't back out now,' he screamed.

'Look, I'm sorry, I really am,' I told him, 'but I've got my future to think about, I'm entitled to that.'

'You're entitled to nothing except the commitment you made to me on Friday.'

'I'm sorry, if you'd had the forms ready, I would have signed on Friday.'

'Nobody does this to me, nobody does this to Kenny

Dalglish. You're a wee bastard and you won't get away with this.' Kenny wasn't cool any longer.

I felt very uneasy about the situation. But I'd seen enough in my short time in professional football to know that honouring deals that were made was rarely a consideration for the various parties involved. Players screwed managers, managers screwed players – and were in turn screwed by directors – agents were despised for their skulduggery, yet clubs were happy to do business with those very same agents all the time. Here was Kenny Dalglish insisting that I honour a deal I hadn't signed. The same Kenny Dalglish who'd spent several months 'tapping' me up behind Brian Clough's back. The more he swore at me, the less my conscience bothered me.

The next call I received was from Frank Clark. Clark was publicly supposed to be doing everything he could to keep me, but privately he knew I was going and it was his job to get the best deal for Forest. 'What's going on, Roy?' he began. 'I've just had Kenny Dalglish on the phone. He says you've changed your mind.'

I confirmed that after talking to Alex Ferguson I had changed my mind. Clark had also received a call from Ferguson. Unlike Blackburn, who were going to pay £4m, Manchester United would only pay just over £3m. That was unacceptable to Forest, Clark declared. So he wanted me to sign for Dalglish in the interests of Forest. I explained that I had to do what I considered was best for my career.

This argument cut little ice with Clark. He made it clear that there would be no sale to United unless they matched Blackburn's fee. I insisted that United was the club I wanted to join. Stalemate. Until the situation was resolved I would remain a Forest player, which was, after all, what Clark had told fans he wanted!

I was going on holiday with Tony Loughlan, Gary Bowyer and Raymond Byrne, three young players I had played with at Forest, the following day. We were going to Cyprus for some sun. I spoke to Alex Ferguson again. He assured me that the choice was mine. It was up to me which club I joined. If I kept my nerve, everything would work out in the end. Keeping my nerve might mean starting the following season as a Forest player. I resolved to do as Ferguson suggested. Go on holiday and don't worry.

The next morning the phone range at 6.30. I thought something was wrong at home in Cork. It was Kenny Dalglish.

'You won't get away with this,' he began. 'Blackburn Rovers will sue you for every penny you've got.' He and Alex Ferguson had never got on and this more than anything appeared to be bugging him. He called me names. He repeated that nobody 'fucked' with Kenny Dalglish and 'got away with it'. I told him I was going on holiday, that the matter was closed as far as I was concerned.

'Where are you going?' he inquired.

'Somewhere far away and sunny,' I replied.

'We'll find you and sue you,' he retorted. He didn't – and didn't.

I had a fabulous holiday with Tony, Gary and Raymond. No one in Cyprus knew or cared who we were, or who we thought we were. Happy, innocent days.

When I returned to Forest for pre-season training, Frank Clark was determined to apply real pressure. I was forced to train with the reserves and it was made clear that I would be punished for the 'crime' of rejecting Blackburn by being ostracized in every conceivable way. Clark declared me a non-person. Ferguson told me to keep my composure. This was a game of poker between United and Forest. United's latest offer of £3.5m fell half a million short of Blackburn's bid. If I kept my head, Forest were faced with a choice: £3.5m or an asset worth nothing, training with the reserve team.

In three seasons I'd played 154 games for Forest, scoring thirty-three goals from midfield. I'd cost £47,000. The club was due a profit of £3m. Were they happy? No. In their world players were lumps of human carcass, bought and sold like cattle. Thinking for yourself, or deciding – yourself – what was best for your career, was a crime. The newspapers, following Clark's lead, now described me as 'Rebel Roy'. It was OK for managers, directors and journalists to make career moves that suited them. Footballers must do what suited others. If you stood your ground, 'the game' became indignant. Ironically, the question posed was the same one I was used to hearing in the kebab shop in Cork: who does he think he is?

Two weeks into pre-season training, Forest blinked. Manchester United's bid of £3.75m was accepted. Now I had to negotiate my own deal with United. Their offer of £250,000 per year was £150,000 short of Blackburn's. Brendan Batson from the PFA couldn't force United any higher. I felt the gap was too big. Remembering my conversation with Dave O'Leary, I called Michael Kennedy.

Michael arrived in Manchester to deal with Martin Edwards. He managed to move United up to £350,000 a year. I was happy to sign. A thousand pounds a week was a small price to pay to be a Manchester United player. I loved Old Trafford from the moment I set foot inside it.

5

The size of my transfer fee caused much comment in the media. Nowadays £3.75m is peanuts; in 1993 it seemed a huge sum. Even for Manchester United, the new Premier League champions. Some newspapers referred to a bad omen: three previous Forest players who'd cost United substantial sums had done badly at Old Trafford. The move from small club to big had proved too much for Peter Davenport, Garry Birtles and Neil Webb.

I was conscious of being Britain's most expensive player but not overawed by it. I was convinced that playing with top players would improve my game. My only major concern when I arrived in Manchester was getting in the side!

The day after I signed we were due to fly out to South Africa for a ten-day pre-season tour. I suggested to Alex Ferguson that I stay behind to work on my fitness. But he insisted that I travel. Having only trained with the reserves at Forest – sometimes on my own – I felt I was short of work.

'Don't worry,' Ferguson assured me, 'the training and matches will get you fit and the trip will allow you to get to know the lads,' he insisted.

Looking around the coach on the way to Manchester airport the thing that struck me most was the maturity and confidence of the United players. At Forest Stuart Pearce stood out, a man among boys. Here was a team of men. Bryan Robson, Eric Cantona, Steve Bruce, Gary Pallister, Paul Ince, Peter Schmeichel, Brian McClair, Denis Irwin and Mark Hughes.

All imposing characters, seasoned professionals. Strong men oozing self-belief. I felt young. I was young, a couple of weeks short of my twenty-second birthday. Task number one, I reminded myself, was getting in the team.

The second thing that struck me about United was the buzz created wherever the team showed up. That first morning leaving for the airport I glimpsed what it meant to be a Manchester United player. On a weekday morning Old Trafford was a hive of activity. People queued for future match tickets. The souvenir shop was crowded. Tourists posed for pictures with the stadium – which seemed vast – as a backdrop. Tourists from all over the world – Irish, Chinese, Americans, Londoners, men and women, young and old. Many just standing in the forecourt of Old Trafford gazing at the Munich memorial clock. I was staring too! This place was big. And full of history, the clock reminding all who stood beneath it of the Munich air crash in which eight of Matt Busby's great young team died. As I would discover, even the greatest players, the most hardened professionals, would never be indifferent to, or immune from, the history of the club. Living with the demands imposed by the history was a constant challenge, the constant challenge of being a Manchester United player.

At Manchester airport a crowd gathered to see us board the plane. When we arrived in Johannesburg several hundred people and a couple of television crews were waiting. At our hotel the buzz remained in the air, staff and guests stopping everything to have a peep at the famous Manchester United players. Stepping into this was like walking into a movie. Lights, action, stars. And of course crowd scenes. I played dumb and took it all in. Manchester United was clearly more than a football club.

As I knew Denis Irwin from the Irish squad, I roomed with him. He was also from Cork, albeit from the wrong side of the city. Neither of us were big talkers. Denis was quiet, intelligent, composed, sensible. I was quiet. We got on well.

We trained harder than I'd ever trained before. Brian Kidd took the training sessions. Kiddo had been a top player, a member of the 1968 European Cup-winning team. The players clearly respected him. He was also liked. A Mancunian with a droll sense of humour, Kidd was human and approachable. The training was interesting, the routine varied from day to day. There was always a sense of purpose to the work, a good footballing reason for the little games and drills we worked on. This was very different from the often idle hours spent on the training ground at Forest.

With so many strong characters in the squad it's perhaps not surprising that there was an edge, a sharp edge, to most of what we did. The five-a-side games at the end of every training session were serious. They often started out light-heartedly before becoming a bit heavy. A tough tackle could be the trigger for all-out war. Someone would start taking the piss; next thing, Brian Kidd would have to step in to stop a fight.

I didn't make a very impressive start. During the first week I hardly got a kick in five-a-sides. All I did was run, working hard to close the gap between myself and the amazingly gifted players around me. Eric Cantona was obviously brilliant. So too was Ryan Giggs. Ryan was two years younger than me, but in terms of ability and maturity light years ahead. He was a real character, funny, cheeky, blessed with extraordinary talent, which he used to devastating effect to take the piss on the training ground.

Although shy and a little intimidated by the levels of skill my new team-mates possessed, I loved the atmosphere around the squad. Before we kicked a ball in anger I could see why United were champions: a team of top players; immaculate preparation on the training ground; the inspirational presence of Alex Ferguson; Brian Kidd's potent blend of football knowledge and earthy humour that kept everyone's feet on the ground; not least, it seemed to me, everyone was happy.

Whingeing wasn't an option here. The demoralization that hung around the dressing room at Forest, the moaning and groaning, the loser-talk that sapped so many spirits at the City Ground was noticeable by its absence. What was there to moan about? These players believed that they were playing for the best club in the world. Ferguson and Kidd were respected, their authority unquestioned. Bryan Robson, the club captain, was the man in the dressing room, but there was never any question of him deciding what day we should have off!

Robson and Steve Bruce took care to make me feel part of things on our pre-season trip. This was important for me for any number of reasons, not the least of them being that, like many other players, I had always tried to raise my game a gear or two against Manchester United. In my case that had often meant steaming into rash tackles. I'd had my run-ins with Robson, Gary Pallister and Paul Ince. A memorable clash also with Peter Schmeichel. But there was no bad vibe now. In fact, although I didn't know it at the time, Ferguson had consulted some of the senior players about potential new signings in the off-season after winning the championship. A number of them had vouched for me when the manager indicated his interest.

If United had a team of Stuart Pearces, the squad also had a few Des Walkers. After the hard training-ground work – and a couple of friendly games – there was time to play. And these men knew how to play. Led by Robson, we enjoyed a couple of spectacular 'sessions' in South Africa. There was nothing furtive about our after-park activity. Ferguson and Kidd had no problem with the idea of players having a few drinks.

That was how we bonded. Discovering that there was a serious drinking subculture at United was delightfully reassuring. 'Work hard, play hard' being my motto, I felt relieved to find myself among kindred spirits. If initially I struggled in the five-a-sides, I wasn't found wanting in the drinking stakes. At least in that respect I felt I belonged by the time we left to return home to Manchester.

The Charity Shield game against Arsenal at Wembley was my first competitive appearance for Manchester United. As Bryan Robson wasn't 100 per cent fit, I partnered Paul Ince in midfield. Although the result didn't really matter, the game was important for me. I wanted to prove myself, to get the question 'Is he worth the £3.75m?' off the agenda as soon as possible. I was also acutely aware that Bryan Robson, Paul Ince and myself were scrapping for two midfield places.

Despite there being nothing at stake, there was a brisk competitive edge to this game. Arsenal were a tough professional proposition. A typical George Graham side, they gave nothing away, fighting for every ball, in every area of the pitch. Anything you got you earned. At the end of the Charity Shield we'd earned a 1-1 draw. We won the penalty shoot-out. If I doubted the quality of English soccer at this level – I didn't as it happens – the two goals scored in this game left no room for doubt. Mark Hughes gave us the lead with a spectacular volley. Ian Wright's equalizer was equally impressive.

I felt I played no better than OK. I knew that OK wouldn't do. Hard work and goals were the target I'd set for myself. I knew I'd get through the work; the goals I hoped would follow.

We played away to Norwich in the first Premier League game of the season. Ryan Giggs and Bryan Robson scored in a comfortable 2-0 win. I made a contribution – crossing for Giggs's opening goal. Three days later I played my first serious match at Old Trafford. On a Tuesday evening the atmosphere was incredible. I'd played at Old Trafford before, but against this crowd. Now I was playing for them. Sheffield United were our opponents.

The occasion inspired me. I felt sharp and focused. Eric Cantona was injured, so Bryan Robson, Paul Ince and I played in midfield. Andrei Kanchelskis and Ryan Giggs played on the flanks, with Mark Hughes up front. With Robson and Ince anchoring midfield, I had a licence to get forward. On some days everything clicks in, and this was one of them for me. I scored my first goal for United when I gambled on a forward run to latch on to a ball that glanced off Ryan Giggs's head. I timed the run perfectly and the finish was relatively simple.

Sometimes the man above looks after you. It was a perfect start, the one I'd dreamed of making. The kind of forward run that produced this chance requires timing and luck. You might make the same run fifty times and never receive the ball. Or receive the ball and miss.

Fate, which I believe in, was on my side that night. I scored a second goal and Mark Hughes got another to give us a handy 3-0 victory. From that night on the burden of being the game's most expensive player eased. Soon it ceased to matter.

We remained unbeaten in our first six League games, winning five, before losing 1-0 at Chelsea. It was a good start but Europe, the big challenge, loomed on the Wednesday after the Chelsea defeat. The Hungarian champions Honved were our opponents, the first leg of the tie away in Budapest. I scored two more goals, Eric Cantona another, in a 3-2 win. Honved weren't the strongest, but a win is a win, especially away from home.

Bryan Robson was increasingly afflicted by injuries, so for many of the early-season games I partnered Paul Ince in midfield. We were similar in some respects, neither of us lost many fifty-fifty challenges, and we were both well up for it if anyone tried to intimidate us. In fact a lot of teams were beaten before they left the dressing room, not just at Old Trafford but at their own grounds. The Manchester United aura was powerful, the reality was pretty potent too.

In our first seven League games that season we conceded only four goals. Peter Schmeichel dominated the eighteen-yard box. Steve Bruce and Gary Pallister gave nothing away. Paul Parker and Denis Irwin could both defend and be comfortable on the ball. Between myself, Ince and Robson we weren't going to lose many midfield battles. And in attack we had pace on both wings with Giggs and Kanchelskis. Mark Hughes held the ball up superbly and scored freely. Eric Cantona completed the package.

Cantona had arrived half-way through the previous season, when, after twenty-six years without a championship, Manchester were desperately seeking the Premier League title. He did the business, providing that extra bit of composure in big games and nine goals that secured Alex Ferguson his first championship. United got Eric for a song – £1.2m – when he fell out with Howard Wilkinson at Leeds. He'd had numerous clubs but had never settled, found a new home. He wouldn't conform, did things his own way, appeared as if he didn't give a fuck.

I was curious about Eric when I joined United. The Cantona enigma was the talk of the game, especially after

United won the title. I liked him immediately. Sure, he was different. He tended to do his own thing in training, an indulgence Alex Ferguson and Brian Kidd permitted. He had his own warm-up routine and stayed out practising his finishing after the five-a-side. Eric also had a fierce temper which sometimes flared up on the training ground. He and Peter Schmeichel in particular frequently found themselves at odds. Fists were raised on one or two occasions.

Behind the enigma Eric was a great pro, very serious about his football and immensely knowledgeable about the game. Collar turned up, back straight, chest stuck out, he glided into the arena as if he owned the fucking place. Any arena, but nowhere more effectively than Old Trafford. This was his stage. He loved it, the crowd loved him.

The players loved him too, for many reasons. Most importantly he got the job done. His finishing was deadly. He didn't exactly put himself about when we were working to win the ball back. Often we'd give him a bollocking for not tracking back. We certainly did more than our share of running for him. Then, just when exasperation was being felt – and expressed – Eric would produce a bit of magic to turn the game our way. He'd seize half a chance, and bang, it was in the back of the net. I'd never seen anyone finish like him. (I still haven't.) On the field Eric played his part. He was different, but bloody brilliant. Not just for the match-winning goals. You could give him the ball in any situation, and he could hold it up – he was a strong bastard – and return the perfectly weighted pass. He made as many goals as he scored.

Off the field Eric played his role to perfection. I'm not surprised he's turned to acting. Cast as the brooding, temperamental prima donna, the man apart, Eric was in reality one of the lads. To strangers he projected the enigma – that was his game, especially with the media. Faced with questions from fans or journalists, Eric shrugged his shoulders and pretended not to understand.

He spoke good English. His command of the language was particularly impressive when it came to swearing. In private he was funny, loved a drink, champagne rather than Heineken, and was great company. Eric was a good lad, one of the best, no real conceit, no bullshit. The eccentric loner was his public mask. Part of what he wanted – professionally – to be.

By the end of October we were well top of the Premier League by a wide margin. I wasn't entirely happy with my performances. One reason which I kept to myself was a recurring hamstring strain that was niggling away at me. I'd always been prepared to play through injuries for pretty selfish reasons: I didn't want to lose my place in any side by missing games. I'd played a Wembley Cup final for Forest with a dodgy ankle.

At United that consideration was more relevant than ever. Despite scoring my share of goals, I was still fighting with Bryan Robson and Paul Ince for a midfield place. I was under no illusion about our eleven-point lead in the League table being down to me. What I was certain of after three months was that this United team was very good and would get better. I wasn't the only first team squad-member conscious of the fact that the club's 1992 and 1993 Youth Cup-winning squads contained several young players who would soon be pushing for places in the side. Young players such as Gary and Phil Neville, David Beckham, Nicky Butt and Paul Scholes were already being talked about around Old Trafford. Time would prove that this speculation was far from idle.

As Alex Ferguson made clear to me when I signed for United, success in Europe was a priority for the club. Europe had been the source of triumph and tragedy for United. They were the first English club to compete in the European Cup, defying the Football Association to do so. Sir Matt Busby realized his dream in 1968, when Manchester United won the European Cup. But the Munich air crash of 1958, when eight United players died, left an indelible mark on the club. European nights at Old Trafford were therefore incredibly emotional occasions.

When we faced Galatasaray, the Turkish champions, in the second round of the European Cup, our excellent start to the season counted for nothing. This was the real test. Over the two legs we failed. After taking a two-goal lead at home, we conceded three. The game ended 3–3, which on the away goals rule gave the Turks a massive advantage. We would have to win away in Istanbul before a crowd notorious for its hostility.

Galatasaray were tough and wily. They pulled every stroke in the book – diving, time-wasting, badgering the referee. With only a draw required, they played it tight, defying every attempt we made to break them down. The game ended scoreless. It had been rough, nasty at times, and at the end all hell broke loose. Eric was sent off. In the tunnel on the way back to the dressing room Bryan Robson was hit on the head by a policeman who was laying into everyone around him. Eric got involved in hand-to-hand combat.

In the dressing room Eric went crazy. While the rest of us just wanted to get out of there, he was determined to go back outside to sort out the rogue cop who'd been wielding his truncheon. Eric was a big, strong lad. He was serious. He insisted he was going out to kill 'that fucker'. It took the combined efforts of the manager, Brian Kidd and a few of the players to restrain him. Normally I wouldn't have backed off a fight, but even I wasn't up for this one. There were a lot of Turks out there! Anyway, the result wouldn't change. We were out.

In early November I played in my first Manchester derby at Maine Road. City had hauled themselves up to a mid-table position in the League after a poor start. But League position and reputations went out the window for derby games. This was a big game, especially for United fans. Failure would condemn them to months of scorn and piss-taking around the city. Victory would provide a shield – and ammunition – for battles fought in shops, factories, offices and pubs over the coming weeks. United and City fans hated each other. For obvious reasons, City fans' bitterness appeared to run deeper. Badly run by a board, a succession of boards, more concerned with feuding and sacking managers than winning football matches, Manchester City enjoyed nothing like United's glamorous international renown. Yet, their fans argued, City was *the* club in Manchester, appealing more to true Mancunians than United, with its wealth and cosmopolitan vibe.

Historically, it was fair to argue that City were Manchester's big club. Before the Second World War and the arrival of Matt Busby in 1945 United was just another football club. For a brief spell in the 1970s Joe Mercer and Malcolm Allison had restored City's glory. But that brief revival apart, United had been top dogs for much of the modern era.

To mark our elimination by Galatasaray, City's fans showered us with hundreds of Turkish Delights when we went out on the field for our warm-up. The game began in typical fashion. The pace was frantic, wild tackles flying in all over the place. City steamed into us, urged on by their supporters, who were, it seemed, even more desperate for a result than the players. They caught us unprepared. Used to controlling the pace of the game away from home, we were unable to withstand the burst of energy hurled at us in the first forty-five minutes. I missed a great chance at 0-0. Then bang, bang, we were two goals down. The half-time whistle was welcome.

The gaffer had warned us that this would happen if we didn't match them for effort from the start. Class doesn't count if you don't win the physical battle first. Taking the field for the second half, we knew exactly what we had to do. First, start winning the tackles, matching them for effort in every individual battle. Then your class will kick in. Although he had a reputation for throwing cups of tea around the dressing room – and sometimes he did – Alex Ferguson was a much more clinical analyst than this stereotype suggested. On this occasion his final half-time words were simple: match them for effort, score a goal, and it's a different game. Win the second half.

We did. Eric got us back in the game early in the second half. A half-chance, buried. After twenty minutes City were gone. They'd blown themselves out in the first half. At 1-2 I knew we'd win. Ninety minutes is a long time. Two-nil is a dangerous lead. If you defend it by dropping back, by losing the inclination to push forward in support of the ball – if you change the things that secured the lead in the first place – the tide turns against you. Contests lasting ninety minutes ebb and flow. Each situation demands a fresh response. You've got to know when to push, when to hold. When to slow the tempo, when to quicken it.

At Maine Road that day it was our understanding of these things – as well as our ability to deliver in practice what we knew in theory – that won the game. Bruce, Cantona, Irwin, Hughes, Ince, Pallister all had an instinctive feel for the ebb and flow of games like this. The idea of 'winners' is casually bandied about in football: 'I'm a winner.' What the fuck does that mean? Anybody can utter the words. The top pros actually prove it. And, as I was only now fully appreciating, the professional character of the team I was now part of was what made them champions. Bryan Robson epitomized the qualities that champions possessed. But he wasn't playing against City. Still, we had enough elsewhere, more than enough, to get the job done.

Eric scored a second goal. Then we knew the three points were there for the taking. There was never a chance that we would settle for getting out of jail with a draw. Another critical point had been reached in the match. Many teams would have settled. Again, experience told us that settling for a point would be the wrong call. With City hanging on, this was the moment to kill them off.

We pushed forward, faced with only nominal resistance. They were going through the motions, most of them anyway. Denis Irwin broke down the left. I started moving forward from midfield. Two things now decided the outcome of this derby game: the quality of Denis's cross and the timing of my run into City's penalty area. Go too soon and I'd either be offside or ahead of the ball. Go too late and I wouldn't reach the cross. If it came at all. You might make a dozen forward runs like this in a game without the ball arriving. Other runs would count for nothing because you got your timing wrong. The point was to keep making the runs. That was my game.

The cross was perfect. Far post, in behind City's defenders, whose concentration had drained away. This time my gamble paid off. The ball dropped in my path and I put it away on the half-volley. I'd earned my corn for another week. Scoring the winning goal, I was temporarily the hero. But the truth was, as it always is in football, that this was a real team effort.

Our victory was the product of any number of things, the single most important factor being the combined experience of the manager and the senior pros in the side, who knew exactly how to approach the task we faced at half-time. We also had the ability to do the job. Manchester City had neither the ability nor the experience. It was men against boys. So we didn't get carried away.

In almost every respect Manchester United was a young player's dream. With such superb professionals, every training session was a challenge and an opportunity to learn. Learning, for example, what real attitude was as opposed to mouthing off and posing. Men like Bruce, Robson, Cantona and Gary Pallister didn't talk big-time, they just got on with it. Paul Ince, 'the guvnor', talked the talk, but he could walk the walk and was never found wanting when the heat was turned up in the big games.

Incey was a character – and a rival – but I got on well with him. He was always in the thick of the banter when we had a few drinks. Peter Schmeichel was a poser. He fancied himself in a big way and played to the crowd. It was all about him. All the finger-pointing and gestures of frustration were designed to convey a message to the fans: look at me, how much longer can I go on performing miracles to save this team! This was an act, mostly, but we didn't really mind, mostly, because his pose was part of what he had to do to gee himself up. To be fair, he did the business. He was as good a goalkeeper as anybody in the world. That, rather than the antics, was what mattered. The fannying-around was a small price to pay.

Even though he was struggling for fitness and in and out of the side Bryan Robson was the main man in the dressing room. He was respected to the point of awe by every other player. Much of this was down to his achievements as a player. On the pitch he was a fantastic warrior, tackling, scoring, defending, great in the air, comfortable on the ball. His courage in the face of injury or any other adversity was bottomless. He and the gaffer and Brian Kidd were close, the bond between them obvious. When Alex Ferguson had struggled in his early years at Old Trafford, Robson had fought like a lion to drive the team forward. He had been a great player for England as well as United. Yet there was no conceit, not a trace, in his behaviour. His enjoyment of life was as evident as his strength of character. He could drink as hard as he trained and played. He was clever and very funny. His zest for life was what made him a great player and a great companion in a drinking session.

As the club captain Robson was the players' shop steward. The gaffer consulted him on most matters concerning the players. Training, travel arrangements, any of the many little things that, if not attended to, might grow to become a problem. Mutual respect was the key to the relationships between Ferguson and Robson – and Robson and the other players.

From my first day at the club Bryan was brilliant with me. I was shy and intense, struggling quietly to come to terms with so many changes in my life – in and out of football – that the odd word of acknowledgement or praise meant a lot.

After the derby game I returned to Dublin to join the Irish squad for the crucial final World Cup qualifying game away to Northern Ireland. Having beaten us 3-1 in Dublin in October, Spain were favourites to qualify. Second place would be decided between Ireland and Denmark. If the Danes beat Spain in their final game – in Spain – they would secure second place in the group. In the more likely event of Denmark losing, we were through if we avoided defeat in Belfast. As we'd beaten Northern Ireland comfortably, 3-0, in Dublin the task we faced didn't seem impossible.

By this time I think it's fair to say I had mixed feelings about playing for Ireland. I relished the ninety minutes of football when match day came, but the rest of it left me cold. Of all the set-ups I'd been part of, going back to Rockmount AFC, through Cobh Ramblers and Forest, the Irish international camp was by far the worst organized. From training facilities to the training itself, travel arrangements, the kit we trained in, medical facilities – you name it, the Football Association of Ireland got it wrong. Finding something as basic as a tracksuit was a problem. If you were lucky, you might end up with an XL top and a small-size pair of tracksuit bottoms. Or vice versa.

Coming back to this shambles from a professional club in England was a shock. Coming from Manchester United, where Alex Ferguson ensured that every detail was attended to with meticulous care, deepened my sense of frustration. Worse than the shambolic preparation was that perverse sense of pride everyone appeared to feel in the fact that the Irish did things 'differently'. Unlike the international teams we were competing against, we could be ill prepared and unprofessional and boast about it!

Nobody seemed to enjoy telling anecdotes about the eccentric FAI set-up more than Jack Charlton. Such tales were a feature of his after-dinner routine, when he'd have the audience rolling in the aisles. Naturally he was the hero of the story, because he conjured great performances out of the team against the odds. While all this was meant affectionately, frankly it was bollocks. Wasn't it his job as manager – as it was Alex Ferguson's at Old Trafford – to make sure the players were properly prepared for football at the highest level? If we did things properly, it would enhance our prospects by 5 or 10 per cent. And that small margin would make a big difference. He didn't seem to care; on the contrary, the 'charming' 'Irish' caricature – doing everything arseways – was grist to his mill.

Faced with yet another duff hotel, rutted training ground, uncomfortable plane journey – sitting down the back beside the fans and journalists, while Jack and the officials enjoyed business class – the absence of decent training kit, or something as simple as strapping for your ankles, confronted by the customary shambles, players would smile wryly, shrug their shoulders and get on with it. Sure, weren't we doing all right. Hadn't Jack – 'Big Jack' – produced the miracle of qualification for Euro '88 and Italia '90?

For most of the Irish players an international week was a welcome break from their everyday existence with their clubs. Playing international football boosted your reputation, added to your value in the transfer market. You'd turn up on Sunday, renew old acquaintances over a session on Sunday night, arse around on the training ground on Monday, do a bit of shopping on Tuesday afternoon and, if the game was in Dublin, meet the family and old friends to talk about the good old days.

It wasn't so much that the coming game was irrelevant, more that there was no real sense of purpose in the atmosphere, no urgency, no feeling that Wednesday's game was the sole reason you were there. Focus on the business only began in earnest on match day. By then we'd endured two days of Maurice Setters on the training ground. I felt Maurice didn't have a clue – his sessions never measured up to what I was used to week in, week out. Jack, sometimes wearing ordinary shoes, would look on until it was time to talk about tactics.

That speech never varied. Preparation for the crucial World Cup qualifier in Belfast was par for the course.

The Troubles provided an added dimension to this important game. Northern Ireland's bitter sectarian divide afflicted football as much as any other aspect of life in the North. Windsor Park, where we were due to play, was the home of Linfield Football Club. Like Rangers in Scotland, Linfield was a Protestant club. For the first time in its history Linfield had recently signed a Catholic, a decision that caused great controversy. The player, who was also black, another major problem for Linfield's bigoted supporters, didn't last long. (Nor did the manager who signed him.)

Windsor Park was, and remains, a no-go area for Catholics, unless travelling in numbers to support a Catholic club. In 1993 no Catholic had managed the Northern Ireland team, although many of their most renowned players were Catholics. For all kinds of reasons to do with ancient hatreds, few Catholic Nationalists supported the Northern Ireland international side. Instead, they pledged allegiance to the team they considered their own: the Republic of Ireland. Many Northern Catholics travelled to Lansdowne Road to support the Republic.

Not surprisingly, the atmosphere in Windsor Park was loaded. Wondering why the BBC had decided to send war correspondent Kate Adie to cover the match, we soon discovered the reason. Hate-fuelled chants about 'Fenian scum' and 'Teague [Catholic] bastards' greeted us when we took the field. The English-born members of our party looked bewildered. Knowing little of the history, lads like Andy Townsend, John Aldridge, Tony Cascarino and Alan McLoughlin were puzzled.

'What's all this about, Roy?' Andy wondered.

'How long have you got?' I replied, with a laugh.

What was striking was that the bile wasn't merely flowing from the terraces. The crowd in the main stand were just as ugly.

The Northern Ireland team had rolled over at Lansdowne Road. Now they were up for it in a big way. I think the strange atmosphere may have broken some of our players' concentration and the level of resistance offered by the Northern lads surprised me. They really didn't want us to qualify. There was nothing much in the game for them, except thwarting our World Cup aspirations. With that objective in mind, they really had a go, and, after seventy-three minutes, Jimmy Quinn put them in the lead.

Luckily, three minutes later, Alan McLoughlin transformed the game with a fantastic strike from outside the box. A corner from the right was cleared. Alan took it on the volley, the 'keeper never had a chance. We hung on, lifted by the news that Spain were in front against Denmark.

We were through to USA '94. I was pleased, of course, to be going to the World Cup finals but, as the champagne flowed in the dressing room, and the party continued on our jubilant midnight flight back to Dublin, I felt slightly detached from the mood around me.

My reservations about Charlton and Setters, the lousy preparations, our primitive way of playing the game, all the bullshitting and backslapping that accompanied this achievement caused me to hold back. I wasn't plugged in to this scene. We'd got the right result despite doing almost everything wrong. I couldn't just forget it all and join the party.

Unless things changed dramatically we'd be found out at the World Cup finals.

6

When I signed for United I lived in the Four Seasons hotel near Manchester airport. It was a temporary arrangement while I searched for a flat or a house. This was a lonely existence. Apart from training and matches there was nothing to do. At least one day a week I'd drive over to Nottingham, where I still had a house and my old friends. But most of my time was spent eating room service meals while watching television. As I was now 'Britain's most expensive footballer' and a 'Manchester United star', eating in the hotel restaurant was difficult.

I found it very difficult to cope with the kind of fame that accompanied my status as a footballer. You could describe this as the Greta Garbo syndrome. I wanted to be alone. Well, not quite as alone as I found myself during the early months in Manchester. Although I couldn't hack small talk and glad-handing, or casual invasion of my space, I actually ached for company at times. Just to go out for a drink or a meal. But the other United players, many of whom lived close by in Hale and Bowdon, had wives, families or girlfriends. So just as I didn't want my space invaded, I tried to stay out of other people's. Therein, perhaps, lies the foundation of the myth that's developed about me being a loner. Stupidity and pride meant that I would never dream of making the first move to initiate a friendship.

Every second weekend friends and family from Cork travelled over for United's games. I'd pick them up at the airport on Friday night, take them to their various hotels and then figure out how to get enough tickets to satisfy demand. Tickets! Every United player lived with the ticket nightmare. Mine was worse than most because of the size of the Keane family – very large – and the many friends, and friends of friends, who were Manchester United fanatics. Word had gone out in Cork: Roy won't let you down!

Desperate to live up to my reputation as the man who remembered old friends – and wouldn't let them down – I spent a significant segment of every week fretting about tickets. Here, Bryan Robson was the man. As club captain Bryan controlled the players' ticket allocation. Even more important were tickets for the players' lounge, the place to be after the game. I cultivated Robbo ruthlessly. He was brilliant. I don't think he ever let me down, however outrageous my demands.

We were entitled to four match tickets and two for the players' lounge. Bryan would give me six or seven when I pleaded that my entourage had 'travelled all the way from Cork'. Sometimes as many as fifteen made that journey. Most weeks I'd end up buying anywhere between ten and fifteen tickets to meet all demands. Problem solved? No. Offering a match ticket without a pass for the players' lounge was regarded as a slight . . . or worse. So back to Robbo. Any spare for the lounge? The players' lounge at Old Trafford is small – it holds about forty people in comfort. After one game I counted eighteen Keane family members and friends! Over time this problem would actually drive me crazy.

At the beginning I loved seeing familiar faces. After the game we'd all go out for a meal and a few drinks. They were as curious about my new life as I was anxious to remain close to those I'd known before I joined the circus!

Steve Bruce, second in rank only to Bryan Robson in the

dressing room, would sometimes join us. Steve sensed my loneliness in those early days. He was experienced enough to appreciate the difficulties a new player faced when joining United, especially a player who'd cost a lot of money and lived with the responsibility of delivery on high expectations from day one. The problems of loneliness, the burden of expectations, hotel life and adjusting to circumstances very different from those you are used to – on and off the field – can cause, and have caused, players to struggle at Manchester United or any other big club. Steve Bruce and Bryan Robson understood this, and in matters great (such as tickets!), or seemingly small, such as an invitation to have a drink or a meal, made the effort to help me settle in Manchester. I felt welcome, part of the club, useful and respected. Things that apparently had nothing to do with football were in fact very important. As a result of the kindness shown to me by Bruce and Robson I acquired more confidence, and a feeling of belonging, and that in turn fed into my performances for the club.

After a weekend spent drinking, eating and talking I'd be knackered on Monday morning.

'An Irish weekend, Roy?' the gaffer would ask me as I appeared on the training ground on Monday mornings obviously the worse for wear.

'Just a few friends and family,' I'd casually reply.

Alex Ferguson was hard and straight. He was also very human. And, if you had a problem, very considerate. Brian Kidd was another sympathetic presence. Kiddo would know if you'd been on the batter and often adjusted the training accordingly. 'I won't be too hard on you this morning.' Again something seemingly unimportant mattered greatly and I believe contributed enormously to our success on the field. In charge of a group of strong characters, Ferguson and Kidd, strong characters themselves, realized they weren't running a boy scout brigade. Boy scouts don't win trophies!

The gaffer was well aware that drinking sessions, serious ones, took place. In fact, as I quickly discovered, Alex Ferguson had a network of informants in the Manchester area who supplied him with information about the social behaviour of his players. Manchester was a village, you couldn't move without the gaffer finding out.

'Roy,' he'd beckon me over of a morning. 'Out last night?' he'd inquire.

'Yes, I went out for a few drinks.'

'What time did you get home?'

'I'm not sure, but it wasn't too late,' I'd say, chancing my arm.

'Not too late . . . didn't you get into a taxi at half two this morning in Deansgate?' Then he'd name the club and precisely what time you'd been dropped off at your front door . . . or, in my case, the Four Seasons.

I soon learned to put my hands up and tell the truth when confronted by the manager. Honesty was the best policy. Over the years this worked in my favour. I owned up when I was out of order and found that when some of the more lurid tabloid stories about my 'nights of shame' were published, most of them containing only a grain of truth, Alex Ferguson believed my version of events.

Drink and the so-called drinking culture at United was a touchy subject with the manager. It was well known that he'd lashed out at the drinking culture at Old Trafford during his difficult early years at the club. Part of the reason Paul McGrath and Norman Whiteside were sold was to make the point that excessive drinking wouldn't be tolerated.

Football is a very different game today. Now, what you eat and drink is carefully measured. Gatorade, fruit and pasta all come highly recommended. Foreign players and coaches, and the dieticians employed by all the top clubs, have convinced us of the need to look after ourselves. Speaking as a convert to this new order, I believe that the disciplines we now follow have led to significant improvement in our fitness levels and general performance. The English game has been transformed . . . for the better. No doubt about that. It scares me looking back at how we were in my early years at Old Trafford.

At the same time I have the fondest memories of that period. I was young, happy, playing for the best club in the country. This, I thought, was the life. After the initial loneliness of hotel life I began to get my bearings. I developed a routine that revolved around drink. After the game on Saturday the whole team would gather at the Four Seasons. For away games this was the pick-up point where players left their cars to join the team coach. After work the coach would drop us off at the hotel and the 'session' would begin in Mulligans, the Irish bar in the Four Seasons. Mulligans was the 'in' place back then. It was perfect for me – I only had to make the lift to get to bed!

The unusual thing about our squad at that time was that there were no cliques. It was rare for a player to go home without having a few drinks. Obviously in exceptional circumstances people had to go straight home, but generally it would be a brave man who declined to participate in our after-match 'session' without a good reason.

When the bar closed we'd move on to the night club which was also on the premises. It was three or four in the morning – sometimes later – before I got to bed.

(Now it's very different. The Four Seasons is still the meeting point for away trips. But when we get back it's straight into our cars and home to our families. The thought often crosses my mind that if I suggested to Becks or Laurent Blanc that we go into Mulligans for a 'session' they'd think that I'd gone mad!)

If United had a midweek game my socializing would end with a night out on Sunday. My Irish visitors gone home, the other players with their families, the loneliness of an English hotel on a Sunday was unbearable. Two local pubs, The Griffin and The Stanford, were my regular haunts. Sometimes I'd travel with Eric or Lee Sharpe, sometimes on my own.

Lee was single and a couple of years older than me. He'd been at United for a couple of seasons since signing from Torquay. Lee was an outstanding player. When not contending for Ryan Giggs's shirt in his natural position, wide on the left, Lee could fill in as a left back or wide on the right. He was a great, bubbly, happy-go-lucky character. He made me laugh . . . and he loved to live life in the fast lane. Lee was a major ladies' man. I've never seen anyone have the effect on women Lee did.

After The Griffin – or The Stanford – we could always find a pub for a late-night drink. Lee loved going into Manchester to hit the clubs, an option that appealed less to me. There was less chance of agro around Hale, Bowdon and Altrincham, where the sight of United players on the batter was not unusual. In the city-centre you were more likely to encounter hassle. You were also much more likely to be 'shopped' by one of the gaffer's 'contacts'.

Going out with Eric Cantona was always funny. Wherever he went he attracted attention. Even in The Griffin, where the regulars were accustomed to seeing anyone from George Best to Bryan Robson, Eric's enigmatic aura made an impact.

While projecting an image of aloofness, the brooding genius, which he did brilliantly, he was privately quite normal. Almost. He never carried money. Always drank champagne. I recall a great fuss at Manchester airport when he offered his gold card to pay for a packet of chewing gum! On a night out Eric loved to talk football. He was very knowledgeable and talked a lot about different tactics and fitness regimes in the European game.

If there was no midweek game I'd extend my social life to Monday, sometimes Tuesday. After training I'd go back to the Four Seasons, try to settle down in my room, grow restless and head for the pub. Robbo or Steve Bruce might be there; if not, I'd drink with one of the regulars, knowing that sooner or later a current or former United player would turn up. Instead of a meal I'd grab a pub sandwich before heading home at closing time. Maybe!

Looking back, I can't believe the way I lived in those days. Most of us in that United team saw nothing wrong with having a few drinks as long as you stopped three or four days before a game.

I felt fine and the season was going well. By the end of January United were sixteen points clear at the top of the Premier League. Blackburn were our nearest challengers with three games in hand. When we beat Norwich in the fourth round of the FA Cup and drew Wimbledon in the next round, people began to speculate about the League and Cup double. The Norwich cup-tie was televised live by the BBC. Eric and I got the goals in a 2-0 victory. Norwich came out fighting and the game quickly became a physical battle. As a team our attitude was simple. If the other side wanted to play football, that was fine. However, if they came out kicking, that was fine too. So when Norwich started coming in late, high and hard we matched them challenge for challenge, with a bit of interest for good measure. It's still the same in the Premiership. You've got to establish your credentials early on. You've got to let the opposition know that if it gets physical they'll lose. Bang, first tackle, is the most effective way to deliver the message.

At Norwich Eric kicked one of their players in the back as he lay on the ground. Several other battles were taking place all over the pitch. After the game Jimmy Hill and the other BBC pundits complained about our attitude. Retaliating was out of order, according to Hill and his pals. Of course, they weren't being kicked. When the gaffer was challenged about our attitude – Eric and I were singled out for special mention – he called Jimmy Hill 'a prat'. The papers had their headline for the following day.

Earlier that month Sir Matt Busby had died. We attended his funeral, along with all the great players from Manchester United's past. Standing in the church listening to the eulogies for Sir Matt sent a chill down my spine. It was a solemn occasion. Although it wasn't personal to me, I could appreciate the sense of loss felt by so many people at Old Trafford and around the city of Manchester. Because of Busby United stood for something that went beyond football. Busby had been a pioneer in his day, the first to place his faith in youth, the first to see the importance of European competition. I didn't have to look any further than my own family to understand the magic spell woven by the words Manchester United.

A couple of days later we played Everton at Old Trafford. A Scottish piper led the two teams out on to the pitch. During the one-minute silence the atmosphere was heavy with emotion. As a United player the history of the club was all around you every day. Always lurking in the back of your mind was the thought that this was like no other football club. There was a lot to live up to. Against Everton we failed miserably to concentrate on the job in hand. The occasion got to us. We played shite but won 1-0 thanks to a Ryan Giggs goal.

One night when we were having a drink, Bryan Robson and I fell into a conversation about football. We didn't always talk shop when we were out, but occasionally one or other of the players let loose about some football issue that was bugging him. The few drinks helped to lessen inhibitions. The thrust of what Robbo had to say to me was that, if I wanted to step up a level in the game, I would have to get more involved in the team's build-up play.

I still saw myself as a goalscoring midfield player, working box to box, tackling, closing people down, grafting to win the ball back. Offensively I believed I was at my most effective running on to the ball to finish moves such as the one that produced the winning goal at Maine Road. This left Paul Ince or Robson to drop deep to receive the ball from the back four, a responsibility which, in truth, I wasn't confident enough to take on. But Robson insisted this was something I had to do. Trust your own ability, was the message. He was right about me copping out of a task I wasn't sure I had the ability or vision to perform. I'd coped with the burden of my transfer fee but after six months at United, surrounded by so many gifted footballers, I still lacked confidence in possession of the ball.

Robson had missed a lot of games through injury. Sitting watching the team play, he'd identified my unwillingness to take responsibility on the ball. Don't leave it to Incey, Robson argued. Get involved in the build-up. That was an important conversation. I don't know if Alex Ferguson prompted Robbo to talk to me, but knowing now how the gaffer operates, it seems a real possibility.

As Blackburn began to close the gap, getting to within six points of us at the end of March, our disciplinary problems continued. Eric was sent off twice in three days – at Swindon for stamping on someone and then at Highbury against Arsenal.

Our FA Cup run continued with wins over Wimbledon and Charlton. We had what looked like a handy semi-final draw against Oldham. The League and Cup double was now a real possibility. Blackburn beat us 2-0 at Ewood Park to open up the championship race. Games against Dalglish's side were always hard and this one was no exception. Alan Shearer scored their goals. In our next two games we then beat Oldham 3-2 before losing 1-0 at Wimbledon.

During this run of games, particularly against the so-called lesser clubs such as Swindon, Oldham and Wimbledon, the reality of being a Manchester United player sank in. For most clubs the United game was the big game of the season. However badly things were going, victory over Manchester United was an end in itself. Grounds that would normally be only three-quarters full, if that, were packed for the United game. The home team's fans were geed up, the players responded, raising their game far above the norm. The old cliché about this being their Cup final was true in these circumstances. Therefore, every game we played demanded 100 per cent concentration, especially in the early stages.

I welcomed the added intensity of every United road game. There was no danger of becoming complacent and I felt this would help me become a better player. But the extra effort made by players from clubs like Norwich, Swindon, Crystal Palace, Oldham and Wimbledon usually led to trouble. Confronted by tackles that were high, late and sometimes crazy, our only option was to meet fire with fire. Eric, Incey, Mark Hughes and myself led the resistance. It was no coincidence that Eric had been sent off at Swindon and identified as the villain after the Norwich cup-tie. Taking him down a peg or two seemed to be objective number one for the opposition hard men. Perhaps part-time hard men would be a better description. For what really bugged us was the thought that these guys were out to make a name for themselves by sorting *us* out. Why the fuck didn't they put the effort in *every* week, then maybe they wouldn't be playing for fucking Norwich or Swindon. So there was no rolling over when faced with this stuff. Meet aggression with aggression, then ability would make the difference at the end of the day.

Criticism on television or elsewhere in the media didn't bother us. United was always a story, our virtues, like our failings, always exaggerated. Coming from the European game, Eric found the Premier League strange. The football was fast and physical, no time was allowed for strolling. 'They're fucking crazy, Roy,' Eric would complain.

At Easter, the decisive period in every Championship season, my personal circumstances improved dramatically when the woman I loved agreed to come to live with me in Manchester. Now she was coming to Manchester, my life outside of football was complete. It had real shape and purpose. Theresa was expecting our first baby, which was a wonderful incentive to grow up. Whether or not I was ready for that was another matter. Some evidence suggested not.

Feeling flush with recently acquired success, and the bonuses that went with it, I decided to treat myself to an expensive watch. Lee Sharpe was the man to see when looking for a good deal on clothes, cars, even watches. Lee always knew a man who'd see you right.

He took me to a select jeweller's in town. This is my mate Roy, he's looking for a watch. No problem, said Lee's pal as he produced a selection from beneath the counter where the unvoiced understanding hinted the good stuff was kept for special customers. The choice narrowed down to three, all nice, all fairly expensive but in my price range. Trying not to appear too concerned about price I nevertheless noted that one cost £2,000, another £1,800, the third £1,100. I was impressed when the jeweller suggested that the £1,100 watch was the one I should choose. Fair play to him, he'd earn less commission selling the least expensive of the three. Well done, Lee, I thought as I produced my credit card.

When Lee's pal returned with the receipt for my signature I felt sick, really sick. The bill was £11,000. I'd misread the price tag. Now, with pride at stake, I didn't bottle it. Not much! I bottled it in a big way. Instead of explaining that there had been an expensive mistake, I signed the receipt like a man. Outside the shop I confessed to Lee. Jesus, my dad's on the dole in Cork and I'm spending £11,000 on a fucking watch. Lee broke up laughing. OK, I begged, don't tell the lads. No Roy, no way, Lee assured me, I won't say a word. He told everyone, couldn't wait, and I couldn't blame him. The story kept the dressing room in good humour for days. How's that watch Roy, keeping time?

It took us two games to see off Oldham in the FA Cup semi-final. Chelsea, who'd beaten us twice in the League, would be our Cup final opponents. After losing 1-0 at Wimbledon, we didn't lose another League game, remaining unbeaten in our last six matches. The most important game was away to Leeds, where we won 2-0. Blackburn's challenge ended when they lost away to Coventry.

We drew 0-0 with Coventry at Old Trafford in our final League game of the season. For Bryan Robson this was an emotional occasion, his last game for Manchester United. Robbo was one of the great players of his generation, a legend at Old Trafford, as loved and respected as any of the great United players of the past. Of course, I remember that day because I won my first Championship medal, but more memorable in a way was the reception Bryan got from the Old Trafford crowd after we had received the Premier League trophy.

The United players, the manager and the staff were as moved by this occasion as the fans. For all of us Bryan Robson stood for everything that a professional footballer should be. He was close to being the complete player – tackling, scoring, passing, good in the air, up for every game, brave, a leader by example. He captained his country and his club, yet there was nothing big-time about Robbo, no bullshit. He was a huge influence on the United team I joined. In matters great and small, on and off the field, he set the tone. The senior players in any dressing room define the character of most teams. And the character of Alex Ferguson's first Championship-winning team was determined by Bryan Robson more than any other player. Now he was off to Middlesbrough as player-manager. He'd be a big loss to Alex Ferguson and the rest of us.

The following Sunday we beat Chelsea 4-0 at Wembley. Eric scored two penalties to put a gloss on a scoreline that flattered us a little. Winning the League and FA Cup double in my first season as a United player blew me away. I contributed, but I'm not sure how much. Since Bryan Robson had urged me to get more involved in the build-up, I'd dropped deeper to a more central midfield role, sharing that task with Paul Ince. I made fewer forward runs and as a result scored fewer goals in the second half of the season. Eight goals altogether, seven before the end of January.

The double was very much a team effort. (It would have been a treble but for losing to Aston Villa in the Coca-Cola Cup final.) Eric scored twenty-five goals, Mark Hughes twenty-one, Ryan Giggs seventeen. Andrei Kanchelskis scored ten times, Paul Ince nine, Lee Sharpe eleven. In the Premier League we conceded thirty-eight goals, less than one a game. The back four – Paul Parker, Steve Bruce, Gary Pallister and Denis Irwin – picked itself, each of the four of them being almost ever-present.

Looking back on the season, I felt my biggest achievement was establishing a regular place in the side. I was also relieved that the record £3.75m transfer fee was no longer an issue. Pleased but not carried away is probably the most accurate description of my mood as I headed off with Denis Irwin to play for Ireland in the World Cup finals in the United States.

Though the professional side of playing for Ireland left a lot to be desired, other aspects of the experience were fine. There was always a good vibe in the dressing room and around the training camp. In a perverse way the Carry On-style organization worked to create team spirit. Like a family gathering, a wedding party that all goes horribly wrong, everyone would decide to muck in together to make the best of a bad day. We didn't expect much and not much was expected from us. Certainly not by the Irish fans, who were fantastic and passionately supportive of their team – win or lose.

Setting out for USA '94 as a young player, I was happy just to be going to the World Cup finals. There was no pressure on me or the team. Qualifying was enough. The only challenge we were expected to meet was to avoid disgrace. Four years earlier a better Irish side had reached the quarter-finals of Italia '90 before losing 1-0 to the host nation. I'd watched on television and, like the whole country, marvelled at the team's achievement, if not at the football that was played.

Lansdowne Road was packed for our final warm-up game against the Czech Republic. We lost, but it didn't matter. We got a great send-off from the fans.

The Irish international experience was different from its English equivalent. England expected to win the World Cup. The players and the manager were the focus of media madness. Reputations were vastly inflated before reality and the inevitable recriminations set in.

I felt the only reputation inflated in Ireland was Jack Charlton's – 'Big Jack', our saviour! As a result he was much in demand for advertising, media work and after-dinner speaking. As coach he didn't impress me at all. I felt the preparation for Ireland games was a bit of a joke, and one shared by most of the players, especially those from the big clubs, where preparing properly was the norm. Although the joke was on us, nobody said a word. One of the reasons for this was that in every Irish squad there were several players who were well pleased to be playing international football at all. Why would they rock the boat? Why would anyone? It would make no difference. Big Jack didn't go in for the kind of consultation that Alex Ferguson did at Old Trafford.

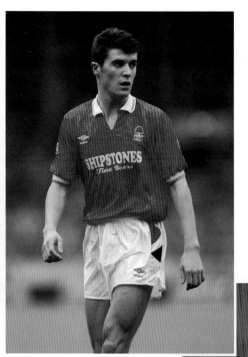

25. With Forest.

26. With Martin Edwards, Manchester United's chairman, signing for the club in summer 1993.

27. The new signing.

28. Playing in my debut game for United the following month.

29. Celebrating my first goal for United against Sheffield United.

30. Training with the Republic of Ireland squad as Jack Charlton looks on.

31. Playing Norway in the 1994 World Cup.

32. Holding off Maldini. Playing for Ireland against Italy in the 1994 World Cup at Giants Stadium, New York.

33. With my wife Theresa on a rare night out.

34. With my daughter Caragh, aged six months.

35. With Caragh and Shannon after winning the Premiership.

36. On holiday in Sardinia with son Aidan ...

37. ... who was then 8 months old.

38. Father's day at Old Trafford!

39. Shannon and Caragh share the spoils. With the FA Cup and Premiership trophies in 1999.

40. With Aidan, aged two, and the PFA Player of the Year trophy.

41. With the kids and the Premiership trophy again – this time with Aidan, who seems more interested in keeping a look-out for real celebrities.

As USA '94 would reveal, there was plenty to complain about, beginning at Dublin airport, where a large crowd gathered to see us off. If in other respects the contrast between the Irish and English approach favoured us in terms of preparation, our Carry On shambles was nothing to be proud of. After humping our luggage through the airport, we checked ourselves in for the special Aer Lingus flight carrying the team, supporters and journalists to the States. On the flight Jack and Maurice, the coaching staff and the FAI officials, and their wives, took their places in first class. We were back in economy class with the fans and the journalists. No space, no privacy, no respect. A small thing? Not really. Shouldn't the whole FAI party, players included, travel together? In first class?

Our opening World Cup game was against Italy in New York. Mexico and Norway were the other two countries in our group. To prepare us for the heat and humidity, our training camp was in Florida at Orlando. The facilities laid on by the Americans were perfect. But I thought the training put on by Maurice Setters was crap. I was used to the well-planned, always interesting and relevant routines put on by Brian Kidd. By comparison, Setters hadn't a clue. One of the keys to a proper training session is not to have players hanging around. Organizational skills are required, which Setters didn't appear to have. We hung around.

The one idea Big Jack and Setters had was to run the bollocks off us every day. The theory was that we'd get used to being knackered and therefore wouldn't wilt during games. The opposing theory, that we might conserve our energy in heat that we'd never encountered before, the idea that we might pass the ball and make the opposition do the running, never seemed to have occurred to Jack and Maurice. (To be fair to Charlton and Setters, I recently heard Johan Cruyff talking about the Dutch team making a similar mistake. But as Big Jack himself had played for England at the 1970 World Cup finals in the heat of Mexico, this was a mistake we really didn't have to make.)

After two or three days of duff training, morale was beginning to dip. One day Jack disappeared, leaving Setters in sole charge. The sun was blazing down. Even walking to the training ground you began to sweat heavily. He ran us into the ground. Then he set up an eleven-a-side game on the full pitch. This became a farce. Knackered, we didn't know whether to laugh or cry. Everyone was pissed off. Andy Townsend, the captain, told Setters we'd had enough. I'll tell you when you've had enough, was Setters's response. We just downed tools. Next thing, Andy walked off the pitch, followed by the rest of us. Mutiny.

The press were there, although at first I don't think they copped what was going on. Setters started shouting at nobody in particular. Andy repeated that we'd had enough. The news finally reached the media. 'Bust-Up in Irish Training Camp' was a hot story. 'Keane in Bust-Up in Irish Training Camp' was an untrue story. I'd simply followed the herd, although I completely supported the walk-out. I was mystified as to how my name came to feature in the story. When he finally returned, Jack called a team meeting to find out what had happened. Then he proposed a solution. Setters and *I* would hold a press conference to clear the air. 'Everything was fine' would be the message.

Instead of saying that *I* hadn't had a bust-up with Setters – that in fact it was skipper Andy Townsend acting on behalf of all the players who'd had the row – I went along with the party line. Good old Roy! Better Roy from Manchester United, controversial Roy, than Big Jack's captain, Andy

Townsend. *That* would reflect badly on Big Jack and Setters. I was a much more convenient patsy. Like a fool I played the role, the anger only rising in me when I walked into the glare of the television lights alongside 'my good friend and ace coach' Maurice Setters. Charlton was clever with the media. On this occasion his plan worked perfectly. I became the story. Nobody asked why *he* had been absent from training.

When we moved to New York for the Italy game, several players complained, quietly, about the size of our hotel rooms. Ray Houghton and John Aldridge, Liverpool players used to the best, joked that there wasn't enough space for them *and* their suitcases. The hotel wasn't the best, but to be honest I would have slept on the street to play in the World Cup finals. You want to test yourself against the best and in 1994 that meant playing in this tournament. (I think an argument can now be made that the knockout stage of the Champions League is a more severe test, with almost all the world's great players playing for top European clubs.)

Italy were many people's favourites to win the tournament. As well as their great defenders Maldini and Baresi, they had the class of Roberto Baggio up front and top players like Dino Baggio and Donadoni in midfield. Many had questioned the wisdom of staging the World Cup in the United States in mid-summer. FIFA were trying to convert Americans to soccer, it was said. Of course FIFA's sponsors were trying to sell their products in the States, which was a more realistic ambition. Any chance of selling soccer to the United States was seriously undermined by FIFA's decision to start most of the games at midday, when the heat was at its unbelievable worst. One thing was certain: this climate would not suit the kick-and-run style Charlton favoured. The only concession he made to the heat and humidity was to make sure we had a large supply of water on the touchline. Drink and run was our game plan.

Still, as always with an Irish team, our spirits were high. On the coach on the way to Giants Stadium we played our rebel songs, which told stories about English oppression and how our Irish heroes fought gallantly. And were shot. Or hanged. The English-born members of the party sang as lustily as the rest of us. Even Setters had a go at the choruses.

Thousands of Irish fans made the journey to America. We expected good support, but as New York had a large Italian-American community many times larger than its Irish equivalent, we expected support in Giants Stadium to split fifty-fifty at best. To our astonishment we were greeted by a stadium decorated wall-to-wall with Irish tricolours when we went out to warm up before the game. It is estimated that an incredible 50,000 Irish fans were in Giants Stadium that Saturday.

Boosted by their presence – it really was like a home crowd – and the inspiration provided by the U2 music that we always played in the dressing room, we took the field in good heart. Giants Stadium was like a furnace. I'd never experienced humidity like this. It was hard to breathe, never mind run.

The Italians began in their familiar cautious style. They were happy to pass the ball and make us work. There was very little shape to the game. But with Roberto Baggio in particular we knew that a moment's lapse in concentration might be costly. On the plus side, we had plenty of experience in our team. Packie Bonner from Italia '90, Denis Irwin, Steve Staunton, John Aldridge and Ray Houghton, Andy Townsend and Paul McGrath, who was then playing the best football of his career for Aston Villa.

As there was no early Italian storm to weather, we slowly got a grip on the game. Our passionate support helped, so did the Italians' obvious nervousness. Out of nothing Ray Houghton produced a goal. A long nothing ball was lumped into the Italian penalty area. Baresi, normally so cool, took a swing at the ball, which only reached Ray thirty yards from goal. Ray controlled it, moved five yards forward and struck it just off-centre. The Italian 'keeper, Pagliuca, had moved off his line anticipating a perfectly struck shot. But Ray had just miscued, and as the ball travelled through the air it dipped over Pagliuca's head and landed in the net. I've never quite figured out that goal. It didn't matter, though, they all count – this one big-time.

The Italians came after us, but in fits and starts and with no real conviction. We didn't exactly forget about the heat, but the combination of the goal, the rousing support and a feeling that the Italians didn't fancy it drove us on.

In the second half Italy got their act together for twenty-five minutes. It was backs to the wall. Packie made a couple of vital saves. I put myself about in front of the back four, paying special attention to Roberto Baggio, who was dropping off his markers. This was the kind of situation real players relish. A battle demanding as much of your mind and spirit as your ability to play. In fact, you can't make any distinction between ability to play and the capacity to meet a challenge such as the one the Italians now laid down. Man for man they were undoubtedly the better footballers. But this was a battle of wills. A footballing brain, able to spot the danger and nip it in the bud, and the desire to keep fighting, winning tackles, latching on to loose balls were the crucial qualities required.

Big Paul McGrath showed all the qualities demanded of us

for half an hour in Giants Stadium that day. For him the word big *is* appropriate. Known for his poise, his ability on the ball, his unique gift for reading the game, Paul displayed all those qualities on this day. One other huge asset was his courage. When the Italians did get sight of the goal, Paul presented a final, insurmountable obstacle. Paul inspired us as much as in the end he demoralized Roberto Baggio and the other Italian players.

Fifteen minutes from the final whistle they'd 'gone'. Jason McAteer came on for Ray Houghton and started running at Maldini. When Jason went for a fifty-fifty tackle with Maldini and came out with the ball, it was game over. We almost got a second goal when John Sheridan hit the crossbar late on.

It was an amazing match, a fantastic beginning to our World Cup. Interestingly, we played some good passing football in between bouts of serious defending. This sometimes happened on good days with Big Jack's Ireland. We'd throw out the game plan and do what came naturally to most of us. Just play the game the way we would for our clubs.

The Irish crowd were in great form after what was probably the best victory in our footballing history. They celebrated as if we'd won the World Cup. My family were there – the whole country was it seemed – and I was pleased for them. I felt good myself, I always did after games like that when I'd been forced to find reserves of energy and commitment it was always good to know were there. But I wasn't under any illusion about what we had done. We'd caught the Italians on a bad day – not the first country to do that – we hadn't won the World Cup. (Of course, Italy recovered, going on to contest the final against Brazil, where they lost when Roberto Baggio missed a penalty in the shoot-out.)

Ireland's World Cup ended that day in Giants Stadium. Beating Italy gave us a great opportunity to top our group and probably meet easier opposition in the tournament's second phase. Although people in our camp talked about this prospect, I don't think many really believed that we were at the World Cup finals for anything other than to make up the numbers and avoid disgrace. Now that we weren't going to be disgraced, we could relax and party. And that was more or less the mood as we travelled back to Florida for our second game against Mexico. No one was happier or more relieved than Jack Charlton. His stock among the Irish was higher than ever. He'd done it again. A large group of English journalists were now sent to cover 'the Irish miracle'. England having failed to qualify, their media sought the secret of Big Jack's success. In contrast to the way he treated many Irish journalists, he was always available to Fleet Street's finest. They were his mates, going back a long way. They wrote his legend up for the English papers. He obliged with the details of *his* success.

The heat in Florida was desperate, much worse than New York. The plan against Mexico involved bombarding the 'little Mexicans' with long balls. Get the ball back to Packie. His long punts deep into enemy territory would sort the Mexicans out. Then we would 'press them', run and scrap for every ball.

We never got a kick. The Mexicans were tough, coped easily with the missiles Packie launched in their direction, and generally played us off the park. They passed the ball, we ran. The temperature was 110 degrees. Our legs were gone. It took guts, which we didn't lack, to chase the game. Seven minutes from the end we pulled a goal back to leave the final score 2-1 to the Mexicans. John Aldridge's goal meant a draw would do against Norway in our last group game.

Back to New York. Our 0-0 draw against Norway may well have been the worst game in the history of the World Cup finals. After a run-in with officials in the previous game, Big Jack was banned from the touchline and watched the game from the ITV television gantry. Setters kept in touch with the national hero by walkie-talkie from the touchline. The Norwegians looked as knackered as us. There was never going to be a goal. That suited us.

Back to Florida. The travelling and the heat were now taking a serious toll on everyone. I wasn't the only player who was beginning to long for home. Arranging football matches to kick off at midday in the Florida heat was a bad joke. It suited television schedules, but it killed the players. Playing the kind of football Charlton wanted simply wasn't possible in these conditions. Nevertheless, he kept faith in himself.

Holland were our opponents. A true world-class team, with players like Dennis Bergkamp, Marc Overmars, Frank Rijkaard, Ronald Koeman and Frank De Boer. We adopted our usual approach against the Dutch. Back to Packie, who hoofed the ball forward to Tommy Coyne, our lone striker. Small for a striker, Tommy wasn't built for the task of getting on the end of Packie's punts.

Terry Phelan's mistake in the twelfth minute enabled Overmars to set up Bergkamp, who finished the job. One down against a team who loved to pass the ball, all we could do was run. It didn't have to be this way. Our midfield, with Andy Townsend, Ray Houghton, John Sheridan, myself and Steve Staunton, was well capable of playing a passing game. Gary Kelly, Phil Babb and Paul McGrath were well able to pass the ball from the back. Sadly, in the Charlton game plan that wasn't an option.

Just before half-time Wim Jonk finished us off when Packie

made a rare error when he failed to hold a speculative twenty-five-yard shot. Two-nil, time to pack our bags. Sure, we battled in the second half, but it was never anything other than a lost cause.

I felt that USA '94 exposed Charlton's crude approach to the game. There was no plan B, nothing. At half-time, when a real manager can earn his corn by adjusting the tactics to meet the demands of any given situation, the great man offered nothing. Except bluster. And even he had run out of bluster by half-time in the Dutch game. Outside, our fans were still singing. They deserved better than another gallant loser story. Which is exactly how our failure was reported to the travelling fans – and the people at home.

After the Holland game I was selected for the FIFA dope test. (I thought the travel arrangements and the midday kick-off *were* the FIFA dope test.) Because I was dehydrated, it took me a couple of hours to pass urine for the test. I was longing to get home to see Theresa and our baby Shannon, who'd been born a short while earlier. Please God, give me an injection and let me wake up in Cork. A tournament I'd looked forward to playing in, dreamed of since I was a kid, had been a bloody nightmare.

I eventually complied with the dope test. I returned to the dressing room to get my gear. It was deserted. The Irish party had fucked off without me. The hotel was a good few miles away. Thanks, Jack, I thought, as I stood outside the stadium trying to hitch a lift. A passing American took pity on me. When I arrived at the hotel the celebrations were well under way. I wasn't accustomed to celebrating failure but joined in anyway. A few drinks offered some consolation.

The news from home was that the nation was proud. The flags were out to honour the team that beat Italy in Giants

Stadium. The rest of USA '94 was wiped from memory. We returned as conquering heroes, Big Jack leading the parade. Struggling with the mother and father of hangovers, I vaguely recall the reception with the President in the Phoenix Park, and afterwards walking across the stage at the homecoming party. Although grateful to the people who turned out to demonstrate their support, I, like most of the other players, had had enough. There was nothing to celebrate. We'd achieved little. The whole thing was a fraud. But nobody was asking questions.

7

The 1994/95 season was regarded as a failure at Old Trafford. We finished second in the Premier League, a point behind Blackburn, and lost to Everton in the FA Cup final. We failed to progress beyond the group qualifying phase of the European Cup, which now had a new format and was known as the Champions League.

If my attitude to the Irish international set-up seems too critical, then the influence of working for Alex Ferguson at Manchester United explains where I was coming from. Forget the double, last season is history, this time it will be harder. This was the manager's message when we reported back for pre-season training. Success in Europe was of course the number-one challenge. To keep that target in our sights, we had to win the Championship. So the pressure was felt from day one. That was no bad thing. Knowing that as champions now for two successive seasons United were expected to win drove our standards higher. Too many people in the game complain about 'the pressures'. But if you want to win the big prizes you have to accept that there will be no free lunches between August and May. Every year. The more you achieve, for example the double, the more demands will be made on you. The more you strive to meet those demands, the better player you become. That's nice pressure. And, of course, the more success United have experienced over the years the more failure is despised and feared. By the players, the fans and most of all by Alex Ferguson. Any player under the illusion that his reputation

– or last season's trophies – offered some kind of guarantee of first team football soon found out that that was not the way things were at United. Season 1994/95 would prove that.

Although established in the side, I was by no means complacent or even particularly satisfied with myself. As the previous season had developed and I heeded Bryan Robson's advice to adopt a playmaker's role, I scored fewer goals. When I watch old games screened by MUTV, as I constantly do these days, I'm shocked by how ordinary I was in some of the games I felt I did well in at the time. I was nowhere near as fit as I should have been – my lifestyle was the reason – and my distribution of the ball lacked subtlety and imagination. Instinctively I knew this at the time . . . but I was in the best team in the country, which seemed to suggest that all was well. Even though, as the tapes of the old matches demonstrate, I had an awful lot to learn.

Another source of pressure in 1994/95 was the talent in the reserve team dressing room. United's Youth Cup final teams of 1992 and 1993 had been the talk of the club for a couple of years. Ryan Giggs graduated to the first team straight away. Others were now ready to join him. People within the club – and fans who followed the progress of the youth and reserve teams, real fans not prawn sandwich merchants – differed as to which of the young United players would go all the way.

Paul Scholes was a superb footballer, a beautiful passer of the ball, a free-scoring midfield player, a tough and resilient lad who never shirked a tackle. Nicky Butt was another touted for a big future. Another midfield player who could dig and play. And score goals. David Beckham was a Londoner – the rest were mostly local lads – who'd been a United fanatic all his life. Becks was a great striker of the ball who could play wide on the right or in midfield.

The Neville brothers, Gary and Phil, caused much argument about which of them was the better player. Gary was a very mature lad – nineteen going on ninety – who could play right back or central defence. Phil was more technically accomplished, able to play in either full back position. Keith Gillespie from Northern Ireland was a brilliant winger.

Sometimes there are doubts about whether gifted young players will train on. But we knew from the beginning that these guys would make it. They trained with the first team and never looked out of place. They were not only good footballers, they were very confident lads. As a group they were inseparable, hanging out together off the field, very obviously a unit when they played against us in the practice matches the gaffer used to sharpen us up from time to time. Those games were fiercely competitive. The tackles flew, the quality of the football was unbelievable. Both sides had something to prove. They were desperate to show that they were ready. We were just as keen to say – 'not yet'. To claim that the test provided by United's emerging reserves was much tougher than most of our Premier League opponents were capable of putting up to us is no exaggeration. The feeling that it was only a matter of time before the names of Beckham, Neville, Butt, Scholes and Gillespie would be on the first team sheet was soon borne out. The identity of the first team players who'd be out to make way for the youngsters remained a matter of speculation.

The first disappointment of the season came in the Champions League. Drawn in a group with Gothenburg, Galatasaray and Barcelona – with two clubs to qualify for the knockout stage – we failed to progress. Barcelona gave us a 4-0 hiding at the Nou Camp. The four goals conceded were crucial, meaning that Barcelona rather than us emerged from the group on goal difference. UEFA's rule that prevented more than three foreign-born (plus two 'assimilated') players from playing in Champions League games provided the manager with serious selection decisions in every tie. The manager was forced to choose from Peter Schmeichel, Eric Cantona, Andrei Kanchelskis, Denis Irwin and myself. Vital experience and ability had to be sacrificed to comply with UEFA rules.

Although the rule on foreign players didn't help, it didn't fully explain our failure. If we were forced to bench some talent, it was no more than was required of other competing clubs. There were two principal reasons for our initial failure to make an impression on Europe.

Firstly, our style of play was geared to the English game, where the pace was manic from start to finish, and lacked the subtlety and tactical fluency we commonly encountered in Europe. The European game was much more sophisticated and punishing than the Premier League. In domestic League games you could afford to be sloppy in attack – where, if you gave possession away, you'd quickly regain it – and in defence, where mistakes were not, as in Europe, severely punished.

The other and more insidious problem was habits, bad habits, acquired, week in, week out, as we began to dominate domestic competitions. Most weeks we didn't have to draw on all our reserves to win. At Old Trafford most visiting teams would throw the towel in at the first smell of defeat. They'd have a go for twenty minutes, but most visiting teams lacked real conviction, were only going through the motions. And even that stopped if we took the lead.

Away from home it was another matter. In front of the home fans the opposition would have a go, but except for places like Anfield, Highbury or Elland Road, or Ewood Park when Dalglish was there and Blackburn were riding high, you only had to stand and fight, and wait for the class of Eric, Ryan or Mark Hughes to kick in. The statistics of my first three seasons at United are revealing. While failing consistently in Europe, we lost only sixteen games out of 122 played in the Premier League. The truth was, and arguably still is, that domestic success came too easily. Relatively easy success breeds bad habits, and they are punished when you step up to meet other countries' champions.

Steve Bruce took over from Bryan Robson as club captain. He was the man I now courted for tickets. Getting tickets for home games was now a growing problem in my life. The Premier League was growing like a monster – a glorious monster, and an increasingly lucrative one for the players, agents, and Sky Television, whose dish sales boomed on the back of its football coverage. In return, Sky pumped more and more money into the game.

I signed my first major non-football commercial contract to sponsor Diadora boots at the beginning of the 1994/95 season. I was now earning more than I had ever dreamed of. Apart from Alex Ferguson, Michael Kennedy was the most important person in my life outside my family. Agents took substantial amounts of footballers' new wealth. In other ways, too, agents could unsettle players, whether it was tempting them to make unsuitable but lucrative (for the agent) moves, or hawking rumours of imminent transfers to newspapers to up the ante in negotiations with your own club. The middle-men were always at it, in some form or another. There were exceptions, but few. With Michael I was totally secure, knowing that his sole concern was what was best for my football. Money mattered to me, but was not the number-one priority. For Michael money didn't count at all. He was a football fan. Every time I tried to get him to send me a bill for his services, Michael fobbed me off. He asked only for match tickets, saying we'd settle 'the other business later'. (Ten years on, that's how things stand. It will be some bill when it finally appears!)

Getting Michael tickets was a pleasure. Naturally this was also the case for my family. However, the Keane family is large, the extended family infinite if the ticket demands are the measure of it. In relation to tickets for immediate and extended family, friends and friends of friends of friends, and people posing as friends, a pattern now developed that would torment me for several years to come. Early in the week of a home game requests for tickets ('one will do' was my favourite) were lodged. It would be a headache from Thursday onwards. The pressure on my family at home in Cork was worse. People would knock on the door of my parents' house asking if there was any chance. Such requests were hard to resist. It was a no-win situation. Saying no caused offence, and being what they were – decent obliging people – my mum and dad, Johnson, Denis, Pat and Hilary invariably said yes. Saying yes meant hassling me, which, of course, I knew was hard for my family. So I pretended it was no bother, no problem at all. Roy the people-pleaser always came up with the goods. By hook or by crook. Mostly in fact by buying around twenty tickets – sometimes more – for every home game. No problem! Good old Roy hadn't changed with all the success. He'd prove it even if it killed him.

In truth I wasn't at risk of anything worse than draining energy and emotion from my body – badly needed energy and emotion – in the twenty-four hours up to kick-off time every second weekend. After several years of coping with demands that grew in direct proportion to my willingness to meet them, this insane subtext to my life took its toll on my parents, both of whom fell seriously ill in the late 1990s. I believe that the insatiable demands made upon Mum and Dad by all and sundry caused them to get sick in the end.

I've stopped it now, but for many years I was a famous mug. There's no other word for it. For, not content with providing tickets, I'd also organize flights, book hotels and meet the visitors when they arrived at Manchester airport, often at different times. Friday night, when I should have been resting and focusing on the next day's game, was airport and hotel night. Looking around the club, I saw no other player doing this kind of thing. Maybe it was an Irish thing . . . although I rarely saw Denis Irwin in the same predicament. Sensible Denis, stupid Roy, I now concluded. But it took a long time for this particular penny to drop.

Two stories illustrate how daft I was in those years. A couple of years ago, I met a guy who greeted me like an old friend. He was from Cork. I didn't recognize him from Adam. So I was surprised when he informed me that he'd stayed overnight in my house in the mid-1990s. I'd been a wonderful host. I felt foolish and ashamed. Could I have inflicted this madness on Theresa? Answer, *yes*.

The second revealing story concerned a group of Denis Irwin's friends visiting from Cork. It was a midweek game. In the players' lounge after the match I was introduced by Denis. We had a few beers. Then the Cork lads suggested a trip around the Manchester nightlife. Denis demurred. He was going home to his wife and family. Roy couldn't say no. Off we went, me now playing host and nice guy to Denis's friends. *I* had a wife and family too. Sadly I was on one of the steepest learning curves in history. I eventually copped myself on. Now it's said I'm a loner. Perhaps some time alone with Theresa and my children was overdue.

Along with the so-called glory of being a Manchester United player there are facts of life such as outlined above that can complicate, even compromise, your career as a player. As the Premier League grew, so did the commercial spin-offs associated with it. Videos, books, sponsorship deals, media interview requests to promote the various commodities in the market place. The Manchester United shop was extended to a superstore, with a chain of similar outlets planned for the future.

Amidst all of this the dressing room and training ground were oases of sanity. The manager's focus and relentless drive were a constant reminder that winning trophies was the number-one priority. Alex Ferguson was first in every morning. He stayed as long as there was work to do. No detail was too small to grab his attention. He monitored every player, always looking for signs of diminished appetite, any slacking in training, any unsettling social habits. Nothing escaped his scrutiny. And it was generally acknowledged in the dressing room that the route to success, peace and prosperity was staying off the gaffer's radar screen. In what would prove to be a troubled season that feat eluded a number of players, three of whom would leave the club.

Failure in Europe meant that winning the Championship was a must. By Christmas we were motoring. We'd lost three of our first nine League games, then didn't lose for two months. After losing at home to Forest in mid-December, we went on a ten-game unbeaten run. Blackburn Rovers were the main contenders for our title. They were there or thereabouts all season. A 3-2 win at Stamford Bridge on Boxing Day morning saw us head the table briefly; then Rovers beat Manchester City at Maine Road to regain top spot by five o'clock that afternoon.

In early January the gaffer bought Andy Cole from New-castle in a £7m deal. Keith Gillespie went to Newcastle as part of the deal. Cole was a prolific goalscorer – for Newcastle. Scoring for United had proved more difficult for any number of top strikers over the years. If Andy could do that, the record transfer fee would be money well spent. Just over eighteen months after I cost £3.75m, transfer fees were rising fast. The Cole fee was almost twice what United had paid for me, and that graph would continue to rise steeply.

Eric and Andrei had been scoring consistently all season. Mark Hughes also chipped in. I'd scored a couple, but my original plan of scoring goals to justify my fee was out the window. Paul Scholes, Nicky Butt and Gary Neville were well on the way to establishing themselves in the first team. David Beckham was knocking on the door. They added a vital dimension to the side: commitment to the club where as footballers they were born and reared.

As transfer fees and wages went through the roof, loyalty became an even more valued asset. Three players in our dressing room were the subject of press speculation. Paul Ince was linked with a move to Italy. Andrei Kanchelskis and Mark Hughes were also periodically rumoured to want away. Andrei's situation was cause for all kinds of rumours, the most alarming concerning interest in him from the Russian mafia. I never knew the truth about this but my ticket problems paled in comparison!

One morning Brucey arrived in the dressing room with a cheque for fifteen grand. The first team squad had contributed to some video and this payment was due to be split eighteen ways. Struggling to work out who was owed what, we decided on a majority vote to hold a draw, winner takes all. The option of taking your cut – about £800 – was available. For the younger lads this was a couple of weeks' wages. They wanted the money. Only Paul Scholes and Nicky Butt opted to play for the jackpot – about twelve grand after the needy were paid out. When the draw was made, Eric Cantona's name came out of the hat. He got his cheque. And plenty of stick. Next morning Eric arrived in with two cheques made out to Paul and Nicky. This was their reward for taking the gamble, Eric explained. This was Eric to a tee. The unexpected, a touch of class, also an appreciation of the plight of two young lads more in need of money than himself. Twelve grand was a lot of money to spend on a gesture, even in those relatively prosperous times.

On the field Eric was really playing well. Against Blackburn at Old Trafford – obviously a six-pointer – he scored the winner. If we won the Premier League that season he'd break the record with four successive Championship wins – three with us, one with Leeds. He and Andy looked like forming a productive partnership. We'd certainly put pressure on Blackburn come Easter and the make-or-break games.

Crystal Palace away, a game we should be looking to win. We beat them easily, 3-0, at home, and the contest is over after Eric scores our first. The gaffer's selected me to play right back, which he's done a few times this year when Gary Neville was needed as central defender. That's fine, I'm in the team. It's a nothing match. No real flow to the game. Their effort cancels out our ability. We're not going to lose, it's just a question of waiting for a break. At 1-1 there's always hope that Eric in particular can steal a chance from nowhere.

But Eric's got involved with his marker, Richard Shaw. It's niggly stuff, not nasty. Shirt-pulling, obstruction, a bit of chat. Stuff you shouldn't bother about, but the purpose is to break your concentration – and with Eric, it can work. This time Palace get a result. Eric loses it and kicks Shaw. He's off.

The crowd goes mad. Selhurst Park is full for a change. Some of the things you hear from the terraces are really sickening. Racist taunts, chants about players' personal lives (Eric's suffered a lot from that), filth that makes you wonder about the people who come to football matches to sing obscene songs about the Munich air crash! What *is* this? Answer: English football.

As Eric walks off towards the dressing room, the game resumes. Ten men. Now it's a battle. No Eric. Suddenly there's commotion on the far touchline from where I am. Something's happened, we don't know what.

What happened will be endlessly replayed on television for weeks to come. Some looper has a go at Eric near the tunnel entrance. Eric doesn't react immediately. But he turns back and launches himself at his tormentor. Bruce Lee would have been proud of Eric's kung-fu kick. It's a good thing he wasn't wearing studs. Never did. Eric could have hurt himself quite badly, broken his fucking back. As it is, he ends up on his feet trading blows with the guy who wound him up.

The game over – a 1-1 draw – the dressing room is quiet. The directors, one of whom, Maurice Watkins, is the club solicitor, are in a huddle with the gaffer. Eric is just sitting there, head bowed. Police are outside in the corridor.

My immediate reaction was: so what? Fair fucking play to Eric. I might have done the same myself. When I got home and saw the television pictures I could see that it was a nasty incident. Out of order, of course. But my attitude didn't change. My heart went out to him. All the lads basically felt the same. We didn't pat him on the back and say well done, but Eric was a good lad and we weren't going to turn our backs on him now.

Obviously, it was serious for the club. The gaffer was pissed off. This was a big test for him, especially when the media got on the case. Ban him for life. Make him leave the country. The media had a field day. For weeks our training ground, The Cliff, was under siege. The gates were locked but they threw rope ladders over the wall to take photographs. Outside the dressing room Eric's story was a sensation. Inside it was a problem.

Eric held his hands up, got a good lawyer and paid his dues – community service, which he did immaculately with some local kids. The club had no choice but to ban him for the rest of the season. End of story. You get on with life.

We won eight of our next nine games, conceding only one League goal at Everton, where we lost 1-0. I scored a rare goal against Ipswich at Old Trafford. Nine-nil was the final score, with Andy getting five. Blackburn were also on a run, the Championship looked sure to go down to the wire.

The Cantona affair lingered on. He had yet to face the FA disciplinary committee and the courts on an assault charge. We were drawn to face Crystal Palace in the FA Cup semi-final. We didn't play well in the first game at Villa Park. Palace were long-ball specialists – the Jack Charlton method – which can be hard to play against, especially if it's combined with the effort Palace put in to try and keep us on the back foot. The shadow of Cantona was present, no doubt about it. That worked for them more than us. We finished 2-2 after extra-time.

I played centre-half alongside Gary Pallister because Steve Bruce was injured. Gary dealt with the aerial bombs, I picked up the runners and the bits and pieces. 'Pally' is amazing. A terrific pro. He looks knackered in the warm-up. You think, he'll never last ninety minutes. Yet he's always there at the end, attacking the ball, cool under fire, a good footballing brain. He and Brucey are huge for us. You never have to worry about soft goals. With Schmeichel they form the perfect defensive triangle – certainly, the way the game is played in the Premier League, where pumping in long balls is the first resort for many teams.

Manchester United are back on the front pages of the newspapers after this game. A row between United and Palace supporters outside a pub results in the death of a Crystal Palace fan. A tragedy for some family, a consequence of a game of football. Do we search our souls? The truthful answer is no.

Before the replay the manager, referring to this tragedy, and Eric's moment of madness, warns us to be careful. Behave yourselves. You know Palace are aggressive, don't get involved. That's easier said than done. Aggression is what we do. English football is aggressive, often against sides like Palace the assaults are naked, uninhibited, driven by fear. Desire perhaps. Fear, desire, it amounts to the same thing. Aggression must be met with aggression. Once you've made the point, that kicking us isn't going to work, *then* we can play. That's the harsh reality, as I discover before half-time. Darren Pitcher comes in and catches me hard. He's done my ankle. It hurts. I receive seven stitches from the doctor at half-time. The gaffer asks if I'm OK. Ryan Giggs has tweaked his hamstring. I'm struggling but I can manage. Let me see how it goes early on, I tell him. It's the Cup semi-final, I tell myself, get a grip. Desire? Fear? Madness? I don't know. Lose here and the season could slip away. That's the thought in the front of my mind. Got to keep the season going, get something back for all the work. Not be on that fucking coach on the motorway going home with nothing except what-might-have-beens.

If only? If only you'd made that tackle, covered that run,

passed instead of shooting, shot instead of passing? Every game you make scores of decisions. The mental side of the game, the really difficult hidden part of football. The easiest person to fool? Yourself. Fool yourself too often and you'll be out of Old Trafford. I can see it in others, little things in every game, a cop-out here, a cop-out there. I can feel it in myself. That urge to stay in the comfort zone, especially dangerous for a United player, where there's always the probability that some-one else will do the business for you.

After five minutes of the second half the gaffer asks if I'm OK. I'm not but I think I can run through the pain. Five more minutes? He agrees. Gareth Southgate's challenge is fair but he catches me right on the ankle bone, the ankle just stitched. Fuck you. I get up and stamp on him. Pain, anger, dismay. I know I'm out of the game. I know I'm wrong. 'What the fuck were you thinking of?' the gaffer asks after the game. I could only say sorry.

My first red card in English football added considerably to Alex Ferguson's troubles. Although we beat Palace 2-0, the result was overshadowed by another 'day of shame' for Manchester United. The papers urged the FA to make an example of me. The usual three-match ban for being sent off wouldn't do on this occasion. I had brought the game into disrepute, and should be charged accordingly. No mention of Darren Pitcher, or my ankle with its seven stitches. No recognition that it takes two to tango, and at Villa Park it was Crystal Palace not United that wanted to turn the game into a physical battle. At this stage everything was coloured by Eric's kung-fu kick and the club's reaction to it.

As well as being banned for the rest of the season, Eric was also fined two weeks' wages – £20,000, the maximum allowed. But Alex Ferguson resisted the pressure to sell Eric, or cancel his contract. The media – and not just the sports sections – were baying for blood. If the gaffer wouldn't do Eric, the media would do the gaffer. He demanded character from his players, now he demonstrated what character really was. He stuck to his beliefs, which the dressing room shared, that while Eric had been seriously out of order, he'd done nothing to warrant his career being ended.

Despite bollocking me in private, publicly Alex Ferguson stood by me, claiming that Southgate's challenge had been nasty (it hadn't). On the Friday after the game I joined the gaffer at a press conference. I apologized for the Villa Park incident. I also showed the journalists the damaged ankle. They didn't appear to be impressed.

The FA did not resist the clamour for my head. I was charged with bringing the game into disrepute. When I appeared before the disciplinary hearing in London, I received the statutory three-match ban and a £5,000 fine. United fined me a week's wages. At least I would be available for the FA Cup final. I'd required a hernia operation for a while and the suspension allowed me to have it.

The race for the Championship remained tight. We were unbeaten in our last eight League games. Blackburn appeared to be hanging on. Man. City beat them 3-2 on Easter Monday, a surprise defeat. But earlier in the day we'd dropped two vital points at home to Chelsea, when we could only draw 0-0, a game I missed thanks to what happened at Palace.

The Premier League title was decided on the last day of the season. If we won at West Ham, Blackburn would need three points at Anfield. With twenty minutes to go, both Blackburn and ourselves were 1-1. We pinned West Ham in their own half in the closing stages of the game. An incredible sequence of chances was created. One after the other chances were squandered. It wasn't our day, 1-1 being the final score. At Anfield Liverpool scored a winner in the final minutes. Blackburn had 'bottled' it, as the gaffer had insisted they would, but we failed to do our own business.

Everton beat us 1-0 in the Cup final.

If only Eric had kept his head at Selhurst Park. There's no doubt in my mind that with Eric we would have claimed our second double. Even without him, we might have done the job, had our energies not been sapped in the aftermath of the Cantona incident by the ceaseless controversy that followed.

8

Although this is my story, it is impossible to tell it as it truly is without constantly referring to the people and circumstances that shaped my world as a professional player. My most certain belief is that football is a team game. To be a great manager you need great players, at least great pros. To achieve things as a player you need to be playing for the right club at the right time, alongside other good players. So if readers feel that this is more Alex Ferguson's story than Roy Keane's, they are right. It *is* more Alex Ferguson's story than mine for it was – and remains – his decisions that determined our destinies as Manchester United players. Without a structure, a club, a team, the *right* set-up, neither Roy Keane, David Beckham, Eric Cantona nor any other 'star' would shine as brightly, if at all.

Most managers don't really manage at all. They pick the team, buy players, dictate tactics, placate the directors and court the media. Then they get the sack. Ferguson is different. He knows Manchester United from top to bottom; watches A team and reserve matches as keenly as the first team; will know as much about a youth team player, his habits, strengths and weaknesses, as about the first team players upon whom the club's success depends. For now. He is renowned for his attention to detail. But what does *that* mean?

It means everything that will impact on the club: where you were last night; what kind of company you're keeping; when to rest a player who's showing signs of tiredness on the training ground; when to throw a young player into the

Premiership, when an older player isn't doing it any longer; who to buy, who to sell; when to travel to away games; which hotel offers peace and quiet, with enough distraction to prevent the players getting bored; adjusting your diet; keeping tabs on the latest medical developments; dealing with the players' personal problems – sensitively; making sure that everything at Manchester United is geared to provide *his* players with maximum support so that they can concentrate on the thing that matters most in every football club – getting results. The scale of this operation at Old Trafford is immense. Examples abound, here's just one. Understanding the ever-growing pressures on United players and their families and how potentially disruptive those pressures can be, Ferguson last season ordered that a crèche be built at Old Trafford to enable wives and kids to attend home games in a comfortable family environment. An apparently small yet very important gesture which acknowledged the critical supportive role of wives and partners. A situation *managed*, improved.

Similarly, in matters more easily connected to football, the search for improvement was constant. Brian Kidd scoured Europe, visiting the top clubs in Spain and Italy and went to the French National Training Centre, seeking new and better ways to prepare for games. You only spend ninety or 180 minutes a week performing in public; the bulk of your work is done in private on the training ground. This is the work that counts. You find out all you need to know about a player, Monday to Friday in training. Here form can be lost or found. Confidence lost on Saturday afternoon can be regained on cold weekday mornings. The reverse is also true. One thing is certain: if the training is wrong, the results won't be right. Kiddo was superb at his job, which wasn't only to do with fitness routines or tactics.

Players' attitudes to training vary. I loved it, felt it was essential to prepare as if your life depended on it. I loved the graft and the banter, resenting only the boredom and bluster of the Irish sessions. Other players had different, perhaps no less valid, ideas. Some needed the charged atmosphere of match day to get geed up. Others worried in case they'd leave their performance on the training ground. And there were players who were just bad trainers. Kiddo's skill was to accommodate all the different types, to harness the varying moods to form some kind of collective purpose. This he accomplished without appearing to try. At The Cliff, and subsequently at Carrington, you knew that the coach and the manager had put as much thought into each day's training routine as they would for every game.

First in every morning, Alex Ferguson was always there. His presence was felt even when he was out of sight in his office. He'd come out on the prowl, laughing, joking, on his mobile phone. Yet always watching, looking for signs, good or bad, in players that were the object of his immediate concern. Two or three, or more, always were in the forefront of his mind. Who to leave out, who to put in? Who needed a kick up the arse? Who required a pat on the back?

Managing.

Managing the Eric Cantona affair, while dealing also with scores of other pressing matters, revealed almost everything you needed to know about the art of management and Alex Ferguson. Eric had committed a serious offence. The circumstances were unprecedented in football. No manager anywhere had ever faced a test such as this. So for starters you could throw away the textbooks on management techniques. Ferguson had only his instinct to guide him. Managing means making decisions and Ferguson's first decision, the one that would inform all his subsequent actions, was that although Eric was out of order, his offence did not merit a life sentence. Whatever punishment was meted out, Eric Cantona would remain a Manchester United player.

Eric had done more than any other player to deliver two Championships and a double for Ferguson. Loyalty being a cornerstone of the gaffer's character, he would defy everyone outside the club, rescue Eric's career and rehabilitate him. It was the right thing to do. Also it was hugely in Manchester United's interests to have Eric's talent at our disposal. In this hard game self-interest should never be discounted.

Faced with the nation's outrage, Eric fled to France. The manager followed and persuaded Eric that the problem could be solved. *Managed!*

This was a decisive moment for Manchester United football club. This was a decisive moment in my career, and is in my story. I don't believe any other football man would have demonstrated the skill, resolve and strength of character that Alex Ferguson did *managing* the Cantona affair. We were all to be major beneficiaries of the result Ferguson achieved. All of us, that is, who met the standards Ferguson set for us – and lived by himself.

The gaffer again found himself under fire this time from United fans as well as the media in the summer of 1995 when he decided to sell Andrei Kanchelskis, Mark Hughes and Paul Ince. Andrei, Mark and Paul had been the subject of media speculation for months. The arrival of Andy Cole obviously made life tougher for Hughes, who was no longer guaranteed first team football. He was an outstanding player. Though not as prolific a goalscorer as some strikers, Mark had other qualities that contributed massively to the side. He had good control and the strength to hold the ball up. He was also a tough bastard, never found wanting in a battle. A quiet man, 'Sparky' did his work and went home. Which is not to say he didn't like a drink with the lads. He was transferred to Chelsea. United fans with whom he was a particular favourite weren't happy. (For some reason he's had two or three 'pops' at me on the field over the past couple of seasons. I haven't responded. Now he's retired, it doesn't look like I'll get the chance now, either!)

There had been a number of stories in the papers about Paul Ince moving to Italy. There was no doubt you could earn a fortune in Italy or Spain, set yourself up for life with one big move and earn more than in five seasons at Old Trafford. United weren't the best of payers – at that stage – and we were all conscious that to some extent we were trading off larger salaries for the privilege of playing for a great club.

At the time people thought Incey was sold because he was getting too big for his boots. The word 'Guv' was now on his car registration plate. But I don't think that was the case. Paul was a good lad, popular in the dressing room, who generally did his stuff on the park. He and I shared the midfield responsibility and got on very well. I'm guessing, but I think the manager over time, on the training ground, saw Paul's commitment level drop a percentage point or two and sensed that he wasn't as hungry as he should be. With Nicky Butt and Paul Scholes now proven Premier League players, selling Incey was good business.

Andrei's financial business was a much-discussed mystery. Stories at the time suggested he and the manager didn't see eye to eye, or that he needed to move for money. Either way, he was off to Everton and later to several other clubs.

The decision to sell three seasoned Premier League players, all internationals, was brave. The fact that Eric couldn't return until the end of September because of an additional FA ban, and no one could be sure how much of a mark eight months without football would leave, increased the early-season pressure on Alex Ferguson. It seems incredible that a manager who'd delivered two championships, an FA Cup (plus two losing appearances in League and FA Cup finals) and a double in the previous three seasons could have his judgement questioned so savagely. But such were the expectations of Manchester United now – from the media and supporters – that nothing less than total supremacy over our rivals appeared to be acceptable.

Alex Ferguson was attempting something that football history showed to be the most difficult of all tasks: completing a smooth transition from one Championship-winning side to another without any loss of momentum. This was a trick only Liverpool had successfully managed. From Bill Shankly through Bob Paisley, Joe Fagan and Kenny Dalglish, Liverpool had enjoyed near-unbroken success through the 1960s, 1970s and 1980s. With his record Alex Ferguson could have taken the easy options: do nothing or attempt to buy success. The hard, risky option, the one he chose, was to place his trust in Nicky Butt, Paul Scholes, Gary and Phil Neville and David Beckham. He liked a punt, but this was less of a gamble to those of us within the club than it seemed to fans and critics outside. Had this *management* decision failed, the manager would undoubtedly have paid the ultimate price.

We know this from reaction to our opening game of the 1995/96 season. Away to Aston Villa, we lost 3-1. The game was shown on *Match of the Day* that night, when Alan Hansen famously observed 'You don't win anything with kids.' The newspapers were equally derisive. 'Fergie's gamble fails,' one headline declared. Hold on, guys!

The criticism hurt. The following Wednesday night we

played West Ham at home. Normally a breeze, this fixture now became a huge challenge. We had something important to prove in front of our own fans. Liverpool would have been easier than West Ham in the circumstances. Looking back at our team for that West Ham game, it is clear that, contrary to the popular perception that we fielded a team of 'kids', there was plenty of experience in the side. Peter Schmeichel, Gary Pallister and Steve Bruce (who'd been injured for the Villa game) formed the key defensive triangle. Denis Irwin, Brian McClair, Lee Sharpe and myself hardly qualified as 'kids'. Nicky Butt and Paul Scholes had enough Premier League experience. Only Gary Neville and David Beckham, who was starting his seventh first team game for United, properly fitted the 'kids' description.

Still, the pressure was on, and for once West Ham were up for an Old Trafford contest. I wasn't 100 per cent fit for this game. A knee ligament problem had dogged me throughout pre-season. As usual, I wouldn't do the sensible thing, which was to have the recommended operation. Playing through injuries – hernias, knees and ankles – had been a recurring feature of the recent past. Being so desperate to play wasn't smart. But . . .

In two seasons as a United player I'd learned a lot. The most important development in my football was an ever-growing appreciation of the tempo of a contest. A game ebbs and flows, the rhythm constantly changes, and with these changes you have to be in tune. The best teams and players impose their tempo on the opposition. There's a time to quicken to the pace of the game, a time to slow it down. A time to tackle, a time to hold off. A time to play the ball long, a time to play it short. A moment in a game where someone needs a wake-up call – a bollocking – or some words of encouragement.

Football at the highest level was not a game of running, tackling and bursting guts. Not always. There were, in English football, matches against the Arsenals, Liverpools and Leeds where the game descended into trench warfare, where it was do or die, and you were pushed to your limit, physically and emotionally. Chasing a game against the better sides was occasionally what you had to do. But basically I'd learned to play within myself, reading situations, influencing the contest with the kind of pass, challenge or interception required in any given circumstances. I wasn't much of a goalscorer any longer. I'd scored eleven goals in two seasons, only three the season just past. Essentially, I tried to do whatever we had to do as a team. Defend when necessary, push forward when that was called for. My real job was to dominate midfield, to break opponents' hearts and minds, by denying them possession of the ball and blocking the route forward. Get it and pass it. United had enough outstanding attacking players – Cantona, Giggs, Hughes, Sharpe, Kanchelskis, Cole and Beckham – to finish the job. Protect and support might be a fair description of my role. Ideally, in my mind there would always be something left in the tank, something that was available if necessary, a goal at one end – a last-ditch saving tackle at the other.

Against West Ham that little extra was required. In a tight game I scored the goal that made the difference between a disappointing 1-1 draw – and more critical scorn – and the relief of a 2-1 victory. Of course, 2-1 at home to West Ham proved nothing. Wimbledon at Old Trafford on the Saturday was another no-win game – *if* we won. Anything less would allow the 'judges' another outing. Again, it was a bit of a struggle. Again, I scored two of our goals in a 3-1 win.

Against Blackburn two days later I was sent off for a second bookable offence. The ref claimed that I'd dived in the penalty area following Colin Hendry's tackle. There was no love lost between Blackburn and ourselves – or me and Hendry. Television replays proved that he had made contact. It should have been a penalty. Knowing the score, Hendry tried it on, successfully, with the referee. The reputation I had acquired in the previous season's Cup semi-final made it easier to send bad boy Roy for an early bath. The good news was a 2-1 victory over the side that held the title.

Two games off, but I was far from indispensable. The team continued to complete a ten-game unbeaten run that only ended when we lost at Highbury, 1-0, in early November.

Eric returned on 1 October with a goal from the penalty spot to salvage a point at home to Liverpool. He was as good as ever, remarkable testimony to his professionalism, indeed his character, for few players, especially a foreign player, could have endured the stick he'd taken for his Bruce Lee impression (and would take for the rest of the season).

Newcastle were the team setting the League alight. Kevin Keegan had them playing seat-of-the-pants attacking football. Cynics in the game mocked Keegan's cavalier approach to football. I must admit I admired his passion.

In October I was sent off for a second time that season in the home game against Middlesbrough. Now was the time to have another hernia operation, that I badly needed, but had been trying to ignore. Six weeks out. In December it began to look as if we might have blown the Championship. Peter, Pally and Steve Bruce all went down with injuries. Nicky Butt accumulated twenty-one points and missed three games. United took only three points from five matches between 27 November and Christmas Eve, the last of which was a 3-1 defeat at home to Leeds on my comeback. Meanwhile, Newcastle had shot ten points clear.

Our next home game against Newcastle was now massive. A hell of a game, end to end for ninety minutes. Andy Cole and I got the goals in a 2-0 win. Unfortunately, the ground made up was lost when Spurs gave us a 4-1 hiding on New Year's Day at White Hart Lane. Newcastle were now four points clear. The next day, they beat Arsenal to open a seven-point gap. Was it over? Yes, unless they blew it. We could only plug on. And hope.

Criticism of the manager was sharp: United have gone, we're not the team we were, the summer sales were a mistake, no longer a Championship-winning side.

After that loss to Spurs we went on a sensational run of twenty-three League and FA Cup games, losing only once away to Southampton. Eric caught fire, scoring ten goals in the last fifteen League games, seven of them in the final ten games, with another five in the FA Cup for good measure.

The gap on Newcastle is closing, but when we visit St James's Park in early March they have a chance to put us away. This is a real contest – end to end again, but in front of Newcastle's incredibly passionate supporters, who deserve a Championship, but not this one – and it's more our end than theirs. Eric scores a fabulous winner against the run of play.

After that defeat Newcastle were never going to win the Championship. Unless we slipped up, it was ours. For all the talk about kids – there's no evidence to suggest Gary Neville was *ever* a kid – there was more than enough experience in the side to ensure that we didn't 'bottle' it or become complacent.

The trip to Leeds in April was now the most dangerous game on the run-in. Newcastle were wilting badly. Kevin Keegan had discovered that talking about 'winners' is easier than winning. They must have been praying that the rivalry between ourselves and Leeds would produce a result for them. We emerged with a precious three points after a bruising ninety minutes. I had to go to the reserve tank to score the winner.

After the match the gaffer had a go at the Leeds players, asking why they didn't battle against every opponent the way they did against Manchester United. Their manager, Howard Wilkinson, deserved better, the gaffer insisted. He ended his press conference hoping that Leeds would produce a similarly spirited display against Newcastle the following week!

What a wind-up – an Alex Ferguson special. Of course, the manager denies he's at it, so I must believe him! Anyway, Keegan bit and the controversy couldn't have done anything for Newcastle's concentration. As if they weren't under enough pressure. They'd have something to think of now – other than winning – going into the Leeds game.

We were hungry fighters. After the Cantona business and the stick he'd taken for selling Kanchelskis, Hughes and Paul Ince, the manager was a man on a mission. He had a more personal agenda as well. Although he would only go public with his discontent when the season ended, Alex Ferguson was negotiating a new contract. The talks with the United board weren't going well. It was unbelievable but true that the players were earning more money than the man more responsible than anybody for the club's success. Another double would strengthen his hand in the negotiations. At least in theory.

I was also in talks about a new contract. Michael Kennedy was handling that business. Michael was quiet but resolute. All our options were open. The Bosman Ruling meant that players had a strong hand in such talks, provided that hand was played properly. Provided also that the club understood that leaving was one of the options not ruled out. I would demonstrate my loyalty to Manchester United on the pitch. At the negotiating table Michael would establish the price of that commitment.

We finished our League campaign with two comfortable victories, beating Forest 5-0 at home and Middlesbrough 3-0 away. The double was on – only Liverpool stood in our way.

From my first visit with Forest, Wembley had never turned me on. The crowd was too far away to create real atmosphere. Compared to Old Trafford, Anfield or Elland Road, Wembley was like playing in a vacuum. The pitch was slow, a drag on your strength. The pre-match ceremonial bullshit was a distraction. Shaking hands with the dignitaries, they seem as uninterested in you as you were in them. But we were up for Liverpool. Not winning the double after getting this far would feel like failure, leave a sour taste in our mouths. Beating Liverpool was always enough incentive on its own. For us and for United fans this game – League or Cup – mattered more than most. In professional terms victory in this game to complete a double was essential for all kinds of reasons, one being that the great Liverpool sides of the recent past had set standards, domestically and in Europe, by which greatness could be measured.

In the League they'd beaten us at Anfield and been unlucky not to do the same at Old Trafford in Eric's comeback game, where we scraped a draw. They were a useful team, especially if they were allowed to play their passing game. Robbie Fowler and Stan Collymore provided the goalscoring threat, John Barnes, Steve McManaman and Jamie Redknapp the attacking fluency.

The manager left Steve Bruce out of the side, a tough decision which hurt Brucey. He'd struggled with niggling injuries all season, and was carrying a hamstring that could not be guaranteed to survive the Wembley pitch. Having played – badly – in a Wembley final when less than 100 per cent fit myself I understood the gaffer's sentiment. Which is why David May was the right choice for this game.

Neutrals said the 1996 Cup final was a bore. Not if you were playing. It was grim all right, demanding every ounce of concentration, every last gasp of breath. My job was to anchor midfield, to deny Liverpool time and space, to break up their rhythm, basically to destroy any notions they might have had about passing us to defeat. There's a lot of ground to cover at Wembley, but I covered it, got my tackles in, delivered the message: this is going to be hard work, boys, fucking hard work. Along with Nicky Butt I won the midfield battle. Nicky was a tough lad, and an ideal partner for this kind of operation.

With five minutes to go we were on top with nothing to show on the scoresheet. Eric had been quiet, as he sometimes was. We won a corner on the right. David James reached the cross but only punched it towards the edge of the penalty area. In flight it took a deflection, before reaching Eric. Somehow he manoeuvred his body to create enough space to take the ball on the volley. The next thing I saw was the net bulging, and Liverpool heads sagging. *Yes.*

Another double. This time with 'kids'. The moment of victory is short – it has to be, you have to move on – but on this occasion very sweet. It's not the glory, what *is* glory anyway? What does it look like, feel like, taste like? Can you spend it, kiss it, embrace it? No, what's worth savouring is the vindication. The double of 1995/96 vindicated the manager. He had won something with 'kids'.

Eric had captained the side in Brucey's absence. After the final whistle he tried to persuade Steve to join him receiving

the trophy in the Royal Box. It was a typically generous
Cantona gesture which typically Steve, the club captain, passed
on. One of the great things about that United team was that
most of the players saw through the 'glory' that accompanied
achievement. We'd won the Cup, nobody really cared who
picked it up.

That summer Steve accepted a serious amount of money
to join Birmingham City. He had been a great player for
Manchester United, a huge positive influence in the dressing
room, a great pro, his nice, self-deprecating sense of humour
concealing a steely resolve to get the job done. Steve was up
for every game. He was also a keen social animal, and quietly
made sure that everyone else enjoyed their pint, and the banter
that went with it. Everybody at Old Trafford, the gaffer most
of all, was sorry to see Steve Bruce leave. If you were to create
the perfect club captain, who wasn't Bryan Robson, it would
be Brucey. In my early days at United he'd gone out of his
way to help me feel I belonged. Strictly speaking, that wasn't
his job. But he made it his business.

Four days after the Cup final the *Manchester Evening News*
carried a banner headline: 'Fergie: I'll quit in pay wrangle'.
Unless his new deal was agreed before he left for his holidays,
the gaffer was set to leave. Nothing surprises me in football.
Here was the man who'd delivered everything in the domestic
game to United over almost ten years, forced to go public to
get a contract. That could hardly be just reward for all that
he'd done. He was on a pittance, £300,000 a year, in a game
overflowing with television money. He got the deal: double
the pittance, with a bonus if he was successful!

When Alex Ferguson returned from holiday I signed the
new contract Michael Kennedy had negotiated. I was committed for four more years, and glad to be.

Lee Sharpe's was another significant departure from Old Trafford that summer. He was a smashing lad, but too fond of the good life for the manager's liking. Lee was transferred to Leeds at a knockdown price. He was a very good player, versatile and devastating on his day. He just wasn't hard enough, mentally, for what was becoming a much harder business.

9

A year later Eric was gone. A week after we won our fourth Premier League title he announced his retirement from football. After his love affair with Manchester United he could never play for another club: 'I have played professional football for thirteen years, which is a long time. I now wish to do other things. I always planned to retire when I was at the top and at Manchester United I have reached the pinnacle of my career. In the last four and a half years I have enjoyed my best football and had a wonderful time. I have had a marvellous relationship with the manager, coach, staff and players and not least the fans. I wish Manchester United even more success in the future.'

Martin Edwards and Alex Ferguson paid tribute to Eric. The chairman said: 'I am extremely sorry Eric has arrived at this decision but understand and respect his reasons. Many of us believe that Eric has been the catalyst for the most successful period in our history. It has truly been a magical time.' And in his statement Alex Ferguson commented: 'Eric has had a huge impact on the development of our younger players. He has been a model professional in the way he conducted himself and a joy to manage. He is certainly one of the most gifted and dedicated players I have had the pleasure of working with. He leaves with our best wishes and will always be welcome at Old Trafford. He has given us so many wonderful memories.'

At the time some of us felt that there may have been more to Eric's departure than revealed in the press releases. (Eric was already in France when the news broke.) We knew he'd been talking to the manager, and wondered if it was about money and an extension to his contract which had a year left to run. If those talks had been unsatisfactory from both sides' point of view, an amicable parting of the ways made sense for Eric and the club.

The fans were shocked. They loved Eric for, as Martin Edwards said, he had been the captain for a magical spell, having arrived when a Championship was desperately needed. The scenes around Old Trafford and The Cliff after the story broke were unbelievable. Hundreds of United fans clutching Eric's number 7 shirt stood in mourning on the forecourt at Old Trafford. Many were tearful. Like the Busby funeral, or the more emotional of the European nights at Old Trafford, this occasion reminded me that Manchester United was more than a football club. It was impossible to imagine scenes like these at any other football club in Britain.

The depth of feeling at Eric's leaving had to be managed. If the fans had any inkling of a possible dispute over money, it would have caused trouble. For a bad start to the following season could have led to accusations of penny-pinching. As had happened after Andrei, 'Sparky' and Incey left, the manager would have felt the heat.

Yet something Eric said earlier this year about United wishing to use him as a commodity, and the increasingly commercial nature of the club, provided a clue, perhaps, to the reason he chose to retire when he did. Eric was a proud man. I think he decided that if he couldn't play for United, he wouldn't play at all. I admired that.

We won the Championship in Eric's last season. We began with a nine-game unbeaten run, then lost three on the trot, receiving hidings, 0-5 at Newcastle and 3-6 at the Dell (again), and losing narrowly at Stamford Bridge, 1-2, before going undefeated for sixteen league games until we lost 1-2 away to Sunderland. In our opening game against Wimbledon at Selhurst Park David Beckham scored that incredible goal, chipping Neil Sullivan from inside his own half. The game was a stroll in the sun; too many of our League games were now easily won in the manner of this one.

At the beginning of the season the manager made it clear that the Champions League was our priority. Strolling through Premier League games was a less than ideal preparation for matches against the best sides in Europe. Personally, my season was screwed up by injuries and suspension. After the Wimbledon game I went in for a knee operation. Out for at least a month. When I got back in the team for the scoreless draw at Villa Park, the knee played up again. Returning after missing three more games, I was sent off for a second bookable offence in the 3-6 slaughter at Southampton.

On this occasion, as so many before and since, it wasn't so much spite felt for the opposition as anger at myself and my team-mates that caused me to lose my head. Southampton was a good example of our team going through the motions, thinking our ability gave us a divine right to win the game. These lapses into the comfort zone drove me crazy. So with a rash challenge or a crunching tackle I'd try to inject some angry urgency into the contest. I could take defeat, but not surrender. If we lost at Southampton, what fucking chance would we have against Juventus (who were, as it happened, one of our opponents in the opening phase of the Champions League). Knowing that you couldn't switch form on and off like a light bulb caused me intense frustration in League games like the one at the Dell. The result was sometimes an early bath, sometimes a row with my team-mates.

Any top-class player can get himself 'up' for Anfield or

Highbury. Being ready for battle against the Southamptons of the Premier League was a different matter. Mentally you've awarded yourself the three points when you first looked at the fixture list. Anfield: that will be tough. Highbury: another big game. Coventry: that's OK. Southampton: no bother. West Ham: should be all right. Sunderland: a breeze.

Juventus!

The first leg of the Juventus tie demonstrated exactly what the danger was. The Saturday before the European match we hammered Leeds 4-0 at Elland Road. The Saturday after we cruised in 4-1 at home to Nottingham Forest. In Turin on the Wednesday in between the no-bother Premier League encounters we lost 1-0, a good performance as it happens. Injury meant that I missed that game. But increasingly as I watched football, I learned.

Eric struggled in Europe – to be fair, we all did. As I've acknowledged, he was superb in the domestic game, perfect for English football, where his poise and technical brilliance meant he was always one step ahead of the chaos around him. With bodies and tackles flying everywhere, Eric's sang froid was a major asset. And because we were so strong around the park we could indulge him, spare him the chasing back, the graft, the tackling we happily did on his behalf. Sometimes I'd think, fuck it, Eric, you lazy bastard, and then before, or even after, the words were out of my mouth he'd weave a magic spell to score or set up a goal.

That was the pattern that served us so well in England. Europe was another game, far more demanding. Even the more modest of the teams we met in Europe were champions in their own territory. That's a head thing. They were used to winning, to getting results away from home. Against the Rapid Viennas and the Brondbys you could get away with

Eric. But not facing Juventus, Bayern, Dortmund, or an unexceptional but professional side like Gothenburg, who'd beaten us 3-1 to put us out of the competition a couple of seasons earlier.

A magical asset at home, a match-winner countless times in the Premier League and the FA Cup, Eric didn't shine so brightly in Europe. I can't recall one important European game that he turned for us. In Europe you moved up a level or two. It was not just the real quality attacking players like Zidane or Del Piero that captured everyone's imagination, but tough, wily defenders, guys nobody had ever heard of, who closed space down, timed their tackles to perfection, were instinctively in the right cover positions, had pace and read the game superbly. Eric never conquered this. And conquering Europe was now what Alex Ferguson's Manchester United was all about.

Our progress through a group consisting of Rapid Vienna, Fenerbahce, Juventus and ourselves was less than smooth. After losing in Turin we beat Rapid at home and Fenerbahce away. Then the Turkish champions came and won at Old Trafford. This defeat ended United's forty-year unbeaten home record in Europe. Victory meant an almost certain place in the quarter-finals. But Fenerbahce gave us nothing. They were a good example of the so-called ordinary European sides I referred to earlier – no big names, but tough, seasoned pros who took no prisoners, especially at the back. The soft chances offered up in the Premier League were noticeably absent. Fenerbahce kept the ball, making us work hard to get it back. They were only champions of Turkey! Yet they refused to roll over like so many English sides who visited Old Trafford. Chasing the win like driven men, we were hit on the break with twelve minutes left on the clock. A nothing shot deflected off David

May – Schmeichel had no chance. One-nil. Over. Now we had to travel to Juventus and Rapid hoping for a result.

There was a lot of head-shaking, 'how could this happen to us?' shit in the dressing room afterwards. The last thing footballers will do is look at themselves. Yet sometimes – no, always – that's where the answer lies. If you're good enough, and here in terms of ability we were, defeat is usually down to yourself. Not the referee, or luck, or a deflection, comforting though all those excuses are. This is where the real pros, the likes of Bryan Robson, Steve Bruce or Denis Irwin, are invaluable. They know where to look for answers. The gaffer knows as well. That's why he's accomplished what he has.

After Fenerbahce he defended us outside to the media. Bad luck, blah, blah, blah, blah. Record had to go some time, it's been a burden anyway. We'll get back, blah, blah, blah, blah. We could have thrown away the chance of a quarter-final place four days before. At Southampton. Six fucking three. Before that 0–5 at Newcastle. Why did I lose my mind at the Dell and get the red card? Because I saw it coming. I knew in my bones that you couldn't fuck around at Southampton and turn the tap on against a proper team four days later. Can't be done. Maybe now and again. But Manchester United is not in the now-and-again business. We're in – or supposed to be in – the every-time-you-pull-the-shirt-on-get-the-job-done business.

I knew this from looking at my own family and friends. United fanatics. Six-three at Southampton! They couldn't leave the house. People taking the piss out of them at work. Kids who followed us getting it at school, in the street. The jeering, the mocking, the sneering. Too many players forget what defeat means for the people who pay our wages. We were being paid to play. Paid. To play for Manchester United.

The fans, the real hard-core fans were forking out their money to support us. And we can't be bothered to pick our legs up against Matt le Tissier! In his book Jaap Stam wrote that I was 'on another planet'. Yes, Jaap. Planet Manchester United, where I always wanted to be, where you dream of being some day when you're a kid kicking a ball around.

A 0-1 loss in Turin meant we had to beat Rapid in Vienna while hoping that Juventus didn't lose at home to Fenerbahce. This time we don't do a 'Southampton', putting Leicester away 3-1 on the Saturday before the game against Rapid, Nicky Butt (twice) and Ole Gunnar Solskjaer scoring the goals. We play like a good team should against the Austrians. The gaffer's given me a marking job to do on Rapid's danger man Kuhbauer. Task achieved, at 2-0 (goals from Ryan and Eric) I'm still sensing danger, a goal that might spark a come-back, when Kuhbauer breaks forward to threaten our goal. I track him back and make the tackle. Successfully. His studs rake down my leg. Just below the knee I have a wound requiring nineteen stitches. Another month off. Juventus do the biz. We're through. To play Porto in the quarter-final.

Now another problem surfaces. Relieved to be through to the Champions League knockout stage, we can only draw our next two League games against West Ham and Sheffield Wednesday. Then we are defeated by Sunderland, just three days after we stuff Porto 4-0 at home in the first leg of our quarter-final tie. We're as good as through to the Champions League semi-final, but we've created a Premier League crisis. As if to underline this, we lose 2-3 at home to Derby just four days before the first leg of the semi-final away to Borussia Dortmund.

This is where we want to be, one step away from a chance to win the Champions League. Yet I can sense one or two of

42. Theresa, with Caragh, Aidan and Shannon, holding baby daughter Leah - just home from hospital on the day she was born.

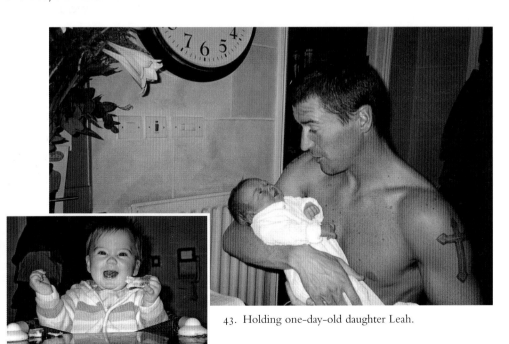

43. Holding one-day-old daughter Leah.

44. Leah, nine months later.

45. At home with all four children.

46. In my study being kept company by my dog Triggs.

47. With the manager.

48. Celebrating with Eric Cantona after he'd scored in the 1996 derby game with Manchester City.

49. The now infamous kung-fu kick.

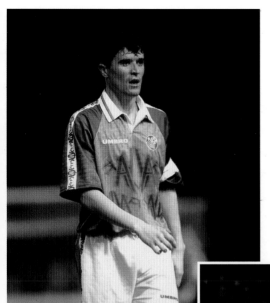

50. My first appearance as captain of Ireland against Russia.

51. And sent off in the ninetieth minute in the same game.

52. Excuse me, Mr Poll, could you repeat that, please ... ?

53. Holding the Premiership trophy.

54. Congratulations from the manager after winning the FA Cup as part of 1999's treble.

55. Celebrations with the 1999 FA Cup.

56. Booked in the 1999 Champions League semi-final against Juventus.

57. Leaving the field after winning the game. Dwight Yorke celebrates reaching the final, while I know I won't be playing.

58. Holding the Champions League trophy in 1999 with Paul Scholes – a player who didn't deserve to miss the game.

59. Celebrating the team's victory in the Champions League with the manager. Despite appearances, I'd rather have been somewhere else.

our players backing off. Surprisingly, or maybe not, Eric is one of them. For all that he's done for us, Eric hasn't got a look in with the French national team, which is not exactly pulling up trees at this stage. Great for United, but unless we win in Europe Eric's reputation will never rank alongside the truly great European players. This is the stage that really counts. Maybe Eric's not capable of it. Never will be.

Still, we're well in the game. Eric misses a good chance. Nicky Butt hits the post. David Beckham has a great shot saved by a defender on the line, goalkeeper beaten. It looks like a 0-0 draw with the decider to come at Old Trafford. Fourteen minutes from the end, Eric jumps out of a tackle in midfield. His challenger Tretschok breaks forward, shoots, the ball takes a deflection off Gary Pallister's foot. Back of the net. Perhaps that's the moment Eric's future was decided.

Four days before the second leg we completed an important piece of Premier League business at Anfield when we beat Liverpool 3-1. That's their Championship more or less finished. Ours is still on track, unless we screw up again.

The yellow card I picked up in Dortmund meant that I missed the second leg at Old Trafford. Although the Germans were useful, I fancied us to beat them in front of our own crowd. But an early goal conceded meant that under the away goals rule we had to score three to win the tie. That was not on at this level. With the Scot Paul Lambert anchoring midfield, Kohler in the centre of defence and Andreas Möller, their best player, always dangerous, Dortmund were comfortable in the end. It's incredibly frustrating to sit and watch, unable to make a contribution to a game that presents us with a great chance to reach a Champions League final. When Dortmund went on to beat Juventus in the final, we knew at least that we were good enough, almost, to become European champions.

The final test of the season was set for us by the wise men who organize the fixture lists: four games in eight days to clinch the Championship. Fortunately, we managed to avoid defeat against Leicester, Middlesbrough and Newcastle, finishing the job with a 2-0 win at home to West Ham. A week later, the day after Chelsea beat Bryan Robson's Middlesbrough in the FA Cup final, Eric Cantona announced his retirement.

On 29 May 1997, Theresa and I were married at the Church of Our Lady in Mayfield. It was a private occasion, with just fifteen immediate family members present. Theresa's father Nick gave her away, my sister Hilary acted as bridesmaid, my brother Johnson was my best man, with my other brothers Denis and Pat as my groomsmen. It was a wonderful day, marking by far the happiest development in my life.

Eric Cantona had followed Steve Bruce as club captain. Now that role had to be filled. There was some speculation about who the manager would choose. Peter Schmeichel, Gary Pallister, Denis Irwin and Gary Neville were all obvious candidates. I was surprised when Alex Ferguson chose me. To be offered the captaincy of Manchester United was a huge compliment, and of course, an equally large responsibility. On the field I was confident I could meet my obligations. However, the club captaincy also demands diplomatic skills off the field, which I felt might prove a greater challenge. One bonus that came with the job was a mixed blessing. The club captain at Manchester United is responsible for distributing tickets for home games – and the players' lounge. Where once I'd buttered up Bryan Robson, Steve Bruce and Eric, I would now be the man players seeking favours would have to be nice to. The bad news was that it would be more difficult to turn down requests for tickets on the basis that I couldn't lay my hands on the precious commodity. The tickets were in my back pocket!

The departure of Eric Cantona meant that another seasoned professional's voice would be lost. The dressing room was now significantly changed from the one I'd joined four years earlier. Since then Bryan Robson, Steve Bruce, Mark Hughes, Paul Ince and now Eric had left. Each of those senior players had been influential in one way or another, on and off the field. The collective influence of their individual personalities was difficult to quantify, except to note that in their absence our dressing room seemed a younger, less battle-hardened place. One thing was quantifiable: the old drinking culture, which had been the bonding mechanism when I first joined United, was much less evident now.

Teddy Sheringham was signed from Spurs to replace Eric. Teddy arrived for training on his first day at the club in his red Ferrari, every inch the confident Londoner. Teddy and I were acquainted from my Forest days. The chemistry between us was never right. And didn't improve during his spell at Old Trafford. Teddy didn't flourish in his first season for United, but in time proved to be a very good buy for the club. He was a bloody good player, a scorer and creator of goals. The fact that he and I didn't get on personally didn't matter a damn when it came to the business on the field.

We won my first competitive game as captain, beating Chelsea in a penalty shoot-out in the Charity Shield. We remained unbeaten in our first eight League games at the start of the 1997/98 season, and comfortably beat Kosice of Slovakia away in the opening Champions League fixture.

The last of those League games was against Chelsea at Old Trafford. This was a very bad-tempered match. At half-time the fists were flying in the tunnel. In the second half I was booked. The final score, 2–2, meant two points lost at home, a bad result, although looking back and considering Chelsea's overall record at Old Trafford, it wasn't as bad as it seemed that Wednesday night.

With some friends, who were over from Cork, I went for a few drinks at the Chester Court hotel, around the corner from Old Trafford. Normally drinking on a Wednesday night was a no-no even in my work-hard, play-hard phase, which I was still in. But Roy, the people-pleaser, was not going to go home to bed and leave his friends to their own devices. With the adrenaline still pumping from the ninety-minute battle just ended, going home would have been the smart thing to do. However, there was no excuse. After the game I phoned back to Cork to discover that my brother Johnson and his partner (now wife) Linda had had a baby girl. Now, no excuse was required to enjoy a session.

Across the bar a group of United fans, Irish, from Dublin, were rapidly becoming as merry as my mates and I. When I went to the bar to buy a round a few smart remarks were passed. I responded to some derogatory comments about Cork and its people with some equally insulting observations about Dublin and its citizens. It was late, half-past three in the morning. I was more than merry, I was drunk, and somewhere in the back of my mind annoyed with myself for not being at home with Theresa. But I had passed the point of no return, as far as good intentions were concerned. After more drink had been consumed, the belligerence between Cork and Dublin became more personal and heated. Blows were exchanged. I gave as good as I got. It would be wrong to blame anybody but myself for the predicament I now found myself in. It was the old who-do-you-think-you-are trick again. And I fell for it again. Two months after being made Manchester United club captain.

Damn is not the word I used when, as my friends and I were leaving the Chester House, my sparring partner from Dublin shouted from his bedroom window: 'Keane, you Cork bastard, you'll be in the tabloids tomorrow.' He had already made his telephone call to a newspaper.

'Keane in Hotel Brawl' was the story the next day. I had to face the manager. First, of course, I had to face myself. Not for the first time, I felt the mixture of shame and remorse: for letting everybody down – Theresa, my family at home, reading this stuff, the club and Alex Ferguson. As I said, I was on the steepest learning curve in history. When would I finally learn to avoid situations I clearly couldn't handle?

As usual the manager was publicly supportive, privately severe. The obvious question was what was I doing out drunk at 4.30 in the morning, two days before a game. Celebrating Johnson's and Linda's baby girl was hardly an acceptable answer. I was well aware that while the manager was always on his players' side in public, his tolerance had its limits. I'd seen him give up on other persistent offenders, and had no reason to believe that I would be treated any differently.

For Saturday's game away to Leeds I was in no shape at all. Too little sleep, too much emotion spent in my despair. Leeds was a tough place to go anyway. David Wetherall gave Leeds a 1-0 lead. We chased the game with no success, nobody more desperately than me. I was having the nightmare game that I deserved. Bloody awful would be a generous description of my performance. With just over five minutes to go, our unbeaten League run looked set to end.

Throughout the game I'd been having a private feud with Alfie Haaland. He was winding me up from the beginning of the game. The late tackles I could live with, they were a normal part of football. But the other stuff – pulling my shirt, getting digs in off the ball – really bugged me. At times Haaland wasn't even following the play, just concentrating on me. I figured that Leeds's coach Dave O'Leary, who knew how to get to me, had given Haaland that specific job.

Five minutes from time, as we pushed forward into their box, I lunged in desperation at Haaland. I was trying to trip him up rather than kick him. I knew it would probably mean a booking, but fuck it, he'd done his job. He'd done my head in. As I slid in to make the challenge my studs caught the turf. I actually heard my cruciate ligament snap. The pain was instant and agonizing. Haaland stood over me shouting, 'Get up, stop faking it.' His colleague Wetherall was gesturing to the same effect. I knew something very serious had happened. I wasn't sure exactly what. The ref booked me as I was being led to the touchline. Dave Fevre, our physio, tried to get me off the field. But we'd used our three subs, so I stayed on to play out the closing minutes. As I limped off the field, David O'Leary offered his commiserations.

Fuck off, Dave. You sent that bastard out to wind me up, I thought.

The Leeds doctor arrived in the dressing room. The body language suggested the worst, my cruciate had gone. Dave Fevre, who'd been physio at Wigan rugby league club, recognized the symptoms. Cruciates regularly go in rugby league because of the way that game is played.

My night of drinking had taken its toll. Exactly what the price would be remained to be seen. I returned to Manchester for diagnosis at the BUPA hospital in Whalley Range. On the way back across the Pennines on the team coach I prayed that the injury would prove not to be as bad as first feared. That night Dave took me straight to the hospital. The consultant who conducted a preliminary examination didn't seem optimistic. They sent me home with instructions to return on Monday when they'd open the knee to have a look at the damage.

On Sunday Denis Irwin dropped my car back to the house from Old Trafford where I'd left it. The knee had inflated like a balloon. The pain was unreal. I knew I was fucked. Monday's exploratory operation confirmed my worst fears. They sent me away for six weeks' rehab to build my muscles up for my operation. After nine League games my season was over. Possibly my career. Paul Gascoigne was not the only player who was never the same again after an operation to repair the cruciate ligament.

Because of his experience with rugby players in my situation, Dave Fevre knew what, and what not, to do to make a complete recovery. There was a physical and a psychological side to rehabilitation. After my operation I spent three days in hospital. Then I began the long, slow, painful business of regaining full fitness. Fortunately for me Terry Cooke, one of United's reserve team players, had incurred the same injury and was on the same journey as I was.

Dave Fevre began by showing us a video of Gazza's rehab course. When we'd finished watching it, Dave said that he wanted us to do things very differently. Mr Noble, the club's orthopaedic surgeon, also showed us a video which demonstrated exactly what the cruciate ligament was, how it worked and what we had to do to rebuild a shattered knee. Dave believed patience was the key. Gazza had apparently been running in Spain with Jimmy Five Bellies after just six weeks. Three or four days after leaving hospital I began with Dave by simply sitting on a table and flexing my leg to get some movement. Then Dave slowly tried to bend my leg and straighten it. This was very painful. Slowly, very slowly we got some movement. The next stage was step-ups on a bench. This was slow, tedious work, just Terry and me day after day in the gym at The Cliff. Signs of progress were minimal. But Dave Fevre was brilliant, always reassuring us that, if we took time and avoided short-cuts, we'd make it in the end.

We graduated to the bike in the gym. Then a major leap forward: we took our bikes on the roads around Salford. After a couple of months we knew the area around The Cliff like the backs of our hands. Every morning I'd slip a fiver in my tracksuit bottoms for our regular stop for bacon 'butties' at the local café. Against the rules, but we felt we deserved a treat. In the afternoons we worked on weights in the gym.

In the backs of both our minds the question always lurked: how am I doing? The other question of course was never far away: will I ever regain full fitness? And if not . . . ? For Terry these questions were less comfortable than for me. He didn't have the big house, savings, insurance and pension, things I could fall back on if the worse came to the worst. Even at the most depressing moments − and there were some in those early months − I appreciated that relative to many other people I was a very lucky man. Self-pity was a luxury I didn't entertain.

During those endless lonely days in that gym at The Cliff I set myself a goal . . . and made a vow. The goal I was prepared to settle for was one more full game at Old Trafford. Just one, to take in the magic of a life I'd taken so much for granted when it was routine. The vow was never to take my fitness for granted again.

Before my injury I'd go to work, do my training and be off at 12.30 to get my lunch and walk the dog. Then watch a bit of television and pick the kids up from school. Now much more was demanded. This regime set by Dave Fevre was flexible as far as clocking on and clocking off was concerned. But if you came in late you stayed late. The hours had to be put in. So, long after everyone had left I'd be working in the gym till three or maybe four o'clock. Few days passed when I didn't think about Alfie Haaland. More positively, I promised myself that if I got out of this with my career intact, I'd spend more time working on my fitness, be less eager to dash away after training.

Meanwhile, United were winning matches, doing well in the League and making progress in Europe. I went to very few games. I kept out of the way. Didn't really feel a part of things any more. Obviously I wanted the club to do well, but I'd tuned myself out. Nicky Butt and Paul Scholes were doing well in midfield. For the moment I was redundant.

I was also drinking too much. During the week I went diligently about my work. Once I clocked out on Friday afternoon I allowed myself some pleasure. With a friend, Mike Constable, I'd hit the local pub late on Friday afternoon. Sometimes former United players, members of the old drinking club, would join us for a 'session'. I vividly remember drinking with Bryan Robson and a couple of other former players one afternoon early in my rehab. I was still on crutches, my bad leg (the right one) propped up on a bar stool. My mobile phone rang. It was Stuart Matherson of the *Manchester Evening News*. How's it going, Stuart asked. Great, I assured him. You're putting the work in I hear, he continued. Definitely, I replied. As we spoke I was – silently – indicating to the barmaid to set up another round.

Mike and I would finish very late on Friday night. On Saturday Mike and his wife, Theresa and myself would go out for a meal. More drink . . . and banter about the previous night's piss-up. On Sunday we'd head for one of a number of pubs in Altrincham that held Irish music sessions. For all my avowed good intentions – which were real – I was still struggling with a fondness for the warm glow of a comfortable bar – which was also real.

On the occasional Monday morning Dave Fevre, sensing I was the worse for wear, would send me home. Don't worry, relax, it's OK, was the message. Because of the work I was putting in I was almost at the jogging stage, another very significant psychological step forward.

One afternoon Lee Sharpe (now a Leeds player) showed up at the house. He'd also done his cruciate a few weeks after I had done mine. I was anxious to know how he was progressing. Flying, was Lee's answer. Jogging, kicking a ball, nearly ready. While we sat and talked about the good old days for an hour or two I'm thinking, Jesus, I'm way behind where I should be if Lee's jogging and kicking a ball. When he got up off the couch to leave Lee's bad leg gave way beneath him. 'It must have stiffened up,' Lee lied unconvincingly. He limped out, jumped in his Porsche and motored off. Relieved, I told Dave Fevre the story the following morning. Sounds like he may have been taking short-cuts, Roy. Don't worry we're getting there, Dave confirmed.

During this period I had one of my worst rows with Alex Ferguson. It was Christmas, the party season. Because I was injured I decided on a double celebration, joining the reserves for their party on Tuesday and the first team the following night. Unfortunately, I got into a row with a barman who wanted to close his bar (at closing time!) on the reserves' night out. Hearing about this, the gaffer called a first team meeting the following morning. I was banned from the first team party. And just to make sure the ban was observed, the gaffer insisted that he would fine any player caught drinking with me that night two weeks' wages. Outraged, I looked around the dressing room for support. None was forthcoming. Fucking wankers, I thought, before going to the manager's office to protest. The argument became very heated. I got no joy.

Betrayed by the good boys – I would have made a point of ignoring the manager's ban if it had been imposed on anyone else – I went out that night for my own Christmas party. The one-man Christmas party had a ball, meeting various characters along his merry way. Next morning I inquired how the good boys had got on. They admitted they'd had a lousy time. Maybe it was guilt. The atmosphere was frosty for a few weeks.

Eventually, I reached the jogging phase of my recovery. Every new experience on the road back was painful as my new knee – for effectively that's what it was – resisted new demands made upon it. These would have been more worrying moments were it not for the fact that, thanks to Dave and Mr Noble, I understood the process of rehabilitation.

The real test came when I joined the normal training sessions and began kicking a ball in earnest. The first couple of days the pain was unbelievable. But Mr Noble told me when I went to see him that this pain was no cause for concern. I also consulted a second specialist, Mr Ray, who confirmed that I was on the right track.

When I started joining in five-a-sides, the lads went easy on me. Too easy. So Dave Fevre called a meeting to tell the team they were doing me no favours. Tackle him. Soon the tackles were flying in. I was back, just about. In the last week of the season, after Arsenal had secured the Championship, I had a notion that I could play in our final League game at Barnsley. Fortunately, the specialists wouldn't hear of it.

With an extra six weeks under my belt I was flying in

pre-season training for the 1998/99 season. We went to Scand-
inavia on tour. Peter Schmeichel had captained the side in my
absence. The manager told me he wanted Peter to continue
as captain for the tour. I wasn't too pleased. Even less so when,
before our opening game, the Charity Shield against Arsenal
at Wembley, Schmeichel showed no indication that he was
prepared to return my armband. No welcome back Roy,
here's the armband. No fucking chance with Peter. In the end
the gaffer had to order him to stand down. He sulked. Arsenal
got two soft goals on the way to a 3-0 victory. Afterwards the
gaffer called a meeting and told Peter to grow up.

10

The manager's continuing hunger for success was clear when he broke the transfer record for a centre-half to sign Jaap Stam from PSV Eindhoven. He also bought Jesper Blomqvist from Parma. According to rumour Dwight Yorke, the Aston Villa striker, was also on the wanted list. When United broke the British transfer record to buy Yorke for £12.6m there was a real sense of change around the club. This was good for everybody. A strong squad such as we now had in the autumn of 1998 meant that complacency was less likely to set in. Nobody was certain of their place, which I felt was healthy. We had enjoyed so much domestic success at this point, eased through so many Premier League games, that it was hurting us when the real prize – the Champions League – was at issue.

The purchase of Dwight Yorke in particular was a daring decision by Alex Ferguson. It subsequently emerged that Brian Kidd had been sceptical about Dwight's ability to justify the fee, a feeling Kidd was not shy about expressing. Like the manager, Kidd was a straight talker when he felt strongly enough about something. To be honest, I wasn't convinced that Dwight would score goals in the numbers required, although I didn't doubt his ability to hold the ball up and the difficulties opposing defenders faced when trying to mark him.

Jaap Stam provided presence at the back, a quality even more necessary now that Gary Pallister had moved on to Middlesbrough. The Steve Bruce/Gary Pallister partnership had been the rock on which much of our previous success had been built. Stam and Ronnie Johnsen, who'd been signed two years previously to replace Brucey, had big boots to fill.

Ole Gunnar Solskjaer had joined United from Norwegian club Molde at the same time as Johnsen. Costing just £1.5m, Ole is probably the best signing the club ever made. Nicknamed the baby-faced assassin, Ole really was both baby-faced and an assassin. The first morning he arrived for training and joined in a team photograph I thought Ole was a schoolboy fan. He looked about sixteen. But when we got the balls out I realized – everyone did – what an extraordinary finisher he was. Ole could – and did – score from anywhere. He turned out to be one of the most popular players in the dressing room, a really nice man, and an outstanding professional. With Andy Cole, Dwight Yorke and Teddy Sheringham to compete with for a starting place, Ole sat on the bench more often than not, He never complained, and when called upon to do the business obliged more often than not. In a team game, which, for all the hype about individuals, soccer is, and will always be, a professional like Ole is priceless. For us he has been.

It took me several games to rediscover match fitness. I was, though, a different person from the lunatic who'd hunted Alfie Haaland (although I hadn't forgotten his contempt as I lay on the pitch at Elland Road). I now cherished every moment of my football – games and training. I now voluntarily worked on my upper-body strength in the gym. I realized as I'd never really done before my lost season that your time in football is finite. It could end with one tackle, you'd be yesterday's man in an instant.

Another fundamental change was to my lifestyle. The extra time spent with Theresa, Shannon and our second daughter Caragh while I was injured now helped me grow up. Now, with my football career active again, and our son Aidan just born, I decided to bury Roy the Playboy. He might get the odd outing, but the carousing days were – more or less – over. Appreciation of my family life was one reason for this change. A deep desire to make every day of my football career count was the other. A bleak period in my professional life had changed me considerably even if I hadn't been fully aware of what was happening or what it meant. Time spent alone helped me figure myself out. Without the daily bustle and hassle of a season's football, which preoccupies you to the point where you are barely conscious of the world around you, the one outside football where, for example, your family live, I'd clearly identified my own weaknesses. As a result I was less tolerant of me.

Stepping outside the game for a season, as I'd been forced to do, also enabled me to look at football and its excesses with clear eyes. It wasn't just wages that were inflated; in many cases bloated egos were just as much a source of danger to the game. Seen from a windowless gym on a winter afternoon, the game looked like a bad movie, full of spivs, bluffers, bullshitters, hangers-on, media whores and bad actors. If you played your hand correctly you could be a big man without achieving anything. People in the game blamed the media for many of its ills. But the media didn't invent the people in the game who played the parts allotted to them in this bad movie. I had always instinctively hated bullshit – a lot of it associated with my own club. Now my tolerance level was zero. Only one thing counted in football: winning, actually achieving. For that I was hungrier than I'd ever been.

One other important consideration was that I had one year left on my contract. My next contract negotiation with United would probably be my last. Returning from injury, I had a lot more than my fitness to prove.

As the season progressed I began to play the best football of my life. This had much to do with the strength of the team around me. The defence was solid, with Gary Neville and Denis Irwin our full backs and Jaap Stam and Ronnie Johnsen gelling as a central defensive partnership. In midfield Paul Scholes, Nicky Butt and myself didn't lose many battles. David Beckham and Ryan Giggs provided threats of differing kinds from both flanks. Andy Cole and Dwight Yorke became good mates off the field and a potent double act for opposing defences to cope with. In what was now becoming a squad game, Phil Neville, Ole and Teddy Sheringham were all major assets when called upon.

Europe, our Achilles heel, was much more manageable now. Having finished second in the Premier League the previous season we had to qualify against the Polish side LKS Łódź. This we did quite comfortably. That placed us in a strong group against Brondby, Barcelona and Bayern Munich. We hammered Brondby home (5-0) and away (6-2). We drew with Barcelona and Bayern home and away. The 3-3 draw in the Nou Camp proved how far we'd come since the 4-0 thrashing we'd received at the same venue in 1994. Dwight Yorke (2) and Andy Cole scored the goals in this game.

In the League Arsenal, the champions, were our main danger. They beat us 3-0 at Highbury in September and got a point at Old Trafford in the return fixture in February.

In the FA Cup an important victory in the fourth-round tie at Old Trafford kept us in the least important of the three trophies we were chasing. This result came from a classic Ole Gunnar Solksjaer intervention. Michael Owen gave Liverpool the lead after three minutes and we were struggling to get back in the game. Yorke scored an equalizer with just two minutes left. Then Ole, on as sub, finished Liverpool off in the last minute. (A fortnight later Ole came on for the final twenty minutes at Forest and scored four goals in an 8-1 win.)

Four matches in fourteen days in April decided our season.

Juventus at home in the Champions League semi-final first leg was a huge test. We didn't play well. Conte gave them the lead – and a critical away goal – Ryan Giggs bailed us out with a last-minute equalizer. We were on a twenty-game unbeaten League and Cup run, but this was a significant step up in class. With Inzaghi up front, Zidane, Deschamps and Davids in midfield, and a typically mean Italian defence to back them up, we were not talking Nottingham Forest and 8-1 victories here. This was serious no-chinks-in-the-armour opposition. (Well, there are chinks in every team's armour, it's a question of being able to get at them.) The Juventus result could have been worse. Inzaghi had a great chance to put Zidane in for a second goal, but went for glory himself, and missed.

Unusually for a home game the manager had decided on an overnight stay at Mottram Hall hotel about five minutes from where a number of our players lived. Detail. Always thinking. Typical. After the game we returned to the hotel for a meal and a team meeting. Harsh words were spoken. Becks and Giggsy got a bollocking for not working hard enough when we didn't have the ball. I was next. I'd had a right go at Denis Irwin for something that happened in the build-up to their goal. Denis had a go back. The manager suggested that I apologize. No, I was sticking to my guns. If this was an analysis of the game, let's analyse it.

'Apologize.'

'No.'

The atmosphere was hot and heavy for a while. I refused to apologize. Then we went to bed. Denis and I were, as always, sharing a room. There was no problem when we got upstairs.

I didn't apologize but we laughed about it. Are footballers sometimes childish? Of course. They have to be, otherwise they'd just start believing that they were only playing a game! And who knows where that thought might lead us! (Almost certainly not to trophies.)

Four days later we faced Arsenal at Villa Park in the FA Cup semi-final. This was a battle of wills as much as a game of football. Neither side yielded in a 0–0 draw. Extra-time made no difference. I scored later what proved to be a legitimate goal but the linesman, supported by my old friend David Elleray, insisted that Dwight Yorke was interfering with play in an offside position.

The following Wednesday's replay will be remembered for Ryan Giggs's incredible winning goal. Again it was a tight game – English football at its best: heart, skill, resilience, determination. Becks gave us the lead with a beautifully struck Beckham special. Dennis Bergkamp equalized with twenty minutes to go. Nicky Butt and I were involved in a war with Vieira and Petit in midfield. Eight minutes after their goal I was sent off for a desperate tackle on Marc Overmars. It was desperation rather than badness. But I was already on a yellow, so I knew my friend Mr Elleray would do the right thing.

Ten men made it so much harder. Especially as the game went to extra-time again. Then Arsenal got a penalty, which Dennis Bergkamp missed – or perhaps more accurately Peter Schmeichel saved.

Sometimes you invest so much of yourself in a game that it acquires a significance way beyond the prize at stake. This contest was a good example of that. OK, it was the FA Cup semi-final, but that trophy meant nothing like as much to us as the Championship or the Champions League. But it was Arsenal, the reigning League champions, who'd trounced us

3-0 at Highbury, and held us to a 1-1 draw at Old Trafford. Theirs was an important scalp. Beating them on this occasion became an end in itself. How fucking good are we?

Ryan Giggs's goal was amazing. In your very best performances you often find that extra bit of inspiration when you forget the tactics, the game plan, even forget what you're playing for and just play. The way you did when you were a kid on the streets when there was nothing at stake except, in some vague way, personal vindication. When you reach that level of deep, deep concentration it's amazingly liberating. You summon up all you've ever learned about the game from somewhere deep inside and just play. I imagine Becks's last-minute goal against Greece that meant England qualified for the World Cup finals came from that kind of inspiration. We had a lot of players in our side that treble-winning season who were inspired at different times to find resources they weren't sure were there. Dwight Yorke and Andy Cole, individually and as a pair, David Beckham, Ryan Giggs, Paul Scholes, Nicky Butt, Ole and Teddy.

At Villa Park Ryan Giggs dug deep to score that fantastic goal. This was a pivotal moment in our season. Beating Arsenal in such an epic battle, against all the odds with ten men, proved that we were a real side, with rare resilience at our disposal when it was required. Sometimes even Manchester United need the kind of confirmation that comes from a victory like this.

A week later in Turin we faced another acid test of our ability and resolve. All Juventus required was a 0-0 draw. Knowing the way Italians' minds worked, we felt it was a real possibility that they would shut up shop and invite us on to them. That notion was out the window after six minutes. Inzaghi was left free on the far post to score easily. Four minutes later he scored again. Anybody looking to throw the towel in now had the perfect opportunity. Anybody seeking to prove that they were worthy of playing for Manchester United also had the chance to fucking prove it. It is at moments like this that football – any sport for that matter – becomes a mind game. How strong were we mentally? How strong were Juventus?

Of course the goals were bad news. The good news, the positive response to this situation, was that there were eighty minutes of football left to play. We were two goals down in the tie. However, if we equalized, we'd be through on away goals.

As the game restarted after Inzaghi's second goal I had made the calculations. Any idiot can start lunging into crazy tackles, and charging forward in search of a quick-fix goal in a situation such as the one we now faced. That's not the way back against top teams like Juventus. Looking around our side, it was easy to take heart from the quality of our attacking players. Yorke, Cole, Beckham could all score a goal (and Scholes could come off the bench to nick one). Which was all we needed to put the pressure back on the Italians. So let's get the ball and play, quicken the tempo, get a few tackles in, turn the tide.

Slowly, we did. Juventus were content to be two goals ahead. They allowed us to come at them in our measured way. As we upped the rhythm of the play they didn't respond in kind. I sensed them lapsing into the comfort zone. I was convinced that they were content to hold on to what they had rather than go for the killer goal. The momentum was with us. Were they good enough to contain Manchester United?

The more the first half progressed, the more we dominated open play. In a grim kind of way I began to enjoy the chase, which is what this contest now was. We needed a goal before half-time. Becks ran to take a corner on the left. I moved towards the near post. A little gamble – scoring headers from corners hadn't been my game since my Rockmount days. You need luck when timing a run into the box, but you do need to make the run. I did. Becks's cross was perfectly flighted. I just glanced it into the back of the net.

All bets were off. The whole equation of the tie had altered. They were afraid of us now. And we were in that inspirational zone, focused, the momentum on our side. Just before half-time I tried to reach a loose pass from Jesper Blomqvist, but Zidane got there before me. Too late to pull out I caught him, innocuously, and he went down. The yellow card meant I'd miss the final. But I was so much into this battle that the consequences of the card barely registered. As in the Arsenal game, victory here and now became an end in itself. We weren't in the final yet. If we didn't get the right result here, there wouldn't be any final to worry about.

Knowing they were on the brink of chucking it – you could see it in their eyes – drove us on. Yorke and Cole were causing their back four all kinds of problems. The pace and guile of Dwight and Andy now kicked in in a big way. Dwight's equalizing goal was set up by Andy. At 2-2 we were through. They packed it in. Zidane, Deschamps and Davids all went missing. I went for a fifty–fifty ball against Davids. It was no contest.

When Andy Cole scored our third I knew there would be a final to miss. I didn't care at that point (although later I would). I was proud of our team that night. I was for once proud of myself, content that I had justified my existence and honoured my debts to the manager who'd placed so much trust in me. The Champions League final was where I believed

Manchester United should be. I genuinely felt that that was
so much more important than whether or not I would be
there. When that euphoric feeling evaporated (it lasted quite
a while) I was gutted.

Sunday 16 May 1999

The dream treble. It sounds good on paper. In the dressing
room as we prepare for the Spurs game the perspective is quite
different. We are, as everyone knows, only three games from
a treble that would be historic. The deal is simple: beat Spurs
today, Newcastle at Wembley next Saturday and Bayern
Munich in Barcelona on Wednesday week and we have sur-
passed anything achieved by any other team in the modern
game. However, there is an alternative possibility that might
prompt a different headline: UNITED BLOW TREBLE
BID. Or FERGIE'S MEN FAIL THE EUROPEAN
TEST AGAIN. Or THE NEARLY MEN. If I tend to be
rather subdued when it comes to punching the air or ripping
the shirt off my back after scoring a goal it is because I never
forget how fine the line is between success and failure when
you're chasing the greatest prizes in the game. The closer you
come to the Dream (of winning) the closer you are to the
Nightmare (blowing a season's work).

So far this has been a good season for me. A year ago I
wasn't sure I'd play again, the difference between the glory of
captaining Man. United and being a has-been at twenty-seven
was one stupid tackle on Alfie Haaland. I made my mistake
and learned my lesson. Or did I? Well, not really. When the
lads walk out to meet Bayern at the Nou Camp I'll be sitting
in the fucking stand. Why? Another stupid tackle on Zidane

in the Juventus game and a daft booking for arguing when we played Inter Milan! So if the Dream Treble becomes the Nightmare Failure, I'll have something to answer for.

We should beat Spurs today. Coached by George Graham, they will try to play it tight, give nothing back, nick something on the break. But if we play we'll break them down. We know we can match any team for effort, then the class kicks in, Becks, Ryan Giggs, Dwight Yorke, Andy Cole, Paul Scholes, Teddy. We're hungrier than they are, that should be enough.

Still, beneath the palpable determination in the dressing room there is a kind of low-level anxiety you feel in your gut, a lingering fear that this could be one of those days when, legs heavy, mind wandering, touch just that vital fraction off, it doesn't happen. Sometimes the big days are like that. The crowd gets restless, the opposition, sniffing your uncertainty, aren't afraid any more. It happens at Old Trafford once or twice a season and you never know why . . . or when it's coming. Southampton, Middlesbrough, fucking Coventry start playing like Real Madrid. Bang, it's over. One of life's little mysteries! Normally you move on to the next match, get back in the groove and reclaim the lost ground. Today that is not an option.

Life in the dressing room is different. Sometimes – no, always – the gap between what we do – and feel – and other people's reality is alarming. The media hero is not necessarily the Man in here. Ditto the crowd pleaser. I'm not complaining. I wanted to be a footballer. I dreamed of it for as long as I can remember. Then being a footballer wasn't enough. I wanted to be a pro. After becoming a pro, I wanted to win things. And when the chance came I desperately wanted to play for Manchester United, to be part of days like this.

Outside we can hear the crowd. They are in celebration mode, happily anticipating another great Old Trafford occasion, another Premiership title. The writers and broadcasters are primed to tell the good news story, to speak of dreams and glory. Or, if we fail, to damn us as the guys who blew the treble. We must win, otherwise – we must assume – Arsenal will beat Villa and take our title.

We are here to work. Football at the level Manchester United play it is a savage business. For us today is not a party day, it's business – a hard, sometimes dangerous, invariably exacting business. Yes, the rewards are great. You can earn a lot of money and be a hero – whatever that is. But you can also be a failure, humiliated, blasted in the media, jeered by the crowd, or simply left out of the team, a very public slight that hurts not just you but your family, wife, kids, mum, dad, brother, sisters. The stakes are high, other people's judgements merciless. Ask Becks, who was vilified a year ago for a momentary lapse in an England game. He's had to endure the nation's bile, generated by the scribes in the press-box or their pals on the serious pages, many of whom probably never saw a football match. He let the country down. He is a symbol of our moral decline! Give me a break. He was playing a game of football. He flicked a petulant foot at Diego Simeone, who was intent on kicking the shit out of him. The press got on his case, priming the pump that spews out the vile chants Becks has had to listen to up and down the country all season. Stuff about his wife and son that is sick. Who's letting the country down?

Ask Eric about the price he paid for his moment of madness. Jack the Ripper got better press. Ask anyone at the club about the bad times when the fans and commentators are baying for your fucking blood. Bad times are only ninety minutes away.

At this club a moment's weakness can lead to shame. A poor result against Real Madrid or Bayern Munich is failure. To be fair, it is failure. Failure to live up to the standards set by men who came before us at Old Trafford: Matt Busby, Bobby Charlton, George Best, Denis Law, the Munich team, Bryan Robson, Eric Cantona. Because of them I wanted to play for United. They are the reason why wherever Manchester United play there is a buzz. Of expectation. Delivering is our job. It's a tall order. Every time I pull on a red shirt I'm conscious of the responsibility of being a United player. We are all, well, most of us, most of the time. If we forget, the manager will remind us. Ideally, as is the case in this side, we'll remind each other. Those exchanges can be bruising.

The manager is the only Man in here. Yes, he's hard. He radiates purpose. He's intense, focused, driven. His commitment, his insatiable hunger never cease to amaze me. He sets the tone, especially on a day like this when the carnival atmosphere around the place can cause you to forget the objective. A result. Remember who you are, remember that you are Manchester United players. Remember what you did to get here, now go and do it one more time. And you'll win.

As the manager outlines the task ahead of us today, anxiety dissolves. That anxiety – low-level, subconscious – is triggered by the realization that over the next ten days we're facing three games that can lead either to a 'glorious treble' or cause us to be damned as a team of 'losers, in need of radical surgery'. Winning the FA Cup would be enough for some clubs. For us this year victory in the Cup would represent abject failure if we were to let the Premiership and the Champions League slip away. Even the double – League and Cup – would be deemed failure of a kind. Europe is the ultimate goal for Manchester United, a target set by the team of '68. That's why the manager bought me six years ago. So far we've failed that test. We're still striving. At this club striving is a way of life. Striving to meet the manager's relentless demands, striving to reach the objective we've set for ourselves, which is victory in Europe. Until we've won the Champions League this team can never claim success.

You can't win a game in the dressing room, but you can certainly lose it if you walk out with the wrong attitude. This is where the manager is really different class. He knows his players, knows how to gee each of us up. They say God is in the detail; in football that's true. Detail is the manager's speciality. He knows what turns each of us on. As importantly, he's read the opposition: strengths and weaknesses.

Sometimes games are won by a magical goal – a Becks special, or some magic from Giggs or Scholes or Teddy – that's what people remember. But the essence of the game over a sixty-match season is more mundane. Detail. Wearing down the opposition. Winning the psychological battles – man on man – from the moment the ref blows the whistle for kick-off. First tackle, first pass, first touch, everything counts. The Law of Cumulation. A lot of little things add up to the thing that matters: breaking the opposition's hearts – but first their minds, their collective mind. Very few sides can match us at that. Most come to Old Trafford already beaten. The only way we lose at home is when we beat ourselves. Of this the manager constantly reminds us.

Although it's a special occasion, the Spurs game reinforces the manager's view – which I share – that the so-called little things really matter. They are half a yard behind us to every loose ball. There's no conviction in their passing. They tackle but it's a gesture rather than a full-blooded challenge. They take the lead. Les Ferdinand tries a cross, misconnects with the outside of his foot and the ball loops crazily over Peter Schmeichel. One down.

Now we've got to step it up a gear. Again, it's detail. No mad rush, just move into a new rhythm. Do the right things, pass the ball, move them around, make the bastards work, wear them down. And try not to think about what Arsenal are doing to Villa at Highbury. This is where confidence and experience count. Also the class in our side, which is the basis for our conviction that we can play our way back into any game.

Now Becks produces a piece of magic to create a goal out of nothing. Well it appears to be out of nothing; in fact, the goal is the result of fifteen minutes of pressure, applied relentlessly, which Spurs aren't up to coping with. Becks only needs a yard. They allow him five yards. It's a beautiful strike which curls high into the top corner. We're out of jail. Although not playing very well, because the occasion has undermined the iron concentration we possess at our best, we have too much for Spurs.

At half-time the manager replaces Teddy with Andy Cole. We know what we have to do . . . and we know how to do it. My ankle is giving me grief, but not enough to take me out of the game. These are the matches I love. Tight, no going through the motions, the season at stake over forty-five minutes. Men at work.

Two minutes into the second half Andy Cole scores a gem of a goal. Andy has a much better touch than people give him credit for. This he now proves by controlling a difficult pass and looping a perfect lob over Ian Walker, a skill perfectly executed just when required. Relief.

Relief is my strongest emotion at this moment. Fuck it, we've done it. We haven't screwed up. The fear that this could be one of those days – compounded by Ferdinand's flukey goal – is gone. For a moment. Then I glance at the clock. Still a long way to go. It's a long forty minutes. We begin to lose our concentration. Again, it's the little things that start to go wrong. Allowing them an extra half a yard. A little too cautious with our passes. Less inclined to push forward into their territory in support of the ball. The instinct to protect what you have at work. A dangerous instinct.

Another fluke, one dodgy refereeing decision and it will be too late to respond. The crowd are going mad. The final ten minutes are surreal. Your mind is distracted, your emotions running out of control, you realize how desperately you wanted this . . . and how close you are to failure. There's no way back if you blow it now, I think as the game runs into overtime. Blow the fucking whistle, please.

Graham Poll blows the whistle. The sense of relief is overwhelming. Job done. Thank God. My legs have gone. The manager is hugging me. Well done, son. In that moment a certain calm descends upon me. The fear of failure which drives us all is exorcized. I don't play football to be famous or celebrated, none of us does. Happiness is satisfying the demands of your business, repaying the fans' devotion, justifying your wages, indeed, your very existence as a Manchester United player. Happiness is not being afraid.

Now we can have a few drinks!

We had a grand party that night. Theresa and the other wives and girlfriends came, along with everyone at the club who made a contribution to the football team's success in many different ways. Although United have always been relatively poor payers of players' wages – something I'm told that goes back to Matt Busby's days – the club has always been very good at recognizing that everyone, from the ground staff and the laundry ladies to the office staff, tea ladies and those who man the stiles on match days, is part of the Manchester United community. Nothing illustrates better the contribution made by people whose names are never in the paper than the work our physio Dave Fevre did with me when I did my cruciate ligament. Without his skill and dedication I wouldn't be sitting here this evening celebrating a Premiership victory.

The manager is particularly good at nurturing this family atmosphere at Old Trafford. Occasions such as this are the perfect opportunity to pay tribute to people who in their own specialities set standards every bit as accomplished as those we are constantly aiming for on the pitch. The vibe that runs through the club as a consequence, from dressing room to kit room, to the training ground and the ticket office, makes this, for all the glamour associated with United, an essentially homely club. This is precious in a curious kind of way: the comforting and intimate human contact of everyday existence as a Manchester United player being just one of the reasons why players rarely want to leave this club.

Mancunians are lovely, warm and witty people. They bear more than a passing resemblance to Cork people, who are also renowned for their suss and lack of airs and graces. When the manager identified a few big-time Charlies in the squad and promised to get rid of them, it demonstrated how in touch he was with the culture that prevails not just within the club but in this city. Another detail, but a critical one. Dressed–up functions I don't normally enjoy. Too much bullshitting. The blah, blah, blah of idle talk. Every arsehole in the room in your face, invading your space. Most people are great, the more genuine the fan the less likely he or she is to move in on you. But in every room there's a few who have a bone to pick, a point to make (usually to their mates). Up they come.

And if you don't buy in to their act they want to know who you think you are.

I can't handle this kind of thing. If that's a failing, it's cost me dear on more than one occasion. Not tonight, though. This is a safe environment. Ryan Giggs and Nicky Butt are as usual the jokers, taking the piss, winding people up, a dangerous duo to take on at the banter game. Giggsy is a real character, a Salford lad, streetwise and wickedly funny. With his deadpan face and innocent demeanour he projects a fairly bland image. Innocent Giggsy is not. He's got away with murder over the years – and he laughs about it. Sensible Nicky, Mr Dependable, is an equally cruel piss-taker. As usual, tonight he and Giggsy are 'at it'; Becks, Paul Scholes, Gary and Phil Neville aren't far away.

Those six have been together since they were kids. They form the core of the team, on and off the field. And are bonded in a way that excludes the rest of us. There's no problem with that. On the contrary, I think it's a huge factor in the club's success. Apart from Becks they're all Mancunians – and he's been at United since he was twelve – and in the modern game, where money talks, usually in a foreign language, the kind of loyalty and commitment that the six lads personify is a precious commodity. Liverpool have it. Arsenal, Chelsea and Leeds don't. So at the heart of our club there is something solid, something real, something identifiably Mancunian, an attitude created by the Six Amigos, that is fundamental to the team and its success. When players join United, however much they cost, wherever they come from, it is this attitude they must plug in to.

This thing we have rather than glory or dreams is what we are celebrating tonight. It's a genuinely happy evening for a genuinely happy club. Six days away from the Wembley Cup final, ten days away from Bayern Munich at the Nou Camp, we can relax from the disciplines, rigours and fears of the long – too long – English season. It's late when we leave, weary, on a high, content. Tomorrow we've arranged a lads' night out. Then back to work.

Monday 17 May

I woke up feeling great. Hungover, yes. With a sore ankle, which I knew would make it touch and go whether I'd be fit for the Cup final against Newcastle – but that was five days away. As I wouldn't be playing in Barcelona, that meant my season was over bar one game. My feelings were mixed. Relief and disappointment. Relief that we'd won the Premiership, disappointment because I'd miss out on the Bayern game, which meant so much to the club. But I'd cross that bridge when I reached it.

Meanwhile, a day off, the only responsibility an appointment with the physio for some treatment on my ankle. Followed by a session with the lads. United was no longer the drinking club I'd joined. The regular Saturday-night sessions with Bryan Robson, Steve Bruce, Eric, Lee Sharpe and the others, which had been such a feature of club life, had long since ceased. The game had changed, for the better. We'd grown up, we now looked after our bodies, ate pasta, drank creatine, went for quiet meals with our wives. The professional Roy Keane welcomed the new regime, its disciplines and rewards. But we'd had a lot of fun in the drinking era and the part of me that hankered after the rowdy banter and camaraderie of the best drinking sessions missed those gloriously irresponsible nights. Inside professional Roy there was another guy bursting to get out. The guy who loved hanging out with Des Walker, taking the piss, swopping insults, looking for a bit of mischief, living for the moment. Roy the mischief-maker rarely got out. He would today.

The plan was agreed. We'd meet in Mulligans, an Irish bar in Manchester, at five o'clock. By one o'clock I'd finished my treatment. The prognosis was good. I'd be OK for Saturday, not 100 per cent, but fit enough to play what would be my last game of the season. I could have a right go without worrying about being fit for the following week.

Now I had a few hours to kill, a rare luxury. Of course, footballers have plenty of time off, or apparently off. Alas, what appears to be free time isn't generally really free – in the sense that you can do what you like. What may seem like free time, in, say, the afternoons is in fact rest time, recovering from morning training, preparing for tomorrow's work, and always thinking – about the last match, the next match and, increasingly in the modern game, especially at United, of some extra-curricular duty – commercial, media – designed to make money or create good will, for you or the club.

Time off? When I look back on the average season and add up the days when I am actually off, there are very few. As I've got older I have gradually come to appreciate that from day one in July, when you report back for pre-season training, until the end, which may be a World Cup qualifying game in June, there is no time off. You enter the concentration zone, live for the game and its attendant responsibilities to the exclusion of almost everything else. Family life comes second. Social life is non-existent. Football is all-consuming. For a Manchester United player, perpetually chasing results and trophies, there is no respite. It's a selfish existence. Wonderful, yes, exacting, for you and those closest to you, definitely. But not today.

I'd arranged to meet Norman Whiteside in The Griffin in Bowden at twelve. Norman is a good lad. He was an outstanding footballer, the youngest ever to play in the World Cup finals (for Northern Ireland in Spain in 1982) and scored a brilliant winning goal for United in the 1985 FA Cup final. Sadly, his career was cut short by injury. Norman had retrained as a podiatrist. He was still a popular character at Old Trafford. Respected for two reasons (make that three!): his talent; he took no prisoners on the pitch; and he was a leading member of the work-hard, play-hard drinking club that Sir Alex had banished from Old Trafford a couple of years after he arrived.

Norman, Bryan Robson, Paul McGrath and Kevin Moran were all fantastic players – part Stuart Pearce, part Des Walker – but in the best – or worst – of Old Trafford traditions that stretched back to Sir Matt Busby's days – indeed, to the legendary Busby Babes – Norman, Bryan, Paul and Kevin mixed outstanding achievement with some pretty spectacular sessions. That culture was still thriving when I arrived at the club in 1993. And many of my happiest Manchester days were spent enjoying a few pints in The Griffin.

Of course, things have changed dramatically. But the pull of a lazy, inebriated afternoon that stretched way past sunset was strong. Perhaps once a week (or twice) we'd give it a blast. Driven by guilt you'd work like a demon in training the next morning. Pleasure followed by punishment. A fair deal. And a glorious escape from the bullshit of celebrity, fame and associated nonsense, the circus that is the modern game. The beauty of a good session is that there are no stars or heroes. We live in a make-believe world created by the media which is largely, though not entirely, fiction. The fictional hero is often an arsehole. Conceited, greedy, vain, often a cheat on the pitch. We have had one or two in our dressing room, lapping up the applause, milking their fame, playing the game with the media and the fans. You are unlikely to find the stars in a session. But their bullshit ways are frequently discussed, scorned and mocked. The bad boys usually sit at the back of the bus. They are the first to buy their round, and, crucially, as was the case with Norman, Robbo, Paul and Kevin, these are the guys who'll make the difference when it matters on the pitch. Or at least that's the way we justify ourselves in The Griffin.

So today is for me a touch nostalgic. I've spent a few good days in this and neighbouring pubs with Paul Ince, Robbo, Lee Sharpe (who preferred the city-centre), Eric, Steve Bruce and Norman, who commands as much respect and affection as any double-winning star. We can relax and be ourselves. There is no audience, no gallery to play to. It's real, human, normal – men behaving normally, which stars never seem to do.

As the afternoon passes, the office workers drifting back to work, we talk about everything and nothing. Norman is a funny lad, the perfect companion for a carefree session. The gossip is vicious, the judgements passed on various stars we have known severe. Tales of outrageous incidents that never got back to the manager's office – and some that unfortunately did – are told again and seem all the richer for being recycled in the heady atmosphere of late-afternoon drinking. We don't talk about ourselves, or the Meaning of Life, just about how things are, instead of how things are depicted.

I've eaten nothing. I haven't had much sleep. I'm glowing. It's time to move on to meet the lads in Mulligans in Manchester. As we are driven into town, I feel slightly apprehensive. Despite living here for six years I know little of the city-centre. When Lee Sharpe was my guide, I just followed.

From pub to club, down narrow streets, following Lee, who always knew where the action was.

There is a pattern here, the story of me, drink and cities: Cork, Dublin, Nottingham, Manchester. It adds up to aggravation. Ninety per cent of the time there's no problem. But I've learned to my cost that in bars situations can arise that require the kind of guile I don't possess.

For example, a scene in Dublin not long ago when I went out for a drink with Tony Cascarino. It was a Sunday night before a Wednesday international. Cas and I thought we'd kick off with a pint in the hotel bar. Just as we ordered, a guy comes over. His mate has got married that day. The wedding party is in full swing across in the ballroom. The exchange goes as follows:

Stranger: 'Roy, would you mind coming over to have a photo taken with the happy couple?'

Roy: 'We've just ordered a drink, give me five minutes and I'll be over, no problem.'

Stranger: 'We need it now.'

Roy: 'Look, let me get the drinks in, then I'll be over.'

Stranger: 'So it's true what they say about you, you're an arrogant prick.'

Cas: 'Listen, mate, he's said no problem, just give us a few minutes.'

Stranger: 'Fuck off, you, I'm talking to him.'

Fortunately I've no drink taken, otherwise the anger I feel would have erupted. Still, my inclination is to hit the guy, who has been drinking all day by the looks of him.

Cas: 'Roy, let it go. We're out for the night, don't let this fucker spoil it.'

Roy to Stranger: 'Piss off.'

Most people in the public eye experience scenes like this.

Most learn to handle strangers with attitude, most of whom believe they own a part of you. I don't have those skills. Ever since I was a kid, small for my age, my instinct has been to look danger in the eye rather than turn the other cheek. Stand up to bullies, don't be pushed around. Meet aggression with aggression. Cas and I had a good night, but it could have ended up as another Roy Keane brawl story.

Mulligans is a small Irish pub tucked away on a back street, the perfect venue for the kind of night out we want to have, a normal drinking session, such as any other group of workmates enjoy at the end of a normal working week. The downside of fame, of being a United player, is the absence of normality. Which is illustrated by the presence of three bodyguards in Mulligans, courtesy of Ned Kelly Security Force.

That doesn't stop us having a good time. Ryan Giggs and Nicky Butt are looking for victims. Gary Neville is talking. Peter Schmeichel is posing (what's new?) and boring the arse off people. Dwight Yorke is bubbling with good humour and mischief. Becks is listening to Gary. Teddy is being cool. He's from London! Denis Irwin and Paul Scholes, the quiet men, are coming out of their shells.

We decide to move. One of our bodyguards goes across the street to Henry's, a smart bar, to check if it's OK for us to go over. No problem, he reports. Some of the lads are regulars in Henry's, so we can get a couple of tables and continue our celebrations.

For a while all is well but soon trouble appears in the shape of two women and a guy who'd been eyeing us up in Mulligans. I'm talking to Ryan when one of the women asks if we'll buy her a drink. We blank her. But she persists. This time backed up by her pal and the guy who's with them. We move. They follow.

'Aren't you going to buy the girls a drink, you wanker?' The guy is in my face. Meet aggression with aggression. Well, the sensible thing to do at this point would have been to call Ned Kelly's Security Force. Sadly, with drink taken, common sense is not my strongest suit.

'Piss off and leave us alone,' is my response.

'Why don't you piss off? Who the fuck do you think you are?' woman number one replies.

From somewhere a glass flies through the air, hitting me in the face just below my eye. I lunge at the guy. Then all hell breaks loose. What follows is a blur. But subsequent reports established that the two women left the bar to make two phone calls. The first to the *Sun* to claim they had a story (true!), the second to the police to say they'd been assaulted by Roy Keane. This allegation was later denied by the bar manager, who confirmed that initially 'Roy Keane turned away from the girls, who were pestering him, one of them was seen to throw a glass, which hit him in the face. At this point the girls were asked to leave the bar. They had been offensive to both staff and customers and were ejected in line with company policy.'

The police came, lights flashing. A small crowd was gathering. I could see tomorrow's headlines already.

'Come on, Mr Keane.' Polite but firm. I'm in the back of the police van. I thought, 'You prick. Why me, the usual, why me? I wasn't the only one they were bothering, but I was the one who had to get involved. Again.'

At the police station I explained what happened. They listened. Unfortunately, after nine hours on the tear I didn't make a very convincing witness. No food, no sleep, three aggressive punters in a bar: a recipe for disaster. They put me in a cell, to sleep it off. It was a long night. I didn't sleep much.

My first thought was for Theresa and the kids. Remorse and shame soon sober you up. The press would be outside the house when Shannon was going to school. Then there was the club: facing two big games, one of them the biggest in United's history, with the club captain in a cell for drunk and disorderly conduct!

Yes, it was a set-up, but that was no excuse. There was no excuse. I was just a daft fucker. Wild man Keane. I phoned Michael Kennedy, who told me not to worry! I thought about my family at home in Cork, picking up the papers, reading the headlines, fretting, getting looks from the neighbours, having to endure that embarrassment of their Roy. Again. I was some tulip.

The manager arrived the following morning. Michael had called him, although that wouldn't have been necessary. Manchester is a village. If you're offside, the manager will know the following morning. So-and-so was in a club until half-two. He got into a taxi looking well drunk, etc., etc. He'll have you in, and there's no use denying it. I've always been honest with him, held my hands up, which now pays off. For when I explain what happened in Henry's he accepts that I'm telling the truth. 'I'll get you out.' This is the last thing he needs four days before the Cup final. But in these situations the manager has always been brilliant. He knew how bad I felt. The last thing I needed this morning was a bollocking.

I was released on bail with an assurance that if, as seemed certain, the assault allegations proved false, I'd hear nothing more about the matter. Relieved, I went home to Theresa and the kids vowing that I wouldn't make the same mistake again. Of course I'd made that vow before.

Saturday 22 May

Wembley. My last game of the season. Victory over Newcastle would mean a third double in the 1990s and a place in the history books. But I think Henry Ford was correct when he said that history was bunk. I don't believe football teams think in those terms. You shouldn't look back . . . or forward, beyond the ninety minutes ahead of you. Start thinking about records and for sure you'll fail to concentrate on the task at hand. History is for anoraks.

I'd never really bought into the Wembley 'dream'. The facilities for players and spectators were poor. The pitch seemed miles away from the fans – if anything, atmosphere was lacking. And there's no doubt that in an era when the Premiership and the Champions League have become the competitions to win, the FA Cup is nothing more than a consolation prize, an afterthought really.

Warming up before the Newcastle game, I knew my left ankle wasn't right. It was touch and go whether I'd be OK. I was in two minds: I didn't want to let the lads down by playing in circumstances where I couldn't make a proper contribution; at the same time I hoped that with proper strapping and the adrenaline kicking in I'd be OK. Any damage done wouldn't matter, as this was it for the season. In the end the urge to play was irresistible. Fuck it, I'd give it a go.

I lasted eight minutes. Two minutes into the game Gary Speed caught me a beaut. A late tackle. He certainly did me: the ligaments of my good (right) ankle went. If I'd been 100 per cent Speed wouldn't have caught me. After a couple of minutes I hobbled off. I'd see Gary Speed some other day.

The manager put Teddy on, which proved a smart move.

Teddy scored a goal and made one for Paul Scholes. We'd won the double. Despite my scepticism about the wonders of Wembley and the 'dream' of lifting the FA Cup, there was a feeling of real satisfaction as I led the lads up the steps to receive the trophy from Prince Charles. Job done.

Next – although sadly not for me . . .

Monday 24 May

We flew to Spain on Concorde. This was the biggest game for the club since the 1968 European Cup final. Flying Concorde may have been the manager's way of reminding us, and the world, that only the best would do for Manchester United. You never know with Alex Ferguson. He's always looking for an edge.

The season was not exactly ending as I'd hoped. The good news was that we'd won the double and now had a great opportunity to add the Champions League, which had always been the ultimate goal since the day I joined the club. The bad news was, well, that I'd spent a night in jail, been injured in the opening minutes of the Cup final and was now travelling first class as a spare part for the Champions League final.

Ever since that mistimed tackle on Zidane I'd known that this would be a difficult week of mixed emotions. I desperately wanted the lads to win. Although we had dominated the Premiership for years, there was no denying that we'd failed in Europe. And when you considered what Liverpool had achieved in Europe in the 1980s, not to mention Brian Clough and Nottingham Forest, our failure was significant. Reaching the final was a glorious opportunity to get that monkey off our back.

Not having an opportunity to contribute hurt, particularly when I remembered the manager's remark when I joined United in 1993: 'We'll win the Premiership whether you join or not. But with you we'll win the Champions League.' Now, with that achievement within our grasp, I would be a spectator. So too would be Paul Scholes, who'd also been booked in Turin.

We stayed in a beautiful hotel overlooking the sea in Sitges. As usual, I was rooming with Denis. (This would prove more trying for Denis than for me.) For some time I'd questioned the idea that grown men should have to share rooms on the road. There were probably sound economic reasons for the club to book eight rooms instead of sixteen. But this was Manchester United, the largest empire in football. Why not allow each player the space and privacy that, for example, a travelling businessman or woman would feel entitled to? I found room-sharing an embarrassment bordering on insulting. Why did Denis and I have to share? Worse still, at some clubs and in Jack Charlton's days with the Irish team the managers selected your room-mate for you! There are still some things football hasn't worked out, this room-sharing nonsense being one of them. On the one hand, the club expect you to go out and play like a man to win matches for them; on the other, they want to treat you like a kid on a school trip. Which is how you end up with two millionaire professional players, both internationals, sharing a small space for three days. This is mad. Some people like to read, others to watch television. Some are early to bed, others not. Some like a lie-in in the morning, some are up at the crack of dawn.

In Sitges there was a particular problem with the room-sharing arrangement. Denis was playing, I was not. My season was over. I felt pretty useless. Paul Scholes felt the same. It's astonishing how out of things you feel when you're not playing. It's as if a glass partition descends between you and the players who are in the side. And you are on the wrong side of the divide. I was familiar with this feeling from the year I did my cruciate ligaments. No matter how much people try to act sympathetically to you, you remain outside, apart from the action. Utterly redundant.

After training and a meal on Monday night, the players began drifting off to bed. Paul and I were left to our own devices. Some United fans were in the hotel bar. We joined them for a few drinks. Slightly pissed club captain Roy Keane crept quietly to bed in the early hours. Fortunately, Denis didn't wake up. As far as I know.

The following evening we went to the Nou Camp to train on the pitch. Then the reality of my suspension hit me with real force. It's a magnificent stadium. As the lads played a five-a-side, their shouts and laughter echoed around the empty arena. Imagining what it would be like tomorrow night, full of noise and colour, filled me with frustration. The desire to play in a Champions League final – and win – had driven me ever since I'd joined United. Now we were here there was nothing I could do. I would merely be an extra in the movie, part of the noise and colour. I felt almost as sorry for Scholesy as for myself. He was arguably the most gifted player in our squad. He was a Manchester lad, United to the core. Missing this must hurt him badly, especially seeing all his mates from the 1992 and 1993 Youth Cup final teams play for the ultimate prize in the European game. Paul was the perfect pro. Superb on the field, modest and sensible off it. No celebrity bullshit, no self-promotion or glory-hunting, an amazingly gifted player who remained an unaffected human being. Oddly, the fact that he and I were in the same boat took the edge off my disappointment.

Paul and I had another late night. My brothers had arrived after an overland journey from London by minibus! I'd tried to book them flights but a couple of my cousins and a few other friends decided to hire a bloody bus to make the trip. While the working pros were tucked up in bed sleeping, we enjoyed a few drinks in the hotel bar. I was literally drowning my sorrows. It was 4 a.m. when I crept into the room, where Denis was sound asleep.

And I had a few more beers on the Wednesday before we left the hotel to head for the Nou Camp. The normal pre-match banter on the coach was very muted. Even Ryan Giggs and Nicky Butt were quiet. The manager too was palpably uptight. We'd come a long way as a team, breaking most of the domestic records. We'd won three doubles. But everyone on the coach knew that this was the biggest game we'd ever played. We'd been most places, but never here before. Uncharted territory. This was not just another game.

For the manager the stakes were particularly high. He deserved his place in football history along with men like his fellow Scots Busby, Stein and Paisley. I'm certain he felt his lifetime's work wouldn't be complete until we were European champions. I owed him a lot, we all did, this was the night to deliver.

And all I could do was watch. The booking for the foul on Zidane I could live with – there was no option. But the yellow card I got against Inter Milan, for shooting my mouth off, really came back to haunt me as I stood in the dressing room in my club suit wishing the men who had to go out and finish the job good luck.

With Paul and me unavailable the manager had moved Becks into the centre of midfield alongside Nicky Butt. Ryan Giggs was moved to the right wing with Jesper Blomqvist on the left. I sat beside Jimmy Ryan, Henning Berg and Paul. Although I was putting a brave face on it, this was just about the worst experience I'd had in football.

We'd played Bayern home and away in the league phase of the competition. Both games were drawn. They were a good side, but beatable. Bayern were never going to tear you apart as, say, Real Madrid or Barcelona might do. They'd be steady. Defend well, pass the ball around, be patient, wait for their opening. Effenberg in midfield was their main man, he dictated the pace they played at.

Six minutes into the game we gifted them a soft goal. Ronnie Johnsen fouled their big centre-forward, Jancker, and Mario Basler scored with a less than unstoppable free-kick. After that, nothing much happened. Neither side seemed capable of rising to the occasion. Of course, Bayern had the goal and were even more comfortable in their predetermined pattern of play. We had to chase the game, patiently, lest we were caught on the counter-attack. Twice in the second half they hit the woodwork. Curiously, these near misses acted as a spur to our players. This United team is never beaten. We know how to intensify the rhythm of a game. Pass the ball, move, support the player on the ball: fight to win it back if you lose it, the deeper in their half the better.

Slowly, I felt the game turn. Looking at the clock, there were just under fifteen minutes to go. The manager substituted Jesper and Andy Cole throwing on Teddy and Ole. You couldn't choose two better subs. Teddy could drop deep and get on the ball, Ole was just about the best goalscorer in Europe. The tempo of the game was bound to change anyway.

Would the Germans adapt to answer the subtly different questions now being posed?

The answer was no. Watching this, my head was wrecked. Bayern were hanging on. Their back four were no longer out behind the ball. Their midfield players were camped in their own half. 'They've gone,' I said to Jimmy Ryan. 'We've got them.' We desperately needed a break. If you keep doing the right things, you'll get your break in every game. But the Germans were riding their luck, strung out across the edge of their penalty area. For a team with their reputation Bayern Munich were by now a shambles, as bad as bad can be: they were actually 'bottling' it big time. They couldn't possibly win the Champions League playing like this. Or could they? For all the pressure around their goal, we never created a clear-cut chance.

Down on the touchline the fourth official held up his board: three minutes of added time. Another corner for us. Peter Schmeichel was sprinting forward. I'd never seen that particular tactic work! Amazingly, this time it did. Becks swung in a beautifully flighted cross, the ball was half cleared to Ryan on the edge of the box. He mis-hit his shot – straight to Teddy, who poked it past the German keeper.

The Nou Camp erupted. Even now I can't adequately describe the emotion I felt at that moment. Relief, certainly. Satisfaction, for I felt the lads deserved to stay alive just as the Germans had not deserved to win the trophy by default. Most of all, I was pleased for the manager. Not for the first or last time he'd played his substitution cards shrewdly.

There was still a minute to go when Bayern restarted the game. They had now completely lost it. We got the ball back immediately. Back from the dead, we were now unbelievably chasing the winner. Bayern conceded another corner. Becks curled it to the near post, Teddy got the flick on, and Ole guided the ball into the back of the net.

I doubt if we'll ever see three minutes of football like that again. In the end the Champions League of 1998/99 went to the team that wanted it most. Heart won the day. I had played in twelve of the thirteen European games, yet I never felt so drained as I did at the end of those ninety-three minutes in Barcelona. Even at the best of times I've never been one for overdoing the celebrations on the pitch after big games (I usually save myself for the bar). In the Nou Camp that night Paul and I were reluctant to respond when the manager urged us forward to receive our medals. Yes, we had played a part in the European campaign, but the night belonged to the guys who'd done the business against Bayern. Paul and I were in football limbo, examples of the stark truth that lies at the core of professional football: you play for your team, for your club, for the fans, but first and foremost for yourself. Football is a very selfish game. No matter how many people tell me I deserve that Champions League medal, I know I don't. In fact, you could argue that my indiscipline came very close to costing us the treble.

We had a great night back at the hotel. There was a real sense of achievement shared by everyone belonging to the club Alex Ferguson had created. Europe was the acid test and we had passed. Ultimately this was his achievement. I could easily lay aside my personal disappointment at missing the final, for in truth it was an honour to captain the team that delivered for a great manager and a great club. For that reason I sang, laughed and drank the night away. Some of the lads hit the Barcelona nightlife – led by Dwight Yorke – while I stayed in the hotel with my brothers and friends. After ten crazy days of drink, trouble, tabloid hell and trophy heaven, of ups and downs – and lots of places in between – I longed to go home to Theresa and the kids.

We received an extraordinary welcome from the people of Manchester the following day. Much though I love the city and its people, I was too exhausted to enjoy the occasion. Perhaps I'll look at the video some day in the future and tell my grandchildren how wonderful it was. Perhaps.

Midway through the treble-winning season, in December 1998, Brian Kidd left to join Blackburn Rovers as manager. He felt it was time to be his own man, to find out if he could manage a club. Although Kiddo was an integral part of our set-up, I wasn't surprised. Nothing in football surprises me. I'm certain money was one of the reasons Brian left. He had been central to the transformation of United in the 1990s, working as the gaffer's right-hand man. Yet, while we'd become wealthy, his salary wouldn't match the average Nationwide League player's. You'd have to be daft not to think about your wages when all around you were making hay. When Jack Walker offered Brian more than he would earn in a lifetime at Old Trafford, how could he resist? I respected him as a person, and a coach. I was sorry to see him go.

Steve McClaren arrived. A new voice, new ideas, I welcomed that as well. It was another challenge, a chance to learn, an excuse to push myself a little harder in a changed environment.

Money and contracts also occupied my thinking at this stage. I was twenty-eight, in the final year of my contract. Michael Kennedy had been negotiating with the club for several months, Maurice Watkins and Martin Edwards represented the club. Things weren't going well. Money was not the only issue to consider in these circumstances.

I loved playing for Manchester United. As far as I was

concerned, Alex Ferguson was the perfect manager for me. He was dedicated and hungry. He saw through the bluffers and bullshitters in football and resisted whenever that kind of stuff surfaced in our dressing room. Personally, I owed him everything. Whenever life got turbulent, as mine tended to, on and off the park, he was there for me. He didn't want a boy scout, accepted me, the good, the bad, the ugly, for what I was. So leaving him would be a big step.

I also like the dressing room at United. During this period I had the option of going abroad to play. A number of European clubs, big clubs, were sniffing around. As of 1 January 2000 I could officially talk to another club. Then under the Bosman Ruling I could leave on a free transfer in June 2000. The cards were stacked in my favour. And Michael knew how to play the hand.

Juventus and Bayern Munich were the two clubs I seriously thought about. Both were prepared to offer unbelievable money, enough to set me up for life. During my last season I'd come to understand how fleeting a football career was. One day a well-paid hero, the next day Roy who? Juventus was a big club with a good coach (Lippi), great players and a strong tradition. I liked the feel of the place when we played there . . . there was a good vibe off their players the night we beat them in the semi-final. I would go there if I had to. Bayern was another club I admired. Again, a good coach (Hitzfeld) and a great tradition. Also stability, no superstars walking in and out the door every season in exchange for large cheques. In negotiations you've always got to be prepared to walk. I was. But leaving United was hard to contemplate.

Despite the stuff that's written about me being a loser who is semi-detached from the other players at the club, the truth is a bit more complicated. I'm a little older than 'the kids', not one of the gang – Becks, the Nevilles, Nicky Butt, Ryan Giggs and Paul Scholes. They eat meals together, socialize with each other, have their own thing going. My thing is different. I socialized with the lads in the 1994/95 team more. I was into the drinking sessions, the banter with Robbo, Brucey, Incey and Eric. A different team, a different, more carefree time. Those lads were my mates. Now I have colleagues. But I really like them, all of them. We have our fun, each of us plays a different role in the scheme of things. They accept me for what I am, a driven bastard most of the time; I accept them for what they are. Unlike the team of the mid-1990s, our bonds are forged on the field rather than in the bar.

I recognize that 'the kids' are the greatest strength the club possess, potentially. They form a core of United believers that other Premiership clubs don't necessarily have. Arsène Wenger won the double for Arsenal; next thing, Petit and Overmars are going. Vieira may or may not move to Real Madrid or some Italian club. At Leeds and Chelsea the same instability eats away at the fabric of those clubs. Not at Manchester United.

I was happy at Old Trafford. Theresa and I were happy living in Manchester. Our children were settled, Shannon beginning school. The idea of pulling up roots and moving abroad for money, however large the sum, was unattractive. Knowing all of this, United played hardball to protect the club's wage structure. It was up to me to make them understand that, despite everything, I would move unless I got the contract I felt the club could afford. I went public to declare that a European club was an option. United used the media to send their own message: sign or quit. The negotiations went to the wire before an agreement was reached. I was delighted to sign a new four-year deal.

During the opening weeks of the 1999/2000 season Michael conducted the business, while I worked hard to prove my value to the club on the field. I scored two goals at Highbury in a 2-1 victory and the winner in the Inter-Continental Cup against the Brazilian side Palmeiras in Tokyo.

We won six and drew three of our first nine Premiership games. Then Chelsea whacked us 0-5 at Stamford Bridge. Peter Schmeichel had left in the summer. The gaffer had signed two goalkeepers to replace him: Mark Bosnich from Villa and Massimo Taibi from Venezia. Bosnich was a likeable character. You could write a book about him. A gifted keeper, Bosy didn't exactly seem the most dedicated pro. He arrived an hour late for training on his first day. The manager was away somewhere. When Bosy strolled out around eleven o'clock, I asked him where he'd been.

'I got lost on the way from the hotel,' he smirked. He was a bit of a smirker.

'Got fucking lost,' I sneered.

'Yes, mate,' said Bosy.

'Your first fucking day at Manchester United and you turn up an hour late for fucking training,' I said.

It's funny, but this little incident struck a chord with me. Like Bosnich, I'd been billeted in the Four Seasons hotel on my first day six years previously. Anxious lest I be late, I ordered a taxi, told the driver to lead the way to The Cliff, and followed in my car. I was an hour early. The little things matter, usually betraying an attitude to the job. In this instance the signs were telling. I gave him a bollocking to wake him up, to let him know what was expected of a Manchester United player – these days. For Bosy had been at United when he was younger, but failed to get a work permit.

Mark Bosnich stayed at Old Trafford but he never got

the message. My own split personality meant that while Bosy pissed me off with his easy-going approach to the business, I really liked the guy's Jack the Lad character. He and Dwight Yorke were good pals, two of a kind in many ways. Dwight had enjoyed a fabulous season when we won the treble. In fifty-one appearances he scored twenty-nine goals and led the line superbly, setting up countless scoring chances for others. Sadly, for him and us, success on the field led to excess after hours. At this stage he was still able to be a player and a playboy, but the clock was ticking for Dwight.

Massimo Taibi was a really good pro – and a really good lad. He was clearly a good goalkeeper. Unfortunately, Massimo got off to a dreadful start when he got in the side. The week before the Chelsea drubbing, at home to Southampton, he'd allowed a harmless Matt le Tissier shot to slip through his legs. The Chelsea game was the end for Massimo. Bosnich was back the following week. Massimo on his way home to Italy.

It didn't matter. After losing to Spurs 1–3 we went eleven League games unbeaten.

In Europe we progressed steadily. With the contract talks still unresolved, I kept my scoring boots on. Having scored in our wins against Croatia Zagreb (away) and Sturm Graz (home and away) in the first phase, I also got goals in the second-phase games against Valencia, Bordeaux and Fiorentina. On the day before the Valencia game, Michael had called to say that we finally had a deal.

In October 1999 the manager called a meeting to explain that, for reasons outside of United's control, we wouldn't be entering the FA Cup. England was bidding to host the 2006 World Cup finals, a gift that was FIFA's to bestow. And FIFA wanted Manchester United to play in the first Club World

Championship to be held in Brazil in early January 2000. The government and the Football Association were putting pressure on the club to go. For United it was a no-win situation: offend FIFA, the FA and the government . . . or turn their backs on football's oldest competition and offend, well, almost everybody as it turned out.

The truth of this affair, which caused so much controversy, was that the FA Cup had lost its relevance, certainly for me. Sure, it was a day out for our families, and everybody who worked hard behind the scenes at the club. The Wembley myth, the folklore attached to the walk out of the tunnel, the red carpet, meeting the big shots, going up to the Royal Box to receive your medal, a pat on the back from the great and the good (and hopefully the Cup), all of it was bollocks. The Premiership and the Champions League were the only trophies we were concerned about.

Of course you couldn't say that. Tradition dies slowly in the English game. It does, however, die. With the news that the holders of the FA Cup wouldn't be defending the trophy, all hell broke loose. We all put on our sick-as-parrot faces, expressing shock and regret. Privately, I didn't care. Brazil in January sounded great. Even if the so-called FIFA Club World Championship seemed less than a must-have trophy.

We left for Brazil with good intentions. You always want to win. We were representing Manchester United. The manager reminded us of our duty, urging us to prove that we were the best club side in the world.

Rio was hot. The hotel was on the beach. The exact status of the tournament was vague. Necaxa of Mexico, Vasco da Gama of Brazil and the Australian side South Melbourne were our opponents in the group phase. For our opening game against the Mexicans the renowned but distinctly shabby

Maracanã stadium was empty. A vast concrete oval, echoing with the sound of our own voices. Atmosphere nil. Heat beyond belief. Result 1-1.

The stadium was packed for our second game against Vasco, the local champions. However, two bad errors by Gary Neville allowed Vasco two very soft goals. We lost 3-1. Tournament over. Nobody cried. For all kinds of reasons this was mission impossible. The travelling English journalists tried hard to create the impression that we were enjoying a holiday. We were. Secretly. While complying with the wishes of the Football Association, the government and FIFA. The gaffer rested several players for the game against South Melbourne, which we won 2-0.

On our return from holiday it was important to recapture our concentration. Freed of FA Cup distraction, we could focus on the Premiership and the Champions League. We faced two home games, against Arsenal and Middlesbrough. Arsenal was a big game, always. Bigger this time because of the awayday and the criticism it attracted. We were crap – sluggish, second to the ball, losing the crucial tackles and a goal down until Teddy rescued us with a late equalizer. Summing up the game, Sky Sport's Andy Gray made the following observation: 'We were all waiting and watching and wondering how United would perform. Arsenal flew out of the traps and it took Manchester United half an hour to get going. But Roy Keane was absolutely sensational. Anyone who has a video of that game can look back and see just how Keane got his team going. He went out and started kicking a few, started getting in amongst them. Suddenly his team just rose from there and that typifies why Alex Ferguson has decided to pay such a huge salary to keep him at Old Trafford.'

Andy was spot on about one thing: my reaction to the

comfort zone we tried to operate from for a long spell in this game. Fucking going through the motions like we did at Southampton, with the same result, defeat staring us in the face. Yes, I did get in amongst the Arsenal players, but the message was for our own lads – me included – more than Arsenal. This time it worked. I didn't get sent off, Teddy got the goal. Yet we dropped two points.

Next up, Middlesbrough. Another dangerous game if the attitude wasn't right from the off. It wasn't. Our heads were still in Rio. Headlag! Nil–nil and hanging on, Jaap Stam gave away a penalty. In fact, Japp got a touch on the ball as Juninho dribbled past him. Referee Andy D'Urso got it wrong. We ran at him pleading. He backed off, we kept coming. The photographs of this now notorious incident are shocking. The psycho in the middle with veins bulging in his head is me. Later, I would joke that if Mr D'Urso had stopped running – backwards – we'd have stopped chasing. It's not a joke. I know we were wrong, I the worst offender. Now I believe that, although he made a human error, Andy D'Urso should never have been subjected to our venom. It was our fault the score was 0–0. That was why I raged, against our own crippling complacency, which was now compounded by the ref's mistake. Mr D'Urso was just a whipping boy and that is completely out of order.

That's the rational explanation. Unfortunately, you don't contest games in a reasonable frame of mind. At the level Manchester United must compete at football is savage, cruel, relentlessly punishing. There are no free lunches – and there was no soft landing after Brazil. This we learned the hard way. Fortunately, Juninho's penalty was saved by Mark Bosnich. Becks scored the winner three minutes from time.

After that game we woke up, only losing one of our last seventeen League matches. In that sole defeat, 0–3 at

Newcastle, I was sent off for receiving two yellow cards, one
for dissent, the second for a foul I didn't commit. In a way,
justice for Andy D'Urso. Fair enough.

We were odds-on to win the Premiership by the time we
played Real Madrid in the Champions League quarter-final.
In the first leg in Madrid we got a bit of a chasing. They were
good, Raul, Redondo, Roberto Carlos, Morientes, coming
at us from all angles. Tough lads too. This was a game to relish
for anyone who dreamed of playing at the highest level. The
Bernabeu was packed, fiesta time. Nights like this, particularly
in Spain or Italy, were brilliant, the different sights, sounds
and smells creating an exotic atmosphere. I often wondered
what it would be like to play for the big European clubs. In
Madrid we dug in, ran, marked and covered, and played a bit
when we had the ball. The 0-0 draw was a satisfactory result.

Old Trafford was electric for the return leg. There was a
long history between Real and United dating back to the
pre-Munich Busby team. United had beaten Madrid in the
semi-final in 1968. This kind of occasion was what Manchester
United was all about. That night Real proved how good they
were. It was a classic, both sides creating chances. They got
the vital away goal when I stretched to intercept a cross and
knocked the ball past Raimond Van der Gouw into the back
of our own net. We came back at them, but shortly after
half-time Raul nicked a second, then another within a couple
of minutes. We'd given ourselves a mountain to climb.
Although Becks and Paul Scholes pulled two goals back late
on, Real were just too good for us on the night.

Defeat always hurts, but at least we went down to a very
good side. Redondo's forward run and beautiful turn past
Henning Berg to set up one of Raul's killer goals was football
of the highest class. This was the standard we had to aim for,

world class. A number of features of Real's play struck me. The incredible first touch. The economy of movement, no daft running, every move purposeful. Raul's cunning, waiting like a panther to pounce on any half-chance. And burying it when it came. So much poise, even when we tried to get amongst them; they were so technically adroit we were chasing shadows. They were fit and physically strong as well. I watch a lot of Spanish football on television on Saturday nights. They set the standard we should be aiming for, going forward and defending. Yes, it hurts to lose, but there was much to think about after this game. Most importantly about the goals we should be setting for ourselves at Old Trafford. Should be, but weren't as far as I could see.

Some context for this game. On either side of the Real ties we played West Ham, Middlesbrough, Sunderland and Southampton. We beat West Ham 7-1, Boro away 4-3, Sunderland 4-0 and won the Championship with a 3-1 win at Southampton the Saturday after Madrid beat us. Even though we won the Premiership easily, there was a serious danger that we were fooling ourselves.

We had failed to defend the Champions League. To be honest I wasn't surprised. After winning the treble I knew it would be hard to generate the hunger required to go for the Premiership/Champions League double the following season. I felt my first pangs of doubt standing in the dressing room at the Nou Camp after we'd beaten Bayern. The champagne was flowing, people were going fucking crazy. Of course this was understandable, human nature. But my true, unspoken feeling was that we were lucky to beat Bayern on the night. In the circumstances I couldn't say it. I hadn't contributed. That, though, is what I believed. Bayern 'bottled' it, threw it at us. Maybe I was just being sour, hurt at missing out on the great occasion. Don't be bitter, Roy, let the lads savour the achievement. That argument was countered by another thought: we were dead lucky against a team that bottled it.

When I heard the post-game interviews, my doubts increased. A couple of players told the press that after this they didn't care if they never won another trophy! Hello, I thought. Overexcited maybe, but what the fuck are we going to do next year? Is that it? We've made history. Now we pack it in? Don't care if you don't win another trophy? Jesus. Start thinking like that and you won't win another trophy. Don't be bitter, Roy, the little voice in my head insisted.

What has happened to Dwight Yorke since that night is perhaps the most dramatic example of our slide. But others were softened in more subtle and insidious ways. Don't get me wrong, I like Yorkie, big-time, he's a lovely lad. But the rot had set in at Old Trafford, beginning that memorable night when we claimed the treble. For months afterwards the treble haunted us wherever we went. Well into the following season we were being saluted as heroes, history-makers, better than the 1968 team, the team of the century. Signing photographs with the three trophies, talking about that 'great night' that we'll never forget. It doesn't matter what we do now, we'll never be forgotten. It's still going on today! It drove me crazy then, it drives me crazy now. What about the next step, the one that would take us beyond Premiership 'glory' to the level of Real Madrid? We should have enjoyed the night . . . and moved on. We didn't. For that we would pay the price. Never win another fucking trophy. The rot takes a long time to fully set in. Defeat by Real Madrid was OK, because you couldn't do it every year. Why not? Liverpool did. Real did. Juventus did. Bayern did. I kept my mouth shut. Except to family and close friends.

Every Easter the lads from Cork come to Manchester for the weekend. Some from Rockmount, like John Delea, my old mentor, Kièran O'Sullivan, Billy Cronin, Declan Courtney and Jamesie Corcoran, my oldest, dearest friends. Sometimes Denis, Johnson and Pat, or Hilary and her husband came as well. They'd come to the games, we'd go out afterwards for a few drinks and a meal. This is a cherished ritual now, a visit I truly look forward to, an antidote, badly needed, to the celebrity bullshit of everyday existence that can eat away your own soul. We talk about old times, have a singsong if my mam and dad are there.

On these occasions I also remember friends and relatives who have passed away while I've been in England. My dear old granny, Essie Lynch. Essie used to give out yards to me for watching too much soccer on the television on weekends when she came to stay with us. My godfather, Pat Lynch. We were very close; he more than anyone encouraged me to play football and to believe in myself. And the late Gene O'Sullivan, my manager at Rockmount. Fabulous people without whom I wouldn't be where I am today.

Sitting around having a drink with my own at Easter time I also think and talk about three of my closest school friends, all of whom are now dead: Eddie Malone, Alan Barrett and James Courtney. What times we had when it appeared that we had nothing.

Against that background I tell them about the well-known bluffers who are fooling most of the people most of the time. This, and Theresa, Shannon, Caragh, Aidan and our new baby Leah, is the core of my life. These people, and other old friends like Tony Loughlan from my Forest days, who's now a coach at Leicester, and Mike Constable, my carousing buddy from the Roy the Playboy years, laugh at the image of Psycho

Roy the Dark Loner. They laugh at the big house and the cars, and if there was ever any danger that I'd lost the run of myself, I'd soon be reminded. Without my family and friends I wouldn't be able to enjoy what I'm lucky enough to have. In fairness, given my history, there's a good chance I'd go mad. It makes it easier to go to war, which is what I do for a living, when you know there is a warm, natural world to return to.

A couple of weeks after the Real Madrid defeat I got a call from a friend who's a season ticket-holder at Old Trafford. He'd received a letter from the club explaining that the rise in season ticket prices was due to the cost of my new contract. 'Are you sure,' I asked. He was, he had the letter in his hand. It was signed by United's secretary, Ken Merrett.

Next morning I went to see the secretary. I asked if it was true that the season ticket rise was being put down to my new contract. He assured me he didn't think this was the case. I rang my friend and he said, 'Roy, I'll send you the letter.' In one part the letter read: 'there was a huge collective sigh of relief when Roy Keane agreed to a new contract which will ensure he remains a Manchester United player for at least a further three years. In making this commitment to Roy, the directors believe they are also making a commitment to the supporters. Manchester United fans have grown accustomed to the best. It is our duty to ensure that we remain in a position to be able to provide the best. Price increases are never popular but we are sure the supporters will recognize the importance that we place on staying competitive and being able to compete not only in the transfer market but in our endeavours to retain our existing players.'

I was very angry when I went back to Merrett. How could he not see what people would think? I put the letter on his desk. Then I went to see the gaffer. He agreed the club were out of order. Nothing surprises me in football.

Despite the frustrations behind the scenes, at the end of the season I won the PFA and (sports writers') Footballer of the Year awards. This was a double David Ginola had achieved the previous season and I was thrilled, but I knew it would count for little if as a side we were content to rest on our laurels.

Fabien Barthez was the major addition to our side for season 2000/1. Eric had always talked about Fabien, who of course kept goal for France when they won the World Cup and Euro 2000. Watching the Euro 2000 final, I decided to have a bet on Italy. Gambling is not one of my vices, but I really fancied the Italians. I rang Ladbrokes to put £5,000 on Italy. I flashed my gold card. Bet accepted. The next morning the manager gave me a pull.

'I didn't know you were a gambler,' he said.

'I'm not,' I replied.

'Well what were you doing having five grand on Italy yesterday?'

'Well, er, I fancied them, Gaffer.'

'Well, you were wrong, weren't you?' (Italy had been beaten in the final.)

The penny dropped. Mike Dillon of Ladbrokes was the gaffer's pal.

'Anyway, your credit card about stood fifty quid. You don't want to start that game,' he said, ending the conversation. Not with Ladbrokes anyway, I thought.

Against Chelsea in the Charity Shield I was sent off for a bad tackle on Gus Poyet. Jimmy Floyd Hasselbaink had fouled me a few minutes before and got away with it. It was only the Charity Shield, but it was a nasty game. The media went to town on me. Why did Keane get involved, they asked. The answer is simple. You can't allow yourself to be the victim. If they put it up to you, try to intimidate you, to see if you've gone soft, you've got to send the signal back. Still in business, don't even fucking think about it. You've got to protect yourself.

In November we shot eight points clear in the Premiership. In the Champions League we played Dynamo Kiev at Old Trafford. Teddy gave us an early lead. But we struggled. We had to win this game to qualify for the second phase. Kiev were a good side. We'd played Southampton, Coventry and Watford, beating them all easily, in our three previous games. In the second half Kiev were killing us. Five minutes from time we were almost out of the Champions League. They played through us effortlessly to set up an open goal for Demetradze. The Ukrainian missed from five yards. We were glad to get off the pitch.

We went close to being out of the competition. Too close for comfort. The rot had well and truly set in in the dressing room. The Old Trafford crowd was also getting carried away. When we were really under the cosh in the second half, the crowd was curiously quiet. It was as if they resented the absence of the spectacle they'd come to see. A goalfest, beating the shit out of Southampton, three- or four-nil up, and they were swinging off the rafters. What about the hard days and nights, when you needed a lift from your own supporters?

After the game it was my turn to do the media. Asked about the game I gave the following reply: 'A lot of people come here expecting three or four goals, but it's not always the case. Our fans away from home are as good as any, but at home sometimes you must wonder if they understand the game of football. Some people come to Old Trafford and I don't think they can even spell the word football, never mind understand it. At the end of the day you have to get behind the team. Away from home our fans are fantastic, what I would call the hard-core fans, but at home they've had a few drinks and probably their prawn sandwiches and don't realize what is going on out on the pitch. It's right out of order.'

The reference to prawn sandwiches made the headlines. I was deemed to be having a go at the fans in the corporate boxes. In fact, that wasn't exactly true. Corporate hospitality is part and parcel of the deal these days. The club needs the money raised by corporate boxes. That's the way it is. I was actually having a go at United fans in general, on the terraces and elsewhere in the ground, who were in danger of losing the plot. United had no divine right to success. The real knowledgeable fans, the vast majority of United fans, understood this.

Perhaps it wasn't really the fans who were getting under my skin. Somewhere within I felt a real foreboding that we'd gone soft as a team. The feeling around the place wasn't right. Success, Premiership success, was breeding complacency. Too many people round the club were still intoxicated by the treble. Mementoes, tributes, talk of legends and heroes, the greatest ever United team, blah, blah, fucking blah. When Peter Schmeichel claimed that our team would have beaten the 1968 Cup-winning side 10-0, it summed it all up. How the fuck did he know? How could anyone? They were great players in their time: Bobby Charlton, Denis Law, George Best. Who were we to say that they wouldn't have achieved great things in the modern era? When I came to Old Trafford it was argued that history was the monkey on our back. Fair enough, it was to some extent. But history was also a spur, a goal, a challenge. Now the monkey on our back was believing all the things that were being said about us. Our own history.

The treble was history. But people wouldn't let it go. That was undermining us. I knew it. Could see it on the training ground. People turning up late for training, going through the motions, yet still winning against piss-poor Premiership opposition every week. Then, bang, Dynamo Kiev – not Real Madrid – almost put us out. Looking round the dressing room, I see it's not hurting enough, in some cases not at all. It doesn't matter if we never win another match!

By early February we're sixteen points clear at the top of the Premiership. We sort out Panathinaikos and Sturm Graz in the Champions League. Up front all looks good; below the surface things feel bad.

April, thirteen points clear in the title race, a one-horse race. Bayern Munich coming to Old Trafford for the first leg of the quarter-final in the Champions League. The writing is on the wall when Liverpool beat us 2-0 at Anfield three days before the Bayern game.

Bayern are a good, professional team. They will give us nothing we don't earn. Effenberg, Scholl, Jeremies, a tough little grafter in midfield, Elber and Paulo Sergio up front, quality, though not top-quality, Brazilians. No weak links. Brilliantly set up by their coach Hitzfeld. They were too good for us, could have scored a couple of times before Paulo Sergio, their sub, got the winner four minutes from time. They'd gone forward since 1999, we had not taken the next step.

We breezed past Charlton and Coventry before the second leg in Munich. It was no contest when Elber scored after five minutes. We were kidding ourselves. Talking big, but not delivering. The wheels had come off.

We won the Premiership by ten points.

Coming home from Munich, I felt sick to my heart. We

60. The late Sir Matt Busby's son Sandy presents me with a trophy for being United's Player of the Year in the 1998/99 season.

61. Scoring against West Ham in my first appearance as United's captain on 1 April 2000.

62. With David Beckham.

63. On the ball as captain.

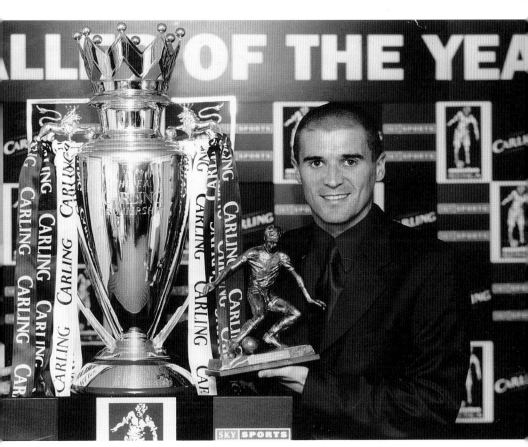

64. With the Premiership trophy and the Football Writers Association Player of the Year award.

65. Reaching boiling point with Alfie Haaland ...

66. ... and being sent off for it.

67. Qualifying for the 2002 World Cup against Portugal ...

68. ... and against Holland. No one rated our chances getting through the group, but we put out one of the pre-tournament favourites.

69. I couldn't believe I'd lost control again.

70. Being carried off during the Deportivo game in the 2001/2002 Champions League.

71. Celebrating scoring the first goal in my return to Champions League duty against Bayer Leverkusen ...

72. ... only to get beaten by them and put out of the competition.

73. Training with Ireland in Saipan. With Mick McCarthy.

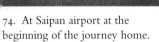

74. At Saipan airport at the beginning of the journey home.

75. An unplanned and unwished-for appearance on national TV.

76. Taking care of business.

should have bought big after the treble, been fucking ruthless, got the best in Europe, freshened things up, attacked complacency, let any who really 'didn't care if they ever won another trophy' leave to join the kind of clubs that never win any trophies. Maybe this team has had it. Me included. I did nothing in the Munich games. I felt flat, empty, angry. I'd been sucked into the Premiership swamp. Be bitter, Roy, otherwise you're going nowhere.

We turned up for training on Friday. Carrington, our new purpose-built training ground, was a professional's dream. Everything you could possibly need to prepare. Everything is fine. Manchester City at home tomorrow. Alfie Haaland has been mouthing off: 'If Roy Keane is so worried about the hard-core fans – and the corporate boxes – why doesn't he take a wage cut?' (This before the Maine Road game earlier in the season.) I hadn't forgotten Alfie. Bryan Robson told me to take my time. You'll get your chance, Roy. Wait.

Another crap performance. They're up for it. We're not. City could have been ahead when Teddy stroked a penalty home with twenty minutes to go. Howey equalized five minutes from the end. I'd waited almost 180 minutes for Alfie, three years if you looked at it another way. Now he had the ball on the far touchline. Alfie was taking the piss. I'd waited long enough. I fucking hit him hard. The ball was there (I think). Take that, you cunt. And don't ever stand over me again sneering about fake injuries. And tell your pal Wetherall there's some for him as well. I didn't wait for Mr Elleray to show the card. I turned and walked to the dressing room.

Shortly after the Bayern game I went to talk to Steve McClaren about the things that were bothering me. Steve was a good coach, an innovator, always looking for a better way to do things. I respected him. He wanted to improve. He was ambitious, hungry. I told him how I felt – that we were 'gone', beating nothing in the Premiership. The Arsenals, Liverpools, Chelseas, Leeds just weren't doing it. It deceived us into thinking we were better than we really were. The gaffer was away that day. But I'd spoken to him anyway. He knew what I was talking about. After the game in Munich I had responded to a journalist's question by suggesting that maybe the 'present team wasn't good enough. Maybe we needed to break it up, get new players, start again.' 'Keane lashes team-mates' was the headline. Actually, I was including myself. I was in or near to the comfort zone myself.

Steve assured me that change was on the way. The gaffer was going to sign some top players. He agreed with my assessment of our Premiership rivals. He also nodded when I argued that with the new Champions League rules allowing the top three in the Championship to enter, we didn't even have to win the title to qualify. If we didn't need to win the Premiership, would we in our present mood?

The dread I felt at the prospect of reaching the comfort zone, aged twenty-nine, was underlined when we received the Carling Premiership trophy, having lost at home to Derby. The crowd cheered. We lapped it up. Loved it. We went on to lose our final two games.

There was one record worth celebrating. Alex Ferguson became the first manager in history to win three successive Championships with the same club. He deserved that place in the history of the game. And he still wasn't satisfied.

The Champions League final in May 2002 would be at Hampden Park, Glasgow. The manager's home town. He set that as our goal for the new season. He also announced that this would be his last season at the club. Negotiations to find another role for him at Old Trafford had broken down.

Nothing surprises me in football. You're here today, gone tomorrow, even this man.

We bought expensive new players and got one real bargain on a free transfer. Juan Sebastian Verón came from Lazio for £28m. Seba was a world-class midfield player. Ruud Van Nistelrooy, who cost £19m from PSV, was a striker with an impressive goalscoring record. Laurent Blanc joined us on a Bosman 'free'. He was a defender I'd always admired, and was outstanding in the French squads that triumphed at France '98 and Euro 2000.

Everyone expected instant results, but football isn't that simple. Especially for foreign players adjusting to the English game – and an unfamiliar culture in everyday life. You can't expect miracles. Unfortunately, a quick fix was what people were looking for. When it didn't come, the criticism was severe.

Jaap Stam had been sold for £15m – a £5m profit. The manager took a hammering for that. More so because Laurent was judged a failure. Too slow, can't cope with the English game. Selling Stam big mistake. Was it because of his book, which alleged the manager had 'tapped' him? I doubt it. I felt that, nice guy though he was, Jaap was limited at the highest level. Great when the ball was there to win, quick and a real physical presence. But his positional play was inadequate. Jaap struggled against the best attacking players. He lacked the cunning instincts the best defenders have. It was just business.

I liked Jaap and his family. He was sincerely devoted to the idea of playing for Manchester United. He bought a house just along the road from us in Wilmslow. He was popular in the dressing room. Interestingly, there's a line in his book about the importance of winning the Premiership, how that was the one trophy he targeted every year. The wrong one.

We struggled in the early part of the season. When we lost

1-0 at home to West Ham in early December it was our sixth defeat of the season. Conventional wisdom said that you couldn't lose more than five or six games and still win the Championship. There was no doubting that this was a crisis. All kinds of theories surfaced.

Much of the criticism focused on Laurent Blanc and Juan Verón. This was desperately unfair. It was said they couldn't adjust to the Premiership. Great world-class players couldn't cope with the muck and bullets? Rubbish. What did people think it was like at the top, a bloody five-a-side? Laurent and Seba are superb professionals, hard enough, more than good enough for the hurly-burly of English football. Sure, there were adjustments required, but top players have faced bigger challenges than the change necessary here. The team was leaking goals. The team. Finger-pointing was useless. We sank or swam. Together. At Arsenal, for example, we all got a chasing. We lost up front, in midfield, everywhere. Fabien had kept us in the game. In the end he cracked. But the trail led to us, me included.

Other observers blamed our loss of form on the manager's declarations that he intended leaving. There may have been something in this, but not enough to explain the slump. Then the fact that Steve McClaren had left to manage Middlesbrough was advanced as the cause of the crisis. Steve was good. But I didn't believe that was the cause.

We weren't hungry fighters any more. That feeling in my gut in Barcelona the night we clinched the treble kept coming back to my mind. An inkling had grown to be an obsession. We'd bought into the glory, the hero stuff, we were living fucking legends. We won the Championship by ten points, what's wrong with you, Roy? I could feel it coming, the desire wasn't there, none of us had it. Not in sufficient quantities. Instead of making things happen we were waiting for one of our hero-colleagues to do it for us. Come on, Becks, win us a game. That's me. Scholesy, your turn. Go on, Ryan. Seba, you cost £28m, can't you win it for us? Ruud, you can do it. Ruud did win us a few. Becks scored some great goals (sixteen in the season), made some others. Ole was always good for a life-saver. And he still did it now and then. Colesy was another you could look to, hoping he'd do the business for you. While we were all waiting for each other, nothing coherent happened.

Nobody rocked the boat. Now and then I'd have a go in the media. Now and then I'd blow up in training or after a game. Jesus, I remembered the United team I joined in 1993. If you lost a game, nobody would speak to each other on Monday mornings. A one-game losing run would be a crisis. Doom and gloom on the training ground, people kicking each other, rows bursting out, the manager effing and blinding, tension building up until you had the chance to go out and fucking put it right the next time. You weren't waiting for anyone else to make it happen, you grabbed it and did it yourself. We'd lost all that. Wall-to-wall doubles, a treble and a hatful of Premierships had taken their toll. You could talk about the new players, the gaffer leaving, Steve McClaren. The core reason was us. One other thing I'd sensed. In the Charity Shield Liverpool had beaten us 2-1. They had closed the gap a little. Arsenal too were upping their game. Now they were hungry, hungrier than us.

We started the season scraping past Fulham 3-2 at home. They took the lead twice before Ruud rode to the rescue. Then we drew at Blackburn, like Fulham just promoted. Another draw at Villa, before blitzing an awful Everton side. Happy days are here again.

Newcastle away in mid-September. We go 3-1 down. Giggsy and Seba get us back to 3-3. Shearer scores the winner eight minutes from the end. Christ. A bloody mess, a shambles, me worse than anyone. I grab the ball to take a throw-in. It's injury-time, deep in our half. Shearer stops me taking the throw-in. He's taking the piss. I lose it, throw the fucking ball at him. 'You prick,' he sneers. The way he says it, I know he really means it. I go for him, try to grab him by the throat. He's grinning. 'You prick.' He gestures dismissively. The red card comes out. Shearer's right. I am a prick. Fell into the trap.

The dressing room is quiet. I've let them down. I can tell by the gaffer's body language that I've let him down to the point where he's hurt and embarrassed. Too hurt to bother having a go at me. I feel empty. Hollow. Nothing in there. Just remorse. Usually, I can excuse myself when I'm wrong. That's me, blah, blah, blah, take me or leave me, I am what I am, self-indulgent crap most of the time. But not this time. I genuinely feel I've let down all the people who've defended me in the past. Theresa, my family at home, the gaffer, the lads in the side, the club. No excuses this time.

Travelling back down the motorway, the coach was quiet. Looking out of the window, I felt numb. I'd done daft things before, but this time there was no excuse. Poyet in the Charity Shield . . . retaliation. The night in jail . . . a set-up. All the red cards, Haaland, Villa Park, Middlesbrough, Southampton, you're only human, Roy, I told myself. But this time I couldn't let myself off the hook. I'd had enough of my own behaviour. I'd had enough – full stop. The silence was probably because everybody else felt the same. It wasn't worth it, I thought. Putting myself and everyone else through this. Driving, always driving. There's only so much people can take.

When we reached the Four Seasons, the gaffer said good-
night. I mumbled my reply.

'Don't do anything stupid, Roy.'

When I got home, Theresa was there. Thank God for her.
For my home and the kids. I didn't have the heart to ring my
parents, again, with the same old story. I went to bed but I
never slept a wink. After the Poyet incident I spoke to the
manager about giving up the captaincy. Maybe that would
help take the pressure off. We decided no.

Some time during the night I decided: give it up, Roy.
You're just turned thirty. Get out, get away, do something
else. You've got to stop hurting yourself, hurting those you
love . . . those you work with. I talked to Theresa. She argued
that I'd miss it. No I wouldn't, I replied. Anything would be
better than this madness. Getting angry and frustrated, lashing
out. I felt I'd lost the argument about the comfort zone in the
dressing room. Too many people were content with what
they had. Let them be. It wasn't for me, so I should go.

Next morning I was waiting for the gaffer at Carrington at
eight o'clock. For once he was late. At 9.15, just as I was about
to go, he turned up. We went in and sat down. I told him I
wanted to pack it in. No, Roy, this is a knee-jerk reaction.
It's not, I explained. I'm not doing my stuff, we're not doing
our stuff, I can't take any more of it. We talked for a long
time, me more than him. He understood, everything. He
agreed about the complacency, things falling apart, where we
were heading if we didn't take the next step. I insisted my
mind was made up and went home. I told him I wouldn't
play against Lille in Tuesday's Champions League game.

Sunday afternoon I walked Triggs a long way. I ran the
options through my head. Another club, abroad, somewhere
sunny. At least I could be miserable in a warm climate. I loved

my football, really loved it. Could I play for another club –
Celtic maybe? I relaxed as I walked and thought of a funny
story. Not long before I'd been injured and gone up to
Glasgow with a couple of friends to see Celtic play, United
fans who followed Celtic as well, I had my baseball cap pulled
well down. It was great. We had a few drinks in a pub near
the ground. No one spotted me. As we were walking up to
the ground two big Scots lads took a second look.

'Are you . . . ? You fucking are.' One guy was about six
foot five, built like a barn. 'Hey, big man, when are you going
to come and play for a big club?'

Big man! He was looking down on me.

My pal shot back: 'He's playing for a big club.'

'Nah,' the big fella replied, 'a really big club.' We laughed.
I loved the Glasgow humour. But my heart was in United.
And if I couldn't play with my heart, I couldn't play.

I felt calm. My mind was settled, a big weight off my
shoulders. I believe in fate. Sometimes things happen for a
reason. I wasn't scared of life without football. Financially
I could survive. I talked to Theresa again. She'd back me
whatever.

Next day I stayed home and walked the dog again. No
regrets, I felt good, off the treadmill, not reading the papers
about my latest disgrace. Peace. The gaffer's secretary rang to
know where I was. Theresa took the call, saying I was out and
didn't want to talk to anybody. The gaffer called round to my
house, Monday afternoon. He sat down with me and Theresa.
Roy, you've been taking too much on board regarding results
and bad performances. You'd be mad to leave football. Think
of your family. I've made my mind up, gaffer. If you walk
away now when you're young and fit you'll regret it for the
rest of your life, he insisted. Theresa backed him up. Play

tomorrow, Roy. We'll solve the problems. Gaffer, my whole being is telling me I'm right. I feel I'm doing the right thing. I can't stand the bluffing and bullshit any more. We're fooling ourselves. Think about it, Roy. Come in tomorrow if you want.

When I thought about it, and talked it through with Theresa, I decided to go back and play against Lille. I did it for Alex Ferguson. He'd stood by me through everything; quitting now would be a slap in the face for him, the last thing he needed when the club was struggling.

We struggled against Lille. Nobody rated them. But after twenty minutes we knew we were in a tough game. Becks nicked one in the ninetieth minute. One-nil against Lille!

A couple of weeks later we travelled to Deportivo La Coruña. The manager decided to use a new formation in the away legs of the Champions League. Ruud up front, on his own, five in midfield with Paul Scholes and Seba breaking forward to support Ruud whenever possible. I'd play a holding role. It worked for eighty-four minutes. Deportivo were useful, but we controlled midfield. Scholesy gave us the lead just before half-time. They pushed on in the second half. We were comfortable. Until six minutes from the end, when they got back on level terms. In the last minute Gary played Naybet onside: 1-2. We should have killed the game at 1-0. We should never have conceded two goals in the last few minutes. Critics blamed the 4-5-1 system. I blamed human error.

We were hanging on now for a place in the second phase. Deportivo at home became a huge game. My knee had been playing up for a while. The same knee, the new one. It went on me as we warmed up for the Deportivo game. I couldn't twist or turn, or kick the ball without a stab of pain. I couldn't start. That was my first thought. I had to start, it was too big a game to miss. I said nothing and pushed myself through the ninety minutes. Fucking mad. Ruud put us in front, but Fabien made two unforced errors and we were beaten 3-2.

But the game that really told a story was at Anfield in November. I was out injured. Liverpool won 3-1, it could have been six. We surrendered. Liverpool now glowed with the kind of purpose we'd shown when we really wanted it. Owen, Gerrard, Murphy, Carragher, all Liverpool lads. They tackled with a real venom, we went through the motions. The gap closed that day.

Then, of course, Highbury. Another whipping, from another team on the up. We struggled badly. Arsenal away, a fucking disaster. We took the lead thanks to Paul Scholes. Then just after half-time Gary Neville gave the ball away near the half-way line. Pires set up Freddy Ljungberg: 1-1. Gary argues, and he's right, that football is a team game, and we had enough opportunity to rectify his mistake. Fabien kept us in the game as Arsenal created chance after chance. Then, with five minutes to go, Fabien mishit a clearance, which Henry slotted home. A long ball from Vieira was fumbled to allow Henry another simple tap-in. Fabien now got the stick.

Speculation continued about the gaffer's successor. Capello, Hitzfeld, Martin O'Neill, Eriksson. We knew nothing. Our principal concern was for Jimmy Ryan and Mickey Phelan, our coaches. They were the gaffer's men. A new manager would doubtless bring in his own staff. What would that mean for Jimmy and Mickey, who'd contributed so much to our success? Too few people gave a fuck about two men who might lose their living at the stroke of a pen. Premiership glory! Bah!

I don't have to restate my respect for Alex Ferguson. I didn't want him to leave the club, couldn't believe that United would let him go. But at the same time I was intrigued by the prospect of a new manager. We needed something dramatic to reverse our decline, for that undoubtedly was what was happening. I needed it as badly as anyone. A new challenge, fresh ideas. Having to prove yourself to, say, Capello, who was supposed to be top-notch . . . and tough. Reputations would count for nothing. Good. The treble would finally be thrown in the bin, yesterday's heroes with it, if they didn't do their stuff. My basic attitude was that at the end of the day, when you walk out on that pitch, it doesn't matter who the manager is. Ultimately you're responsible for your own destiny.

We stayed in contention for the Championship and qualified for the second phase of the Champions League. My knee was a constant worry. I was doing special exercises to strengthen the muscles supporting it. These worked, sometimes.

One day in late February the manager told me he was thinking of reversing his decision to leave. 'Are you mad?' I laughed. He was serious. He'd worked out a new deal with the board. I was delighted. In truth, I could never imagine him going racing on a Saturday afternoon while his team – and it was his team – went out to play. He looked well, he felt fit, he was still uniquely hungry. Why not?

Shortly afterwards he called a team meeting to make his announcement official. Someone wrote that at this meeting a couple of players cried, and that the gaffer got a big round of applause. In fact, a couple of people gave an embarrassed little clap as he was leaving the room. He turned round and said 'fuck off', thinking we were taking the piss. Of course, everybody was very pleased. But emotion of that kind is rarely displayed in dressing rooms.

In fact, when he left, we all turned immediately to Dwight Yorke. Yorkie had been in the papers talking about the post-Ferguson era, how he'd have a new beginning, get a new deal. 'That's you fucked, Yorkie,' someone laughed. He laughed himself, even though it was true.

That turning point came too late to save our season. We had our moments when the class in the side saw us through vital games. Becks scored an amazing goal at just the right time to set up a victory away to Deportivo in the Champions League quarter-final, a beautiful shot that dipped over the keeper and dived into the net. Ruud scored at will throughout the season. Fabien kept us in many games. His errors being so spectacular, though few, detracted from the overall excellence.

Laurent Blanc became more comfortable as the season progressed. It was touch and go whether he'd sign for another season. Personally, I'm thrilled that he did. Laurent is a superb professional. You can tell on the training ground, the way he prepares for matches, that at thirty-six he is still hungry for more success. I've learned from him, about the game, how to prepare, and also critically Laurent directed me to a fitness specialist in France who has helped me sort out my injury problems.

In La Coruña I pulled a hamstring just before half-time. Another four weeks out.

I managed to get back for the semi-final first leg against Bayer Leverkusen, where I came on as a sub. We drew 2-2, which in terms of away goals was bad, but at least we travelled for the second leg with a chance. I started that game, and after twenty-eight minutes got the goal that gave us the lead in the tie. On the stroke of half-time Leverkusen equalized. That was enough to see them home. We had failed to take the next step towards greatness. We've settled for the now reflected glory of the treble year. The complacency that comes with the kind of success we've enjoyed has caught up with us. Last season we got what we deserved. Nothing.

As we stood for the UEFA anthem before the second leg of the Leverkusen game, one of our players was fucking shaking. He was afraid. Played for his country, won championships, big star, fucking afraid of taking the big step up. I thought, Christ, let me enjoy this, the semi-final of the Champions League, what you live for. Relax. This is where we need to be, this is where you have to go.

Afterwards in the dressing room I looked around. It wasn't hurting some of them enough. Laurent was sitting there gutted. I felt sorry for Seba. Cost £28m, became the scapegoat for our season. Some of the others were getting away with murder. Blame Seba. Too easy. Wrong. Glory, believing the publicity, has cost us. Rolex watches, garages full of cars, fucking mansions, set up for life, forgot about the game, lost the hunger that got you the Rolex, the cars, the mansion.

Arsenal at home, second-last game of the season, summed it up. Men against boys. They killed us. Didn't create a chance. Couldn't even put it up to them. On the slide, no doubt about it. That's where we are. Yesterday's heroes.

Raimond Van der Gouw won't get the chance to put it right. Fantastic guy, Raimond. Great pro, fit, really hard worker on the training ground. Played only forty-eight games in six years, yet always prepared, never let us down. Raimond and his family loved Manchester, the club, the place. At thirty-eight he's been let go. Had to tell his wife Marita and kids. They were heartbroken. His wife cried. Cruel is football.

12

Ten years ago, when I began playing for Ireland, it was a joke. I was first capped at senior level in 1991. I was a young lad, just in Forest's first team, Jack Charlton was a legend in Ireland, to a lesser extent in England, where he was known for his role in England's 1996 World Cup victory. In both countries he was admired for his bluff, no-nonsense, call-a-spade-a-spade manner. He was Big Jack, I was little Roy. He'd worked wonders with the Irish team. I don't know how, but somehow he did it. There was nothing I saw to suggest any magic powers. He was like a big, grumpy uncle with strong opinions about football, a bit eccentric, but not the worst. Not nasty. Cunning, though.

When I first played for Ireland, the players humoured him. If we wanted a night out, a few drinks, a day off, we'd chant his name from the back of the bus: 'We love you, Jackie, we do, we love you, Jackie, we do, we love you, Jackie, *we do*, oh, Jackie, we love you.' He'd smile and usually give in.

In 1992 we went to play in the US Cup, a Mickey Mouse non-event which raised a few bob for the Football Association of Ireland, which always needed a few bob. The US Cup was more like a two-week piss-up. The pretext was preparation for USA '94, the next World Cup finals. Some of us found a few good bars, that was the extent of our preparation. In public everyone kept a straight face. The matches took place and were reported on as if they mattered. The journalists were also preparing for USA '94: how to tell the public the convenient part of the story. The full story – about the US Cup – might have caused a fuss.

As an example of the gap between what really goes on in football and the folklore that is fed to the public by the media, Big Jack's story is a classic. It was an eye-opener for me.

After trips with the Irish team, players would go back to their club at the end of an international week and swap stories with English players and those from other nations about the weird but wonderful Irish camp. Everyone had a laugh at the Irish. No one laughed harder than the Irish players telling the stories about cock-ups, piss-ups and the various impediments you faced as a professional player representing your country. When I was young I told stories. And laughed.

Here's a good one from Ireland's qualifying campaign for Euro '96 – towards the end of Big Jack's time as national team manager.

Because of injury I played only three or four games in the qualifiers. But Denis Irwin and Paul McGrath were witnesses to this story. Ireland were at home to Austria in a vital qualifying game. The day before the match, the team went to Lansdowne Road for a training session. On the way they stopped at a branch of Harry Ramsden's on the Naas Road. The photographers were on hand to capture the Irish team tackle their first big challenge of the week: Harry's Challenge, a giant-sized haddock with chips and beans or peas, with a sweet to follow. Eat up, lads, urged Jack. Some of the lads tucked in to Harry's Challenge. Then off to Lansdowne Road for the final training session. Yes, Austria won 3-1. Some of the lads reported that their legs 'went' twenty minutes from the end. Fucked. But they'd passed Harry's Challenge.

The story went down a treat in the dressing rooms around England. Significantly, Ireland failed to qualify for Euro '96 because of that defeat. Holland beat them easily in a play-off game at Anfield. That was Harry's Challenge.

Mick McCarthy succeeded Big Jack as Ireland manager in February 1996. He'd managed Millwall. He was familiar with the Irish scene, he'd do. He and I had never hit it off. McCarthy, Packie Bonner, Gerry Peyton and David O'Leary were senior players in the Irish squad. I was one of the lads down the back of the bus. The big boys would go out for dinner, we'd go for a few jars. McCarthy was part of the Charlton legend. Captain Fantastic. Sometimes he played the role, though he didn't convince me. Still, when he got the job, I thought: let bygones be bygones. Millwall had played good football, maybe he'd encourage Ireland to develop from the primitive Charlton style.

In summer 1996, after McCarthy had taken over, United had just won the double. It had been a gruelling season, ending with a hard Cup final against Liverpool at Wembley. I'd had my share of injuries that season. I was utterly drained. Then the call came from Ireland. After a friendly match against Portugal in Dublin McCarthy planned to take the squad to the United States for the US Cup! Hello!

I talked to our manager. I told him I was knackered, explained about the last US Cup and we agreed I shouldn't go. United informed the FAI of that decision. When I failed to arrive in Dublin, there was trouble. McCarthy said I'd not spoken to him. His pals in the Irish media wrote that I'd let my country down. I didn't want to play for Ireland. Captain Fantastic was angry. Meanwhile, I was at Old Trafford cricket ground as a guest of Lancashire CC along with some other United players. Lancashire were playing Yorkshire, a big game. We were relaxing, having a few scoops, when the English press on a mission to find 'Ireland's missing star' arrived.

It was not much of a story. I wasn't missing. But it was a good opportunity for mischief. As a result I got off to a bad start with McCarthy. He felt I should have spoken to him personally. He expressed this opinion, casting me in a bad light. What he didn't tell the media was that if we'd had that sort of conversation on this occasion, it would have been our first.

I played my first game under McCarthy against Russia at Lansdowne Road. Andy Townsend was captain for this friendly international. When Andy was subbed, I was given the armband. I was sent off for kicking a Russian. 'Keane Disgrace' was the next day's story.

Injuries meant I missed several more games. But the story ran that I didn't care about playing for my country. It wasn't true. What was true was that my first priority was Manchester United, who paid my wages and put the roof over Theresa and my children. I loved Ireland, it was my home, and home to my closest friends and family. I deeply resented this, I'm more Irish than the Irish thing, the patriotic fraud that hung around the Irish team. The bullshitters in the squad were clever about wearing their Irishness like a badge of honour. The super-Irishmen, fucking bluffers and PR men who pandered to the media and the fans as if they'd invented being Irish. Wasn't it obvious I was Irish? From Mayfield in Cork. I didn't need lessons in Irishness. I *was* Irish.

After missing several games, I was selected to play against Iceland at home in a World Cup qualifier. McCarthy played me as a sweeper. Cathal Dervan, a mate of McCarthy's, wrote a column that morning accusing me of betraying my country and urging the crowd to boo me when I appeared that afternoon. Some did, but it seemed half-hearted. We drew o-o. I managed to stifle the renowned Icelandic attack.

We failed to qualify for the 1998 World Cup finals in France, losing to Belgium in a play-off. If we'd beaten Iceland in Dublin we would have qualified. To be fair to McCarthy, he did change the way Ireland played. He encouraged us to pass the ball. The ninety minutes' football was enjoyable. When Andy Townsend retired, he appointed me captain. We came close to qualifying for Euro 2000 in Holland and Belgium, losing out to Turkey in another play-off.

The nearly men.

Denis Irwin retired after that play-off game against Turkey. McCarthy had had a go at Denis, dropped him and told the press he'd have to prove himself. Denis Irwin have to prove himself! He was proving himself every week for the best team in England. Denis had won everything in the domestic game. He was the model professional, one of the best there's ever been. Mick wanted him to *prove* himself.

He cocked it up with Paul McGrath as well. Publicly. Big Paul, an angel of a man, a great player. He was battling the booze. Went to bed one night at nine o'clock. He was dry. Ireland were in Dublin preparing for a World Cup qualifier against Macedonia in October 1996. McCarthy organized a trip to a Bryan Adams concert. His orders were that everyone should go. The bus was leaving the hotel at nine o'clock.

'Where's Paul?' McCarthy asked.

'He's gone to his room, he's not coming,' he was told.

Paul knew the dangers of going out to a gig due to start at ten o'clock. Late night. Temptation. Booze flowing. So he wanted to stay out of the way. Stay at the hotel.

Not appreciating Paul's fears, McCarthy demanded he join his team-mates. Paul pleaded for an early night.

Receiving that message, someone was sent up to Paul's room to get him. 'Come on, we're all going together.' Paul felt he had no choice.

The concert ended after midnight. The lads went for a few drinks (this was Saturday, before a Wednesday game). Paul was sucked in. He arrived back at the Airport hotel at two o'clock the following afternoon. McCarthy dropped him. He wouldn't be travelling to Macedonia. He'd let Captain Fantastic down. 'McGrath's Booze Shame', the headlines read. Public humiliation, the beginning of the end of Paul's international career. Man management.

Ireland lost in Macedonia.

When the draw was made for the 2002 World Cup qualifiers, Ireland were in a tough group. Portugal and Holland were the dangers. We were due to play our first two games away from home against Holland and Portugal.

McCarthy, having played in the Charlton era, was well aware of the shambles that was preparation for the Irish games: the poor training ground at Clonshaugh; the crap gear; the travel arrangements that confined the players to economy class while the big shots sat up in business or first class; the problems with our Dublin headquarters, the Airport hotel. The hotel's food was fine, the staff were brilliant, but it was on a roundabout at the end of a dual carriageway. You couldn't go for a walk. You either stayed in your room or sat in the hotel lobby, which was tiny and so busy with fans, players' families and other guests that you had to fight to get a seat. Privacy was out of the question. Occasionally, when we had a couple of games in Dublin you could be stuck in your room for a week or ten days.

Nothing seemed to change.

England would stay at a luxurious country house hotel, train in the best facilities, have the best medical and dietary advice, travel first class. They did it right, understanding that getting results was the players' job and anything you could do to assist must be done.

I dreaded the prospect of international weeks. I was proud to be Irish, ashamed at the way we went about preparing for games. I kept my mouth shut. Don't rock the boat, Roy. But I knew we were handicapped by giving other footballing nations a head start in preparation. We were also cheating the Irish fans, who passionately followed us around the world.

When the draw for the World Cup was made, I arranged to meet McCarthy in Manchester. He came to the house. As captain I'd decided to level with him, to make the case for a reformed approach. Let's have a go, do it right, sort these little things out. We discussed the problems. He agreed with me. Of course, you're right, he said. It was not an easy conversation – we were not buddy-buddy – but it might be my last World Cup. And his, if we got stuffed.

One of the things we discussed was diet. Harry's Challenge came up. At United, and other top clubs, it was well known at this time that pasta, fruit and cereals were the proper pre-game meal. Also understood was the fact that what you ate the day before a game was more important than what you had on match day itself. The science of preparation was so refined by dieticians at this stage that we knew that it was best to eat your pre-match meal three rather than four hours before kick-off. He agreed with all of this. I thought we had a deal.

If anything, things seemed to get worse.

Our first qualifier was against Holland in Amsterdam. We travelled economy on the flight. Checked ourselves in at the airport. Carried our own bags. Met at the Airport hotel. The day before the game we were due to train at the Ajax stadium, where the match was taking place. It was an evening session. We were having something to eat before we left the hotel. I came downstairs to the restaurant and saw some of the lads sitting at a table eating cheese sandwiches. I couldn't believe it. We'd discussed diet. Fucking cheese sandwiches, an hour and a half before training! Twenty-four hours before a vital World Cup qualifier. Against *Holland*.

I walked over to the staff table.

'Where's the pasta, fruit and cereals?' I asked.

Silence. As I turned away in disgust a voice piped up, 'You should have asked for that stuff.' It was Ian Evans, McCarthy's right-hand man.

I went back to my room. Jesus, I thought, was I wasting my time or what? At Old Trafford the manager would listen to everything, actually seek your opinion about everything, any little thing that might give the smallest advantage. 'You should have asked for that stuff.' As it happens, I did. I had told McCarthy and Mick Byrne, the team physio, about the pre-match developments.

I ordered a pizza, a takeaway pizza, as the hotel didn't have any means of rustling up anything better in the time now available.

When we got to the stadium McCarthy gave me a pull. 'What's up with you?' he asked.

'What's up with me?' I responded. 'What's up with me? We're fucking playing Holland tomorrow in a World Cup qualifier! Do you think Jimmy Floyd Hasselbaink is eating fucking cheese sandwiches or a takeaway fucking pizza tonight?'

We went 2-0 up in the match. They were squabbling amongst themselves, as the Dutch tend to do, we had them on the rack. But second half they threw the kitchen sink at us. We held on for a 2-2 draw.

I was gutted. In this group we needed every point we could get. We'd just dropped two. Everybody was celebrating. McCarthy was on the pitch, pleased as punch. He moved in my direction. I walked past him. In my book we'd failed Mick's Challenge – cheese sandwiches. Publicly, I said nothing.

We got a result in Portugal: 1-1. The players kept beating the odds stacked up against them.

Nothing changed behind the scenes. In an interview with the journalist Paul Kimmage I expressed my views about the travel and training arrangements. (I suppressed the cheese sandwich story.) 'Keane Lashes Out', the headlines read. Not Keane points out that we should really approach World Cup qualifiers in a truly patriotic way and do the best for the players, Irish football and the Irish supporters. Just 'Keane Lashes Out'.

We played Cyprus away and were due to play Andorra four days later in Barcelona. Although we struggled against Cyprus, we eventually put them away. I scored a couple of goals. I was into it now. Despite everything, I wanted to go to the World Cup finals. I wanted more than USA '94. We had some good young players – Robbie Keane, Damien Duff, Stephen Carr, Steve Finnan, Shay Given – and some good pros – Mark Kinsella, 'Stan' Staunton, big Quinny, Kenny Cunningham. We had enough to be ambitious. The spirit in the side was great. We'd always have a go, which was half the battle in international football, where the opposition was often over-rated and fragile. The Dutch and the Portuguese proved that. (Other major footballing powers would underline that point in the finals of World Cup 2002.)

After the Cyprus game the lads went for a few drinks. For some it was an all-night job. Nothing wrong with that, I'd drunk more than anyone in my time. The following day by the pool the party continued. Some of them were arsehole drunk. Some of the FAI officials joined in. This was way out of order. We were playing Andorra on Wednesday. We should have been out training, doing our warm-down. This is the World Cup. I said nothing.

We travelled to Barcelona the next day. It was a joke. Our flight was at six o'clock. We left the hotel around one o'clock. Had to get there early to check ourselves in. Like tourists on a cheap package holiday we queued and carried our own bags, checked in – eventually – around three o'clock. The airport was full of Irish fans. We'd three hours to kill. I asked if there was a lounge we might rest in, get a bit of privacy. No.

So we hung around in the crowded public area. If you wanted food or drink you had to buy it yourself. It was inconceivable that any serious international football squad would be treated like this. No respect for the players, none. I kept my mouth shut.

We reached our hotel in Barcelona at ten or eleven o'clock. Economy class: the big lads – Gary Breen, Derek Dunne, Quinny – squeezed up in small seats.

We beat Andorra.

On the way back we were seated up the front. The lads gave me a round of applause. I bowed.

Then we moved hotels. To County Kilkenny, a two-hour drive from Lansdowne Road. Hotel owned by some pal of McCarthy's, good golf course (important). The day before the matches we made the four-hour round trip to train at Lansdowne.

Then we moved to City West hotel near Dublin. Things were looking up. Kind of.

We qualified via a play-off against Iran. I was struggling with my knee. I hadn't played for United for three and a half weeks before the first leg of the play-off at Lansdowne. I told Alex Ferguson I was desperate to play. He was concerned that I would break down and miss out on United's Champions League commitments.

Everything was on the line for the gaffer and the club in the Champions League. But he was great. OK, Roy, I know how badly you want this. Go and play the home game and if you get a good enough result you can miss the second leg. Deal.

We beat Iran 2-0. They weren't much. I couldn't see them beating Ireland by three goals in the return game. My knee played up during the game. Next morning, I was stiff. The gaffer rang. I told him the story. He talked to McCarthy. No problem, they agreed, I could go back to Old Trafford for treatment.

I got a flight back to Manchester. But obviously some felt the injury was too convenient and had the impression I'd done a runner. Had Ireland lost out on qualifying, no doubt my absence would have been advanced as a reason. We didn't. Got the result we needed. But the rumours still left a sour taste. Anyway, we were going to the World Cup finals.

It was touch and go to make the finals. My knee was ropey. I had a hip injury that had persisted for months. My back was fucked as well. Laurent Blanc found a fitness specialist in France for me. I travelled over a few times. He was brilliant. I was on the mend, but only just. Niall Quinn had a benefit game at Sunderland the week before we were due to leave for

Saipan, our training base. Ireland against Sunderland. I told Niall I was struggling to play. And the previous Friday I informed Mick Byrne. No problem, Quinny said. He asked me if I'd sign a message for the programme. A journalist called Cathal Dervan would draft the message for me. Cathal Dervan was McCarthy's mate, the guy who urged the Lansdowne crowd to boo me because I didn't care about Ireland. I declined Niall's request. As far as I was concerned, Dervan was a waste of space.

I arrived in Dublin to play our farewell game against Nigeria. It was Tuesday, two days before the game. I'd stayed at home to have treatment at Old Trafford until the last possible minute. On the plane from Manchester I got the Irish papers. 'Keane Snubs Charity Benefit'. This was a lie. And I even heard suggestions that McCarthy had no idea where I was. That's a good start, I thought. 'Keane Snubs Sick Kids'. Maybe Keane keeps his contributions to charities – including sick kids – private.

We lose to Nigeria. No big deal.

Friday, we set off to Saipan. The trip is a shambles from the beginning. Dublin Airport is packed. You can't move. We hump a month's luggage through the main concourse. Check ourselves in. We're travelling KLM, going the scenic route, via Amsterdam and Tokyo. Fans, journalists, players, officials all mingle together. The package tour image comes to mind again. Amid the chaos, the Taoiseach, Bertie Ahern, arrives to give us a send-off.

At Amsterdam on the stopover I spot a couple of the journalists who wrote the 'Keane Snubs Kids' stuff. Words are exchanged. I know. I know I shouldn't have. It's pointless getting involved.

There's a bit of a vibe on the journey, no doubt about it.

On the plane to Tokyo I watch a movie. It's the story of Muhammad Ali's life. Will Smith plays Ali. There's an amazing scene when Ali is refusing the draft for the Vietnam war. He's in a room surrounded by family, friends and his Muslim mentors. They're all urging him to give in. Take the draft. You won't have to fight. Just go through the motions, play the game, screw the things you believe in. Ali resists them all. I'm doing what I think is right. *It matters.* You don't compromise on your principles. Watching this is very moving. I hadn't known this about Ali. Something in this scene strikes a chord with me. Don't put up with shit. I'm not fighting a white man's war. It's an inspiring notion, a demonstration of conviction that I understand very clearly, and relate to my own life.

Don't compromise on the things you believe in.

We arrive in Saipan. The hotel is beautiful. Sunday is a rest day. In the evening McCarthy calls a meeting. There's been a problem. The gear hasn't arrived. No training gear, no footballs. No medical equipment. The special drink we need to take to help us acclimatize is missing as well. Nobody knows what time we're going to train on Monday. McCarthy says, we'll just do some running. Because the gear hasn't arrived we'll have to use the tracksuits we wear around the hotel. They're heavy, impossible in this kind of heat.

I went to see McCarthy that night. Quietly, in his room.

'What's the story, Mick?'

'They've let me down,' he says. Who are *they*, I'm thinking. I told him the gear should have been here a fortnight ago. We're at the World Cup finals.

The following morning we're hanging around the hotel waiting to find out what's happening. Eventually we get on the coach to go to the training ground. The training pitch is like concrete, pot-holed with loads of loose stones lying around. With my injury problems the pitch is dangerous. Afterwards I went to the FIFA liaison officer, a local guy. I told him the pitch was rock hard. He said he was sorry but nobody told him we'd be training on the pitch today.

'We could have watered it,' he said, 'if anyone had told us you were coming down.'

I said, 'You must have known the Irish team were going to train today.'

'No,' he replied, 'nobody told us.'

I went back to my room. The weekend before we travelled, Tony Loughlan had come to visit me. We'd talked about the World Cup. I was excited. This was the real test for any player. I told him I thought we could go far, maybe reach the quarters or even the semi-finals. I'd only one fear, I told Tony: we'd go there in happy camper mode with no real ambition, settling for second best. USA '94 was in my mind.

Now this, the nightmare scenario.

The gear arrived on Monday night. Next morning, we arrived at the training ground. There was a truck there with a water hose. About twenty yards of the pitch were flooded, the rest was as rock hard as the day before. It looked dangerous. I laughed. We trained anyway. I thought the training was badly organized. Always did. We'd play possession games. But with Evans the area was either too big or two small. Fucking basics. A farce. The usual farce.

We ended training with a game. There were no small five-a-side goals, only big goals. Big goals, but no 'keepers. With five-a-side goals you don't need 'keepers, but with big goals you do. So I asked about the 'keepers. Evans told me they were tired. They were out working with Packie for half an hour before us. But I said we needed 'keepers to have a proper game. Jesus, even Rockmount, Cohb, the FÁS course, we'd have 'keepers for the game at the end of training. We're at the World Cup finals!

'They're tired,' Evans insisted.

'We're all fucking tired,' I replied.

The game went on. No 'keepers. After training I went over to Packie Bonner, our goalkeeping coach.

'Could the 'keepers not have played?' I asked.

'They worked hard this morning,' he answered.

'I bet they'll be all right for the golf course in the morning,' I said. (Golf was on the menu the next day. After the barbecue for the media.)

Then Alan Kelly chipped in: 'What have you got a problem with, Roy?'

'I've got a problem with you,' I said. 'Could you not fucking get in goal for the game?'

'We've worked hard this morning,' he said.

'Well, do you want a fucking medal for that? You've come to the World Cup finals, you expect to work hard. You've only worked for an hour.'

'Yes, yes,' he went on, 'but we'd had enough.'

'I'll bet you'll have recovered for your golf tomorrow,' I said.

'Just fucking calm down, Roy,' he said.

'Are you going to make me?'

It's funny, Kells is one of the guys I really get on with. But he and Packie have been players. Kells still is, they know what it's like, what I'm on about.

McCarthy and Evans watched all this. Never said a word. There were a couple of journalists there as well.

I got back up on the coach. I was angry. I'd put up with our Third World approach to the game throughout my international career. We all had. Packie and McCarthy, both players. Now with the power to put it right, they were presiding over the same old joke. Sponsoring it. Excusing it. Always blaming someone else. They.

They were they, now.

Lee Carsley and Steve Finnan had picked up injuries on the so-called pitch. This wasn't preparation for the biggest challenge of our lives. Could you imagine the Germans, the French, the Italians, the English working in these conditions? Or the Spanish, Paraguay . . . any other nation but the Irish? By the time I got back to the hotel I'd had enough. This wasn't for me. This is not what I trained my balls off for all season.

Back at the hotel I had a quick shower to cool me down. Leaving the room, I met McCarthy in the corridor.

'Can I have a word with you, Mick?'

'Yeah, yeah, what's it about?'

'I've had enough. I want to go home.'

'What do you mean?'

'I'm going home.'

'Oh yeah. Are you sure you know what you're doing?'

'Yeah, and don't try to persuade me. Just let me go.'

'What is it? Is it me, the training, the pitch?'

Of course, I should have said yes, it is you, the training, the preparation. This whole thing is a disgrace. I didn't.

'No, it's just me. I've had enough.'

'All right, all right,' he said. 'What will I tell the press?'

'Tell them . . . personal problems.'

We agreed Eddie Corcoran (who was in charge of logistics) would book my flights. We shook hands.

'Don't let it go beyond the three of us,' I asked.

'Sure,' he agreed.

I knew the consequences, for my family, my mam and dad, and Johnson, Pat, Denis and my cousin John, who I'd spent 30,000 euros booking a dream World Cup trip for. But I was thinking of my sanity. We were only two days in – I couldn't stand another two or three weeks of the Carry On nonsense.

I met Kells and apologized for the row at training.

'No problem, Roy.'

I went for a walk. When I got back Mick Byrne came to the room.

'What going on, Roy?'

'I've had enough, Mick. I can't stick it any more. It's not even a bad dream, it's my worst nightmare. I like to train hard, work hard. I enjoy a bit of fun, a night off, a drink. But this is the World Cup. We're playing Cameroon in a week and a half and we've got a warm-up match on Saturday. And look at us, Jesus, Mick, look at us.' We sat in silence for a few minutes. 'I know, Mick, I should have waited until after the World Cup, bit my tongue.'

'Roy, just wait until after the tournament. Come on, let me fix it.'

'Fuck it,' I said. 'Go on then. Tell Mick I'll wait until after the World Cup.'

'Brilliant,' Mick said.

Two minutes later Mick came back with McCarthy. McCarthy walked in quite aggressively.

'What's going on, Roy?'

'I thought I should wait until after the tournament. I want to stay.'

'I've rung Colin Healy to come out and replace you,' he said.

That was quick, I thought. There was a moment's silence.

Now I was embarrassed. I like Colin, he's a good lad. Maybe he deserves his chance.

'OK,' I said. 'Maybe you're right. I'll go. Leave it as it is.'

'I wish you'd have thought about me in all of this,' he said.

'Mick, I'm embarrassed by it all. I can tell by your body language that you're happy with the decision. Leave it. OK?'

'Well, people are always walking on eggshells around you,' he said.

'Fuck it, Mick, I don't ask people to walk on eggshells around me.'

I felt bad about Colin. But somewhere in the back of my mind I thought maybe I'm entitled to change my mind, maybe I deserve the benefit of the doubt. People change their minds all the time, for God's sake.

'Just leave it then, Mick, leave it. I'll go back.'

'Well,' he said, 'what do you want me to do?'

'You're the manager. You make the decision.'

He said nothing. Walked out.

Yes, I know it's childish, it doesn't reflect particularly well on me. But that's what happened. I feel it's important to tell it straight. I was indecisive. I desperately wanted to play. Yet I couldn't stand the fuck-ups. There is no hero here.

I went to Mick Byrne's room.

'Tell him I'm going.' That was it.

What I really wanted, I thought, was a generous response. You made a mistake, let's forget about it.

The news got out. Michael rang. We talked. I told him the story. He reminded me of the consequences of leaving. I told him there might be consequences if I stayed. I'd go mad. Michael asked me to ring Alex Ferguson. The gaffer had been on to Michael. He'd heard the news. He was on holiday in Malta, Michael said. Ring him on his mobile.

'No, Michael.'

'Roy, you owe him that.'

I spoke to the gaffer for half an hour. I told him the whole story. He agreed it was a joke. That he thought our preparation had been a disgrace. Like Michael, he outlined the consequences. Alex Ferguson also agreed that I was entitled to change my mind.

Just before eight o'clock, there was a knock on the door. It was Mick Byrne.

'Roy, you've got three minutes to make up your mind, we've got to fax the squad to FIFA.'

I said, 'I'll stay.'

The following lunchtime, McCarthy called a meeting.

'A lot's gone on over the last few days. Now let's forget about it and get on with the business.' I thought, yeah, I do want to play in the World Cup. Bite the tongue.

Then Ian Evans butted in: 'What about Packie? Look what Packie's gone through. He's getting a lot of stick in the papers back home.' (He wasn't getting any stick.)

Why was Evans sticking his nose in now?

Packie said, 'No problem, no problem, Roy, I've had bigger rows with my kids over homework.' The voice of sanity. I was grateful. 'No worries, Roy, everything's fine.'

'Of course it is,' I replied.

I'd seen Kells the night before. No problem. I'd met Packie in the lift. We'd smiled at each other. I thought if I was to fall out with everyone I'd had an argument with, I'd be talking to nobody.

The training that morning was disappointing. A game of head tennis. I did my own bit of running afterwards. But, I thought, on Friday we're moving to the mainland, to a proper FIFA-arranged training camp. I could stick it out.

Problem.

I'd agreed to give two interviews, to Tom Humphries and Paul Kimmage. They were two guys I had respect for. It wasn't my turn to give a press conference until Friday. Now the media were all over the story. I made no comment. I talked to Tom and Paul. They're interesting guys to talk to. They come from a different angle, something other than 'Who's going to win? Is so-and-so a good player?' Both were straightforward interviews. They broached the preparations in a general sort of way. I responded in kind. On the same day I also spoke briefly to Gabriel Egan of RTE Radio. That interview too was innocuous.

On Thursday morning I got a phone call from Tom Humphries at about 7.45. Dublin was eight hours behind and the *Irish Times* was about to print.

'Roy, can I see you in reception just to go through this interview with you to be sure it's all right?' I went down, read the article (which is presented in full in the appendix of this book) and said yes, that's fine. I appreciated Tom asking me.

The article appeared on Thursday morning. It expressed exactly what I felt. I believed people at home had a right to know the truth. The Irish fans are celebrated for the support they give the team. Thousands of them were flying out on expensive packages to support us in the World Cup, my own brothers and a cousin were coming. It was the trip of a lifetime for them. Millions more would be watching the matches at home, as I'd done in 1988 and 1990. Were the people to be treated like mugs? They spent their hard-earned money, paid our wages and then we insult them with PR crap about all they've done for us. Maybe we should do something for them to repay the debt we owed them. Like get our act together. And tell them the score now and then.

As captain of Manchester United I've frequently made similar comments when I felt things needed to be said. The conspiracy of silence around the Irish story had gone on for long enough. The media were the worst offenders. They knew the story. But Jack, and now Mick, seemed to have most of them 'on board'.

On Thursday afternoon I went for a walk on the beach. I met the Irish team doctor, Martin Walsh. We sat down and had a nice chat. We talked about all kinds of things. With regard to the trouble of the past few days Martin was sympathetic.

'I understand your frustration, Roy.'

While we were sitting there McCarthy and Evans were walking up and down the beach. They were talking to each other, occasionally looking over at us. I sensed that something was up. Could it be the *Irish Times* article?

At 6.30 I came down for our evening meal. None of the staff were around. We were told there was a team meeting at 7.30. I knew damn well what it was about. Tom's article. As we were finishing dinner the hotel band started playing. Steve Finnan was sitting beside me. I asked him how his ankle was. On the mend, he said, but he might be struggling for the opening game against Cameroon.

'I was lucky, Roy,' Steve said. 'I was walking when I put my foot in the pot-hole. If I'd been running I'd have broken my ankle.' What we'd been faced with out here was, we both agreed, unbelievable. All the players felt the same. They'd been talking about it all week. Come to think of it, Irish players had been talking like this for ever.

At 7.30 McCarthy arrived in the restaurant. The staff were with him.

'OK, lads, we're off at eight o'clock tomorrow morning.

Get your bags packed and tagged. And while we're here,' he went on, 'whoever's not happy with anything, I'd like them to say it to me.' I knew what was coming. But I was cool, my conscience was clear. For one thing I *had* told him privately what I was unhappy with. As team captain I'd said my piece the other day, no need to repeat it. 'I picked this island, and if anybody's not happy, they should tell me now,' he repeated.

Keep cool, Roy, they're dangling the bait for you. Don't bite. The atmosphere was heavy with the sense that trouble was brewing. They all knew now what the meeting was about. He's going to try and sort me out publicly. Be the big man, the Manager.

I was calm.

'Roy, you don't seem to be happy with something.'

It was pathetic.

'Well, Mick,' I said, 'why didn't you say that from the start? We've talked about this in private. Why aren't we having this conversation in private?'

'Well, you've made it public,' he said, whipping the Humphries article from behind his back, like Paul Daniels.

'What do you mean, "made it public"?'

'This interview with the *Times*.'

'Mick, do you not think I've seen the interview? Do you call this set-up man management?'

'You're going against your team-mates now,' he went on.

'Look, I've seen the interview. I promised Tom last Sunday I'd do a piece with him. I spoke to him yesterday. I stand by everything I said. The interview's fine.'

'You've gone against your team-mates,' he repeated. 'You never wanted to play for your country. You were supposed to go to Iran and you didn't, you faked an injury to get out of playing for your country.' He's on a roll now.

'You know that's not true,' I responded. 'You spoke to my manager, you know I wasn't right for the Iran match in Dublin. You thanked me for coming to Dublin. You agreed that 2-0 was a good result.' I was angry now, he was bending the truth. 'You call this man management?' I went on. 'You were there, you know the truth. Mick, you're a liar.'

What was he doing this for? Suddenly I snapped. All the fuck-ups and bullshit I and every other Irish player had put up with for ten years flashed through my mind. Harry's fucking Challenge. The piss-up in the US Cup. In Cyprus. Paul McGrath. Denis Irwin *proving himself*. The dope test at USA '94. The Captain Fantastic myth. Some Captain Fantastic! The duff hotels. The jokes about the Irish in English dressing rooms, which ate into my soul! The cheese sandwiches in Holland. Most of all, the conversation (in my house!) when this prat agreed with me and promised we'd do it right this time!

And here he was playing fucking Big Boss in front of people who knew the story, who'd been there, gone along with this farce. Stan and Quinny, Kells, Packie. They all knew the score. Stand up, lads, give me a dig out. I looked around at them. Sitting there. Stand up? No chance.

In this bad movie *I* was going to be the fall guy. It wasn't me and him, any more. It was everything. Pulling the wool over the eyes of the Irish fans. Charlton, Setters, McCarthy, Evans, the FAI. The journalists who didn't rock the boat. The fucking barbecue for the media. To keep them happy. Stopped them telling the real fucking story. Have a drink, lads. Would you like another chicken wing? Some sauce?

Walking on eggshells round me. *No*. Walking on eggshells round the truth. Taking the piss out of the Irish people. The fans they're supposed to love. 'You'll never beat the Irish.

You'll never beat the Irish.' At ignoring cock-ups, I thought. And I'm the captain of this. Biting my tongue, going along with the bluffers. Was this what I'd worked for all through my career? To come here and go along with the crap, sending coded messages to the fans through the *Irish Times*. My sin? To hint, *hint*, at the reality. Now *I* was in the dock. Captain Fantastic, counsel for the prosecution.

All of this raced through my head as I sat listening to the worst accusation of all. That I had faked injury. No. I'm not having that. From this impostor. McCarthy running on the pitch after we got a draw in Portugal in the qualifiers and grabbing me.

'Just stand with me, Roy, for fifteen seconds. Let the press get a photograph of the two of us together. It'll look great.'

'You're a fucking wanker. I didn't rate you as a player, I don't rate you as a manager, and I don't rate you as a person. You're a fucking wanker and you can stick your World Cup up your arse. I've got no respect for you.'

'Well, if you don't respect me, I don't think you can play for me.'

At that I got up and left the room. People say you'd never speak to Alex Ferguson like that. Wrong. If Alex Ferguson accused me of faking injury to get out of games, I would tell him where to go. My whole career, including the Iran game in Dublin, I pushed myself way too far playing with injuries. It was the worst insult I could think of to suggest I faked injuries.

When I got to my room I knew he'd got what he wanted. It was a set-up. The insult calculated to cause the gravest offence. Humiliation in front of the whole party was the result he was seeking. Maybe he got more than he bargained for.

Shortly afterwards there's a knock on the door. Stan and Quinny. What the fuck do these two muppets want, I wondered.

'Roy, we can't believe what you said, we can't believe what happened,' said Quinn.

Oh no, I think. Who do you think McCarthy is – Alex Ferguson? Both of them had been around long enough to know the score. They knew the difference between proper preparation and the shambles that caused all this. Go with the flow, boys, dead fish.

Quinn again: 'We can't believe you're going to miss the World Cup: we're gutted for you.'

'Thanks, guys, all the best,' I said, ushering them away from my door.

Cowards, I thought. They said fuck-all when they'd had their chance. Little did I know at that stage that they'd already stood beside McCarthy at a press conference – and backed him – *before* coming to tell me how sorry they were. They had mumbled something about the press but provided no detail.

A few minutes later Jason McAteer called up to the room to wish me all the best. Then Ian Harte.

Alan Kelly arrived. 'You went too far, Roy, in my opinion,' Kells said, but he continued, 'You're entitled to your opinion.' As Alan was standing there, the phone went. It was Michael Kennedy.

'You've been kicked out,' Michael said.

'Jesus, Michael, news travels fast.' It was only 8.15.

'It's been on the news bulletins here,' Michael confirmed.

'*What?*' I said. 'Already?' I told Michael I'd call him later. I turned to Kells: 'It's been on the news at home.'

'Yes,' he said, 'we held a press conference – me, Stan and

Niall and Mick – immediately after the meeting. Mick asked us to stand beside him and give him our support. I gave my opinion. I know you mightn't like me for it.'

'No, Alan, you're entitled to your opinion.'

That was it.

I rang United. I explained to Ann Wiley who took my call that I needed to get home as soon as possible. I asked her to ring the FAI in case there would be double bookings. Ann rang back to say that the FAI had told her to do what she wanted. They'd been quite insulting to her. A 'Roy Keane has nothing to do with us' kind of vibe. She said she'd organize my trip.

I phoned Theresa. Then Michael and the gaffer. Then I watched some basketball on the telly. I was fine, better than I'd felt for a long time. I was angry and hurt on one level, relieved on another, to be free of the conspiracy of silence, rid of the pretence that Ireland was preparing properly for the World Cup. Like a lot of other people, I'd kept my mouth shut for ten years, right from the day I first turned up for training with Big Jack. The jokes that were told about the Irish in English dressing rooms had long since ceased to amuse me.

At midnight there was a knock on the door. Who the fuck is that, I wondered. It was Gary Breen and David Connolly, two young lads I'd got to know better on the trip. They both liked to work in the gym, as I did. And we'd got to know each other over the few days.

'Everything all right with you, Roy?' Gary asked.

'Yeah, I'm fine, lads, a little bruised but I'm OK.'

So they said, 'We'd just like to say that we agreed with everything you said about facilities and things. You were dead right, but who are we to say anything?' I was moved by this.

Two young guys with everything to lose showing me support. 'We want to play in the World Cup,' they explained. I understood, 100 per cent.

'But if it's any consolation, when you left the room Quinny stood up and said we all had to stick together now. There was a round of applause. We didn't clap.'

'Fair play, you lads, thanks for coming to see me. And all the best in the tournament.'

That was an emotional moment for me. I knew that many of the people in that room agreed with much, if not all, of what I said. I knew also that it was impossible for most players to come out and confront a man who could determine the course of their careers. I also knew that the senior players, Quinn and Staunton in particular, were content to play the game. With McCarthy, the media, and worst of all with the fans, who never learned the truth. They'd hung me out to dry for speaking their unspoken thoughts.

Eventually I slept.

I woke up next morning to the sound of Mick Byrne's voice rousing the lads from their beds. I heard them make their way laughing and joking downstairs. Mick Byrne knocked to say goodbye. Mick was usually one for hugging. But I didn't want to hug him now. We shook hands. 'Good luck, Mick.'

My flight was at 6 p.m. I watched some DVDs to cheer me up. *Fawlty Towers* – a bit of Basil did the trick.

That's my story, for the moment. A chapter in my life is closed. My World Cup experience deepened my appreciation of the great football club I play for. Also reinforced were friendships, old and new, that are the cornerstones of my life.

In the days that followed the melodramatics in Saipan, many well-meaning people tried to fix what was broken. Some bluffers also got in on the act. They know who they are. And so do I.

Any possibility of reconciliation disappeared when the Irish squad put their names to a statement which insisted I shouldn't return. I would be a distraction. I can only guess – as I'm sure you can – who drafted that statement. And who corralled the younger players in the squad to add their names to it.

I hope some day I'll play for Ireland again. However, it won't be for McCarthy. Like me he's chosen his course. We disagree on fundamental football matters, but he is entitled to his preferences, as I am to mine.

Now I'm back with Manchester United. We have a lot to prove and I'm relishing the challenge. There's a new coach in Carlos Queiroz, who's great. Tough. And I'm hungrier than I've ever been. This time, if we win the treble, we won't make the same mistakes.

Appendix

'People were not happy but life goes on. Nobody died.'

Roy Keane interview: the Ireland captain talks exclusively to Tom Humphries on why he almost quit the World Cup squad and what made him stay in the end.

Q. So, after all the effort you put into getting the team here, what makes you announce that you are going home after a training ground row?

A. Well, it was the tip of the iceberg. I've basically had enough of certain things. I've come over here to do well and I want people around me to want to do well. If I feel we're not all wanting the same things, there's no point. It's been going on a while. It's the whole fact of being away. Like every other footballer. Maybe I should just be OK with it, but enough is enough. I'm banging my head against a brick wall regarding certain issues about this trip. This trip is the tip of the iceberg. From the training facilities to all sorts.

Q. Even here it's not right?

A. You've seen the training pitch and I'm not being a prima donna. Training pitch, travel arrangements, getting through the bloody airport when we were leaving, it's the combination of things. I would never say 'that's the reason or this is the reason', but enough is enough.

Q. Did you have reservations about the idea of flying 17 hours here?

A. Yeah, exactly. Flying 17 hours. It's different if we came here to a top training facility. The hotel is fine, but we've come here to work. You wonder why players get injured? Well, playing on a surface like that. I can't imagine any other country, countries in the world who are far worse off than us, playing on something like that. I don't think it's too much for us to ask, just for a pitch that's even watered. It's so dangerous. It's rock hard. One or two of the lads have picked up injuries. I'm amazed there hasn't been more but give it time. But you know, we're the Irish team, it's a laugh and a joke. We shouldn't expect too much.

Q. Did you talk to people about it before you got here?

A. No, no, I was quite relaxed. Everything was fine. Starting from the airport though, and the farce of trying to get through the airport, and all the press and nothing organised and we get here and the skips (containing the team's training gear) are missing, blah blah blah! Here we go. This is not right. All I want is what's best for me and the team. I mean that. It's not right in anybody's eyes. It's a laugh and a joke, of course, some of it, always has been with us, but now I'm thinking enough is enough.

Q. It's fair to say though that you came on the trip unhappy with coverage of you missing Niall Quinn's testimonial.

A. Yeah. It was straightforward. I was injured, I wasn't fit. Then coming over on Wednesday on the plane I got a couple of complimentary papers and the word 'disrespectful' was mentioned. People said I should have been in the stand in a shirt and tie. Sure. I'm not that daft either. I was going away on Wednesday for five weeks, what was I supposed to do? Sit in the stand? Do you think I would have been left alone up there? Do you think Quinny would have been going 'ah, cheers Roy for coming.'

That wouldn't have been the case. It was a choice. I wasn't fit. To spend the last night with my wife and kids . . . as it happened I went to the pictures with my wife at about nine o'clock after a day with the kids. It was that or be up in Sunderland sitting in the stand. I'd very little time with Theresa and the kids at the end of a long year.

I played Saturday, had treatment on Monday and Tuesday and left for here on Friday. Good luck to Quinny with what he's doing, but I don't need to be involved in the whole hullaballoo. My conscience is clear. Yeah, I wasn't happy, but I forgot about that.

Q. Was it something that could have been handled better by the FIA?

A. Again yeah. Without a doubt. They knew my situation. And Quinny did. They are the most important people, Quinny and Mick. They knew my situation. I've been seeing somebody in France who's been helping with my injuries. Then I picked up two dead legs against Arsenal. It had gone by Saturday (the one in my right leg) so I played against Charlton, but there was no way I could have travelled to France to have even done that work, because he does a lot of stretching on my legs and I wasn't fit. I wouldn't have made Quinny's game.

Either I went to France on Monday and after the stretching I'd have to rest for a day or two, or the dead leg would put me out. So I let them know. My priority was getting ready for the World Cup and, again, no disrespect to Quinny.

If people want to say that . . .

Q. Did you call yourself?

A. I spoke to Mick Byrne, who's the middle man for me, really. I spoke to Mick. If I thought for one minute it would offend, I would have gone up to save the hassle. But the choice of sitting in the stand or being at home with my family, there was only one winner.

Q. But you were asked to write a piece for the programme and declined?

A. Yeah, with Cathal Dervan. No way. Not with Cathal Dervan. The same man who three or four years ago insisted the fans boo for me. Michael Kennedy (Keane's agent) asked me, through Quinny. I said, if they wanted to do it through a different avenue . . . but it was just left. As soon as it happened, I knew the story would be that 'he refused to write a piece'.

Q. So Tuesday, you left for training, you seemed to be in good form. What happened?

A. It's a lot of things. There's a lot of things I don't understand when we come away like this – barbecue with the media, say. I don't understand the purpose of things. Or some of the gear going missing. The barbecue. Training pitch being wrong. No balls. Only two goals. There's differences of opinions about different things. Maybe I just don't get it.

Q. What bugged you about the barbecue? The media?

A. Yeah, I'm thinking, am I supposed to sit down with people, the likes of . . . I'm not going to mention any names because it gives them the satisfaction, but people who've slagged me and my family off. I know papers have to report. I accept criticism, constructive anyway, but not hypocrites. And I'm not talking just about the press there but people who were there with us being pally pally.

Things like that get under my skin. I've come away to train for the World Cup, not to have barbecues with the press but, if I don't go, I'm the only person who didn't turn up. It's all false.

Q. The team went out that night. Had you any problem with that?

A. I didn't fancy going out. We'll be away a long time. No problem at all. They needed to let off a bit of steam. I went to bed. I was tired. I'm getting old.

Q. As captain, do people come to you about these things?

A. The barbecue was mentioned. I questioned it, yeah. Believe it or not, at the time I didn't want to make a fuss. If the other players were comfortable . . .

Q. So what was the final straw then?

A. We'd no goalkeepers for the five-a-side.

Q. I saw you reacting badly to that. Why?

A. Ask any player, any footballer, anyone in the world, anybody – at the end of training you need a little game. Their attitude was that the 'keepers were tired. I completely disagreed with them. Tired? Well, is that not why we are all here? Explain that one to me. We've done about three hours work here, three hours work since Nigeria last Thursday. I know it's a relaxation but we could be in for a big shock next Saturday against Cameroon.

Q. But how does it go from there to you and Alan Kelly having a shouting match?

A. Obviously Alan disagreed. Packie said they'd worked hard. Alan said they worked hard. I said 'do ye want a pat on the back for working hard – is that not why you are here?' I did mention that they wouldn't be too tired to play golf the next day and, fair play, they dragged themselves out! That was my stance and Kells took his stance. Few words, but I've had arguments like that hundreds of times. Unfortunately, there was press there and you could say it got heated between me and Alan, but Alan is a decent lad. I went to speak to Alan later.

   You can laugh about it. These things happen. You get 23 lads away with each other. No big deal. It's over and gone. Done with.

Q. And when you came off the training ground and got on the bus on your own, had you decided then to come home?

A. Yeah. I'd had enough. I'm not asking too much – for everyone to want what's best. If it's a crime, fuck it, I'm guilty. Listen, people show it in different ways. Some people go to their rooms but it plays on me when something can be done about it. It's not being a prima donna. There's things you can't accept. That kind of pitch. No training kit. No balls. A 20-hour flight and there's no skips (containing the team's training gear). They said the skips were supposed to be here on Thursday. They should have been here two weeks ago, so there was no doubt! We're getting advised that we have to drink this stuff. It's not here yet, but when it does come you have to drink it. All the lads feel the same. I react differently. I know that's a downside. I am what I am, warts and all. Maybe you'll say I should have taken a step back. That's hindsight.

Q. So what happened?

A. It was a long night and a lot went through my head. I had to speak to people I respect. Obviously I had my family to think about but if it was up to me I wouldn't still be here. Couldn't have got a flight until four o'clock Wednesday. I spoke to my wife. I spoke to Michael (Kennedy, his agent), I spoke to Alex Ferguson. He's a good man and he gave me good words of advice. You have to listen to these people. The manager (Ferguson) has the same temperament as me. He understood what I was going through. He told me to stick it out, but this is it.

Q. What were the arguments being put to you?

A. I knew I had my family to think about back in Ireland. My poor Dad, my Mam. My three brothers and sisters. It would be all very well for me going back to Manchester. I knew all that. I was seeing straight, you know, but I just couldn't justify myself being here. Not just this trip, there's the constant, negative criticism over the years chipping away. I'm 31, I've had my few injuries. I travelled more than other players because of my commitments to United. That's not a complaint, it's just a fact and I just got to a stage where I said, I don't need this. So I spoke to the manager and I'll stick it out till after the World Cup and that will be it for me. Without a doubt.

Q. And how do you feel now that you are staying?

A. Today I'm thinking that the first game is next Saturday. I've got some of my family coming out before then to relax with. They're people I can switch off with and relax with. Obviously

I room on my own and I'm in here (in his room) quite a bit, which is what I want anyway. If there was a flight yesterday, I'd have been gone.

Q. Being on your own on these trips, does it make you lower?

A. If I did want to room with somebody, maybe. On the whole, I prefer rooming on my own. We do it at United, pre-season we'd be away 10, 12 days. I know club level is different, the bonds are different but you can't have everything. I prefer to be on my own as regards using the telephone, getting up, reading, using the bath, whatever you might want. I could do something about it but I do accept I'm on my own. I've nobody to bounce things off or have a laugh with. That's the downside.

Q. So you spoke to Theresa (his wife), to Alex Ferguson and Michael Kennedy. Was there anyone from the team coming up to your room by this stage?

A. No. To be fair, I'd made my mind up. They were giving me breathing space. I didn't want to speak to anyone else. I spoke to Theresa and she said Michael was under pressure. It had been out on the news in Ireland. I don't know how that happened, only one or two people knew, but a ticket was booked for me, so maybe that way things got out. It's no good trying to blame any one person, it's a combination of things and myself. Enough was enough.

I spoke to Michael, he said the manager (Ferguson) had been on. He was on holidays but he'd seen the news. I had a good chat with him. He's someone I respect. In football, he's the only person I would listen to. We spoke about my family. I knew what he was saying but it helps when you get other people saying it. We'd discussed it before because of my injuries curtailing my international football. He said hang in there because of my family.

Q. What impact has it all had on the lads on the team?

A. Not sure, to be honest. I think when you are away things happen. To me it's gone now, what happened. I need to get my head down for two or three weeks. Get my head down for the country, enjoy it and leave with my head held high.

Q. How have you dealt with it in terms of your relationship with the team?

A. It's gone now. Me and Kells spoke, even. We had a laugh. We are grown men. I've had hundreds of thousands of those heated discussions. Every day in training at United. Really. I had lunch with Kells on the day it happened and – this is funny – we were saying how we were both the sort of people who fly off the handle easily and how we had to learn to control that. Then three hours later we had that row. Then today at lunch we were saying 'remember that discussion we had yesterday!' It's forgotten about. We want what's best for each other. I'll get my head down for the next three weeks. I want to do well for the people of Ireland, for my family and for me personally.

Q. Do you think though that you exist as an island apart from the team? Take the Iran game, the players were baffled that you left the morning after the first leg without saying anything?

A. It was straightforward. Sunday morning, the manager (Ferguson) spoke to Mick McCarthy. I hadn't played for three weeks before that game. After the match I was feeling my knee, especially in the last 20 minutes. We were 2-0 up having not played that well. I felt the job was done. So, it was Sunday and the manager rang me. Mick Byrne and Mick McCarthy were there. It was agreed I'd go home. I just couldn't see us losing 3-0, but I probably would have taken the blame for it anyway if we did! The lads were having a warm-down, they were all in the rooms. It's not my scene. If I passed somebody in the corridor, I'd say goodbye. I didn't go round door to door. Even here, if I was leaving I wouldn't have gone door to door. That's not my scene.

Q. Do you know anyone else who gets as intense about football and getting it right?

A. Our manager, Alex Ferguson. Look, I just want what's best.

Realistically, I didn't expect to come over here and find High-bury or Anfield waiting but I expected the pitch to be at least watered. We've had two injuries. Players are tired, fatigued after a long hard season and it would be softer out there on the hotel car park. If there is something wrong with wanting that, then what chance have we got? All the players feel the same. They react differently. Some people accept it easier. Maybe that's why some of our players are playing where they are. You have to want the best. You need to prepare. It's hard enough as it is, playing Cameroon next Saturday it's going to be so bloody hard. We could be in for a shock. Everybody could be in for a shock.

Q. Apart from facilities, is it too laid-back here for you?

A. To be fair, the hotel is nice, the sun is nice but it's a long way to come for that. That's my opinion. I think we've come to train hard, to get ready for the World Cup. Look at the facilities. We need to be taking it easy a little bit, I know. To be fair, I don't see anything wrong with the golf or the night out but, when we are working hard, can we not work for three hours solid on a good pitch? Instead, we've done three one-hour sessions.

Q. Why are the highs higher for you and the lows lower?

A. I try not to be like that, believe it or not. I'm trying to get level pegging. I don't want that, the highs and lows. I react. That's the way I am. That's what's made me what I am, good and bad, but I like me. I do like me. I don't think I'm a bad person. In my life, I'm trying to get things level. When I was younger I was up and down like a roller coaster. I was up, out and in headlines, injured and winning trophies. High up, low down. I'm trying to get things down, accepting things, but there's only so much you can accept.

Q. Do you get depressed?

A. No. I wouldn't say depressed. I can't go back to my room and switch off. It plays on my mind. I accept a lot of things, especially with the Irish team. People say I'm always moaning but, if I moaned about everything you'd have about 40 tapes there. I like my life simple, I really do. I didn't want the hassle I had yesterday, far from it. I didn't want the night I had last night. Do you think I slept like a baby? I slept okay in the end last night but that happens when you drain yourself taking things on board. I've decided I'm here for myself and the people of Ireland and my family. Sod everybody else. This will be my last trip. I can't go banging my head against a brick wall. I can't. Sometimes you have to take a stance. If there was a flight yesterday I'd be home now and I wouldn't have felt bad about it.

Q. When you went asleep, did you know you were staying?

A. At that stage, I was still going back. I woke at about 6.30 and I rang my wife. She said Michael Kennedy had been on, he was under pressure from the press. I rang him and he said to ring the manager (Ferguson). He'd been ringing me but couldn't get through to the hotel because of the phones here. I spoke to the gaffer, he said his piece. I decided. I think there was all sorts going on in the background. A lot of people were not happy but life goes on. Nobody died.

Q. What did you say to Mick McCarthy after training?

A. I told Mick I'd had enough. Basically that was it. We've had discussions already the other night about training facilities. You've got to prepare properly is my attitude . . .

Q. You hate the lovable Irish thing, don't you?

A. I suppose so. I accept it, I'm as Irish as anybody, but this has been going on for years. Training facilities, travel arrangements. It's easy to pass the buck. Everyone here does it. You got to prepare properly though, it's hard enough as it is. If I opened my mouth every time there's something wrong, I'd need my own newspaper.

Q. Had you any idea coming away that this was the end of your international career?

A. No. I was definitely going to the European Championships. Without a doubt. Maybe no friendly internationals but . . . It gets harder, no matter what you are doing. That's all. I had no intentions of quitting. I do love the 90 minutes, it's the rest of the crap. I'm sure the other players love their kids, but I can't worry about the other players. I have to worry about me. I travel a lot, I have four kids. I miss them. Everyone is different. All I can do is look after me and my family. The European Championships would have been my swansong. It's just come early.

Q. Any going back?

A. Unless there's drastic changes. No.

Q. Who are your friends in football?

A. There isn't anyone I wouldn't class as a friend. There's a lot of people I like. The Irish lads are all decent, good lads but I wouldn't be one to pick up the phone or send Christmas cards. A lot of people are like that. I have my family. I can go out with them and relax and switch off. It won't go beyond them. I've been that way for a long time. It's nothing to do with having a high profile. I've been a bit wary of people for a long time. It's a good thing.

Q. What's that song you've been heard to sing, Positively 4th Street?

A. My singing days are over. How does that one go again?

Q. You know. 'You've got a lot of nerve to say you are my friend, you just want to be on the side that's winning.'

A. Oh yeah, that one. In my defence, I was only joining in. Yeah, that would sum it up for me but there's people away from football I'd be comfortable with. You have to be like that, have to be a bit wary. People talk. I read things about myself. Players even. Niall Quinn did something, with Paul Kimmage I think, a few months ago. Jason did something too. Niall said, if Roy was buttering his toast it would have to be perfect. I'm thinking, what's Niall talking about? People think they know you. Daft things like that. I don't want to get on the PR machine though.

I don't want it. I do like my life simple. People will laugh at that but people who know me . . . I was in UCC last week and it was a huge honour for me and my family, but a day like that it takes its toll on me. I don't feel comfortable in places like that. I'm so grateful for it – that goes without saying – but give me my kids and walking my dog any day of the week. I do like my life simple and I have to laugh at myself because . . .

Q. Do you think you'll manage or would you prefer to walk away from football altogether?

A. It could go either way. I'd be very capable of walking away but I see the challenge of being a manager, I'd love to pull the strings of a big club, players, listen to people. I look at our manager and I think about it. I know it's stressful. People will say, if I'm going to walk away from this, what chance do I have of being a manager. I don't know. I think I'd enjoy that challenge. At the end of the day, I enjoy managing myself regarding looking after myself, stretching, weights. I'd enjoy stretching that. Good players and good people with me, people I could trust. I'd like that. On the other hand, getting away from it, to a life where people leave you alone. I suppose the longer you're out of it . . . I'd love the idea of holidays at Christmas with my family, summers in Australia, doing courses or whatever. It's hard to imagine.

I have a four-year contract at United, though. That has its challenges. I'm hungry, I've probably never been as hungry as I am now for success. It still hurts me what happened at United this season. I need people around me to be hungry, too. It's the same with Ireland. I need people pulling the same way and wanting what's best.

Q. But isn't there more than one way to skin a cat?

A. Possibly. People do it different ways. Some people need an arm put around them. Yeah, I'm sure there are other ways. I watch people who I respect and if you know football it's about the different needs of different players.

People think because I go away with the Irish team I'm moaning, because it's not as good as Manchester United. That's nonsense. I want to have a good training pitch. At Manchester United they want the best of everything. That's the difference, they want it. Everybody. When we travel the treatment is fantastic because of that. People in the laundrette, the canteen, feel that way at United . . . A bad result and there's doom and gloom. Otherwise what are you playing the game for? I accept a lot of things. I know the FAI haven't got millions in the bank, but it's cost a lot of money to come out here and look . . . It's preparation. Fail to prepare. Prepare to fail.

Q. Why do you think Saipan was chosen as a venue for preparation?

A. Haven't a clue. Somebody came here once and it looked nice once. They thought they were making an effort because it's really far away. The important things weren't looked at. Travel, of course. A training pitch.

We had a lovely day yesterday, we went up to Suicide Cliff and learned the history. I enjoyed that, that's the nice side of it, but I keep saying to everybody we're here to prepare for the World Cup.

I was going to go back up there today to that cliff! Add an Irishman to the list (laughs). It's gone now, this business. We'll just get on with it. Maybe it's the vibe I sent out, the monster that's been built, some of it through my own doing but I don't expect anybody here to tiptoe around me. Alan Kelly took the piss out of things today. He came out at training with a balaclava on. I was glad. Alan would be a player I would talk to a lot. I don't want to be burning my bridges there! I'd be down to zero!

Q. How do you think you've come out of this whole thing?

A. I come off the worst, no matter what! Eventually the penny has to drop but you need to put the penny in. I'm learning but I'm only human. These things happen for a reason. You have to learn from these things, the bad things. Without a doubt. I think the best has still to come. I've made mistakes. I'm better for the mistakes. Introduce me to somebody who hasn't made mistakes and I'll shake his hand. Things happen for a reason, I'm sure the man upstairs is guiding me along the way, putting a few obstacles in the way but I feel very happy with life. I do. I just don't want us going home saying 'if only we'd prepared better'.

Q. And what have you learned?

A. Well, it's brought a decision that enough is enough. At this moment in time, I know this is my swansong. Not sure I'll be missed.

Q. It'll be duller!

A. It might be!

Q. You could be player-manager in the future?

A. Yeah. Nobody would play for me but we'd have great facilities!

Q. Well, you'd be the media choice.

A. Yeah? Right. That's that then!

23 May 2002

Index

References to club and international games can be found under the name of the opposition.

Adie, Kate 102
Ahern, Bertie 255
Ajax stadium, Amsterdam 251
Albania 73, 77
Aldridge, John 52, 75, 102, 121, 122, 125
Ali, Muhammad 256
Allison, Malcolm 95
Andorra 252, 253
Anfield, Liverpool 30, 31, 32, 56, 132, 143, 144, 156, 162, 163, 167, 230, 240, 246
Arnold Town FC 28, 29, 30
Arsenal FC 5, 45, 55, 62, 77, 89, 113, 154, 177, 178, 182, 184–5, 190, 196, 216, 220, 234, 235, 240, 243, 274
Aston Villa FC 12, 62, 117, 123, 150, 151, 179, 190, 193, 217, 235
Austria 245

Babb, Phil 126
Baggio, Dino 121
Baggio, Roberto 121–4
Barcelona 26, 27, 131–2, 182, 210
Baresi, Franco 121, 123
Barnes, John 31, 156
Barnsley FC 40, 177
Barrett, Alan 225
Barthez, Fabien 227, 234, 240
Basler, Mario 210
Batson, Brendan 79, 84
Bayer Leverkusen 242–3
Bayern Munich 164, 182, 188, 191, 197, 210–12, 215, 223, 224, 230
Beardsley, Peter 31, 32

Beckham, David 93, 109, 130, 131, 137, 145, 150, 151, 162, 167, 182–7, 189, 192, 193, 196, 202, 210, 211–12, 216, 221, 222, 235, 239, 242
Belgium 248
Belvedere Boys 19
Berg, Henning 210, 222
Bergkamp, Dennis 126, 184
Bernabeu, Madrid 222
Best, George 109, 191, 229
Birmingham City 158
Birtles, Garry 85
Blackburn Rovers FC 62, 63, 65, 77–84, 110, 113, 116, 129, 132, 136, 138, 140, 143, 144, 152–3, 214, 235
Blanc, Laurent 109, 233, 234, 242, 243, 254
Blomqvist, Jesper 179, 187, 210
Bonner, Pat ('Packie') 122, 123, 125, 126–7, 257, 258, 259, 262, 266, 276
Bordeaux 218
Borussia Dortmund 164, 166, 167
Bosman Ruling 215, 233
Bosnich, Mark 217–18, 221
Bowyer, Gary 24, 83
Brady, Liam 53, 75
Bramall Lane, Sheffield 37
Brazil 124, 219–20
Breen, Gary 253, 269
Brian Dillon's Boxing Club, Dillon's Cross 3
Brighton FC 10, 20
Brondby 182
Bruce, Steve 85, 88, 91, 96,

98, 110, 117, 141, 165, 169, 197, 200, 216
helps RK settle at United 105–6, 158
club captain 133, 158
ticket allocation 133, 168
injuries 140, 151, 153, 156–7
Cantona's generous gesture 157–8
transfer to Birmingham City 158
personality 158
Cantona succeeds as captain 168
Bruce/Pallister partnership 179–80
Buckley, Derek 22, 37, 41, 50
Busby, Sir Matt 86, 94, 95, 111, 161, 191, 194, 199, 209, 222
Busby Babes 199
Butt, Nicky 93, 130, 131, 137, 138, 149–51, 153, 157, 166, 167, 175, 182, 184, 185, 196, 202, 209, 210, 216
Byrne, Mick 251, 255, 260–62, 270, 274, 279
Byrne, Raymond 24, 83

Cameroon 260, 264, 276, 280
Cantona, Eric 85, 87, 98, 114, 132, 133, 137, 145, 152, 154, 156, 190, 191, 197, 200, 216, 227
injury 90
transferred to United 91
Cantona enigma 91–3, 109–10
and Schmeichel 92

Cantona, Eric – (*contd*)
 his finishing 92
 Istanbul incident 94
 derby with Manchester
   City 96, 97
 Norwich incident 111
 sent off twice in three days
   113
 goal-scoring for the
   double 116, 117, 148
 generosity to younger
   players 138
 Championship wins 138,
   148
 'kung-fu' kick 138–44,
   147–8, 153, 155
 professionalism 153
 generous gesture to Bruce
   157–8
 in Europe 163–4, 167
 succeeds Bruce as captain
   168
 retirement 160–61, 168,
   169
Capello, Fabio 240, 241
Carlos, Roberto 222
Carr, Stephen 252
Carragher, Jamie 240
Carrow Road, Norwich 40
Carsley, Lee 259
Cascarino, Tony 52, 102,
   201, 202
Celtic FC 238
Champions League 121, 129,
   131–3, 162–7, 169, 179,
   183, 184, 187–8, 191–2,
   219, 220, 222, 228, 230,
   237, 241–3
 United wins 206–13, 223
 new rules 232
 final at Hampden Park
   (2002) 232
 United's new formation
   239
Charity Shield 89, 169, 178,
   227, 235, 236
Charles, Gary 44, 45, 48
Charles, HRH The Prince of
   Wales 47, 206
Charlton, Bobby 191, 229
Charlton, Jack 2, 16, 41,
   49–50, 100–101, 103,
   207, 245, 266, 269
 Irish national hero 35, 37,
   126, 244
 approach to football
   49–50, 52–4, 73, 74, 76,
   77, 118, 140

in the USA 60
confrontation with RK 61
compared with Clough
   76–7
and USA '94 119–22,
   125–8
and journalists 125, 264
McCarthy succeeds 246
Charlton Athletic FC 113,
   230, 274
Chelsea FC 12, 90, 115, 143,
   149, 168–70, 196,
   216–18, 227
Chile 49
City Ground, Nottingham
   24, 30, 33–5, 38, 56, 65,
   70, 78, 88
Clark, Frank 72, 78–9, 82, 83
Clough, Brian 20, 25, 26, 29,
   37, 82
 and RK's Forest contract
   21–2
 and RK's first pre-season
   game for Forest reserves
   28
 and RK's First Division
   debut 30–32
 and RK's home debut for
   Forest 34
 RK's debt to 34, 56, 66
 personality 34–5
 and RK's visits home 36,
   56
 RK's company car 38
 punching incident 38
 and the FA Cup 1991
   38–40, 44, 45, 47
 and Stuart Pearce 39, 57
 RK's new contract 51
 mixed opinions about him
   56
 knowledge of the game
   57–8
 grand gesture to the
   north-east 59
 public criticism of RK 63,
   64, 66
 and the Forest board 64,
   71
 and Graham Taylor 67
 fines RK in Jersey 69
 announces his resignation
   70
 and Forest's relegation 71,
   72
Clark succeeds 72
compared with Jack
   Charlton 76–7

achievement in Europe
   206
Clough, Nigel 24, 39, 55, 67,
   70
Club World Championship
   218–19
Cobh Ramblers 14, 15,
   17–19, 21, 25, 28, 34,
   100, 258
Coca-Cola (League) Cup
   117
Cole, Andy 137, 138, 140,
   148, 151, 180, 182,
   185–7, 189, 192, 210,
   235
Collymore, Stan 156
Connolly, David 269
Constable, Mike 175, 225
Conte, Antonio 183
Cooke, Terry 173, 174
Corcoran, Eddie 259
Corcoran, Jamie 225
Cork City FC 14
Courtney, Declan 225
Courtney, James 225
Coventry City FC 33, 116,
   163, 189, 228, 230
Coyne, Tommy 126
Croatia Zagreb 218
Crofton Celtic junior club,
   Cork 2
Cronin, Billy 225
Crosby, Gary 44, 45
Crossley, Mark 38, 48
Cruyff, Johan 119
Crystal Palace FC 38, 39,
   114, 138, 140–42
Cunningham, Kenny 252
Czech Republic 118

Dalglish, Kenny 63, 77, 79,
   81–2, 83, 113, 132, 150
Davenport, Peter 85
Davids, Edgar 183, 187
De Boer, Frank 126
Del Piero, Alessandro 164
Delea, John 6, 12, 225
Dell, The, Southampton 161,
   162, 165
Demetradze, Giorgi 228
Denmark 72–4, 99, 103
Deportivo La Coruña
   239–40, 242
Derby County FC 12, 29,
   167, 232
Dervan, Cathal 247, 255,
   274–5
Deschamps, Didier 183, 187

Dillon, Mike 227
Donadoni, Roberto 121
Downey, Len 6, 8–10, 14–16
Doyle, Nick (RK's father-in-law) 168
Duff, Damien 252
Dunne, Derek 253
D'Urso, Andy 221, 222
Dynamo Kiev 228, 230

Edwards, Martin 84, 160, 161, 214
Effenberg, Stefan 210, 230
Egan, Gabriel 263
Elber, Giovane 230
Elland Road, Leeds 64, 132, 156, 163, 180
Elleray, David 184, 231
England team 16, 74, 75, 118, 125, 250
Eriksson, Sven-Göran 240
European Championships
Euro '88 16, 50, 52, 101
Euro '92 51–2
Euro '96 245, 246
Euro '2000 227, 233, 248, 282
European Cup 29, 56, 87, 90–91, 129
  Manchester United wins (1968) 94, 206
Evans, Ian 251, 257, 258, 262, 264, 266
Evening Echo 9, 10
Everton FC 111–12, 129, 140, 144, 149, 235
Ewood Park, Blackburn 79, 113, 132

FA Cup 150, 164, 191
  1981 5, 18
  1985 199
  1991 38–40, 44–9, 93
  1994 110, 113, 115–17
  1995 129, 140
  1996 157–8
  1997 168
  1999 182, 188, 196–7, 205–6
  2000 218–20
Fagan, Joe 150
FAI *see* Football Association of Ireland
Fairview Park, Dublin 19, 34
Fenerbahce 164–5
Fenton, Ronnie 20–22, 30, 45, 63, 65

Ferdinand, Les 192–3, 194
Ferguson, Sir Alex 89, 92, 96, 112–13, 118, 129, 133, 171, 267
  talks with RK 80–81, 83
  RK's South African trip 85
  inspirational presence 88
  respected 88, 240
  first Championship 91
  and success in Europe 93
  and Bryan Robson 99, 116
  attention to detail 100, 136, 145–6, 183, 192
  personality 106, 191, 277
  and United's drinking culture 107, 199
  Cantona affair 139–40, 142–3, 147–8
  Southgate incident 142, 143
  his gamble 150
  negotiates a new contract 155
  vindicated by double of 1995/96 157
  pay dispute 158
  on Cantona 160
  row with RK 176
  and Schmeichel 178
  signs Stam, Yorke and Blomqvist 179
  and RK's arrest 204
  Champions League win 206, 209, 210, 212
  the 'perfect manager' 215
  achievement with United 232
  announces leaving United 232, 240–41
  RK discusses his future 237–9
  decision to stay at United 241
  and RK's World Cup walk-out 261–2, 269, 277–9, 281
Fevre, Dave 172–4, 176, 177, 195
FIFA 121, 127, 218–20, 257, 262
Finnan, Steve 252, 259, 264
Finney, Tom 3
Fiorentina 218
First Division 29, 30, 54, 55, 70
  RK's debut 31–3
Football Association (FA) 94, 142, 150

  disciplinary committee 140, 143
  and the Club World Championship 218–19, 220
Football Association of Ireland (FAI) 2, 14, 40, 54, 60, 100, 118, 119, 246, 253, 266, 269, 274, 284
Football League 56
Football League Championship 56
Fowler, Robbie 156
French National Training Centre 146
Fulham FC 235
FÁS (Foras Áiseanna Saothair; Training and Employment Authority) scheme 13–17, 25, 40, 45, 258

Galatasaray 94–5, 131
Gale, Tony 44
Gardner, Jimmy 'Five Bellies' 173
Gascoigne, Paul 35, 37, 47–9, 68, 173
Gemmill, Archie 20, 25, 26, 28, 29, 33, 34, 68
Gemmill, Scot 25, 27, 28
Gerrard, Steven 240
Giants Stadium, New York 122, 124, 125, 127–8
Giggs, Ryan 87, 90, 91, 109, 112, 117, 130, 133, 141, 151, 182–5, 189, 192, 196, 202, 209, 210, 216, 235, 236
Gillespie, Keith 131, 137
Ginola, David 227
Gothenburg 131, 164
Graham, George 89, 189
Gray, Andy 220

Haaland, Alfie 171–2, 175, 180, 188, 231, 236
Haarlem FC 26–7
Hampden Park, Glasgow 232
Hansen, Alan 150
Harford, Ray 63
Harte, Ian 268
Hasselbaink, Jimmy Floyd 227, 251
Haughey, Charles 13, 75
Healy, Colin 260, 261
Hendry, Colin 153

Henry, Thierry 240
Highbury, London 113, 132,
    153, 163, 182, 185, 193,
    217, 240
Hill, Alan 21, 68
Hill, Jimmy 111
Hitzfeld, Ottmar 215, 230,
    240
Hoddle, Glenn 5, 18
Hodge, Steve 24, 30, 44, 45
Holland x, 119, 126–7, 246,
    249–52, 266
Hollins, John 21
Honved 90, 91
Houghton, Ray 31, 32, 52,
    75, 121–4, 126
Howey, Steve 231
Hughes, Mark ('Sparky') 85,
    89–91, 96, 114, 117,
    133, 137, 148–9, 151,
    155, 161, 169
Humphries, Tom 262–5,
    272–85

Iceland 247–8
Ince, Paul 85, 88, 93, 96,
    114, 169, 200, 216
    partnered by RK in
        midfield 89–91, 117,
        149
    a rival of RK 98
    and RK's lack of
        involvement in build-
        up play 112
    rumours of move to Italy
        137, 149
    leaves United 148, 149,
        155, 161
Inter Milan 189, 209
Inter-Continental Cup 217
Inzaghi, Filippo 183, 185–6
Ipswich Town FC 69, 140
Iran 254, 265–6, 267
Ireland 6, 7, 10, 36, 122
Ireland team
    defeats England at
        Stuttgart (1988) 16
    successful Italia '90 37, 50,
        75, 118
    RK turns down Algeria
        trip 39–40, 41
    RK's first international
        game 49
    in Euro '88 50
    RK plays his first
        competitive game 51–3
    and Charlton's game plan
        49–50, 52–4

World Cup qualifiers
    (1993) 72–7, 99–103
    RK's mixed feelings about
        playing for Ireland 100
    USA '94 117–28
    Harry's Challenge 245,
        246, 250, 266
    McCarthy replaces
        Charlton as manager
        246
    World Cup 2002 249–71,
        275, 278–80
Irish Novice League 3
Irish Supporters' Club 68
Irish Times 263, 264, 265
Irish under-15 international
    team 8
Irish under-21 international
    team 35
Irwin, Denis 3, 52, 85, 87,
    91, 96, 97, 117, 122,
    132, 135, 151, 165, 168,
    173, 182–4, 202, 207–9,
    245, 248, 266
Italia '90 *see* World Cup
Italy 185–6, 227
    USA '94 119, 121–4,
        127–8

James, David 157
Jancker, Carsten 210
Jemson, Nigel 30, 40, 44
Jeremies, Jens 230
Johnsen, Ronnie 180, 182,
    210
Jonk, Wim 126–7
Juninho Paulista 221
Juventus 162–7, 183, 185,
    186, 189, 215, 224

Kanchelskis, Andrei 90, 91,
    117, 132, 137, 148, 149,
    151, 155, 161
Keane, Aidan (RK's son) x,
    180–81, 225
Keane, Caragh (RK's
    daughter) x, 180,
    225
Keane, Denis (RK's brother)
    x, 1, 4, 11, 23, 37, 41,
    46, 50, 80, 134, 168,
    209, 225, 260, 277
Keane, Hilary (RK's sister) 1,
    23, 80, 134, 168, 225,
    277
Keane, Johnson (RK's
    brother) x, 1, 4, 6, 11,
    23, 37, 41, 46, 50, 80,

    134, 168, 170, 171, 209,
    225, 260, 277
Keane, Leah (RK's daughter)
    x, 225
Keane, Linda (RK's sister-in-
    law) 170, 171
Keane, Marie (née Lynch;
    RK's mother) 1, 23, 33,
    42, 80, 134–5, 260, 277
Keane, Maurice (Mossie;
    RK's father) 1, 23, 33,
    37, 42, 80, 134–5, 260,
    277
Keane, Pat (RK's brother) x,
    1, 23, 80, 134, 168, 209,
    225, 260, 277
Keane, Robbie 252
Keane, Roy Maurice
    birth (10 August 1971) 1
    education 1–2, 6–10
    hurling and boxing 3–4
    joins Rockmount AFC
        4–5
    turned down at Dublin
        trials 9–10
    temporary jobs 11–12
    trademark determination
        13
    role model (Bryan
        Robson) 18
    signed for Nottingham
        Forest 19–23
    contract with Forest 22,
        51, 62–5, 69–70, 78, 79
    First Division debut 31–3
    home debut at Forest 34
    and Gazza 35
    first League goal 37
    the price of fame 41, 42,
        50–51, 68, 104, 202
    incident at Sidetrax Disco
        42–3
    injuries 45, 93, 151, 162,
        163, 166, 172–7, 181,
        195, 205, 238–40, 242,
        245, 246, 254, 267, 274
    in Cup Final of 1991 47–9
    first international game for
        Ireland 49
    fined for Jersey incident 69
    voted Player of the Year at
        Forest 72
    terms agreed with
        Blackburn 79
    changes mind about
        joining Blackburn 81–2
    talks with Alex Ferguson
        80–81, 83

signs for Manchester
    United 84, 85
Britain's most expensive
    player 85, 117
South African trip 85–9
first competitive
    appearance for United
    89
scores first goal for United
    90
important conversation
    with Robson 112–13,
    117
first Championship medal
    116
first non-football
    commercial contract
    133
Southgate incident 142,
    143
hernia operations 143, 153
contract commitment 158
sent off at Southampton
    162
marries Theresa 168
becomes captain of United
    168–9, 170
hotel brawl 170–71
returns to training after
    injury 177–8
incident at Henry's 202–4,
    236
unable to play in the
    Champions League final
    206–12
new contract 214, 218, 226
sent off at Newcastle 222
awards 227
bad tackle on Gus Poyet
    227–8, 236, 237
and 'prawn sandwiches'
    comments 229
discusses his future with
    Ferguson 237–9
bad start with McCarthy
    247
appointed captain of
    Ireland 248
walks out of World Cup
    Finals 2002 ix-xii,
    259–71
Irish Times interview
    263–5, 272–85
Keane, Shannon (RK's
    daughter) 127, 204, 216,
    225
Keane, Theresa (née Doyle;
    RK's wife) 127, 135,

171, 180, 194, 204, 213,
    225, 236–8, 247, 273–4
RK meets 59–60
moves in with RK 114
marries RK 168
happy living in
    Manchester 216
told of RK's withdrawal
    from the World Cup
    269
and RK's return home
    from the World Cup
    2002 x, xii 278, 281
Keane family 104–5, 111,
    134, 165, 204, 260
Keegan, Kevin 153–5
Kelly, Alan 258, 260, 262,
    266, 268–9, 276, 279,
    284
Kelly, David 49
Kelly, Gary 126
Kenneally, Anthony 7
Kennedy, Michael xi, xii, 77,
    78, 84, 133–4, 155, 158,
    204, 214, 215, 217, 218,
    261–2, 268, 269, 275,
    277, 278, 281
Kidd, Brian 80, 87–9, 92, 94,
    99, 106–7, 119, 146,
    179, 214
Kimmage, Paul 252, 263, 282
Koeman, Ronald 126
Kohler, Jürgen 167
Kosice 169
Kuhbauer, Dietmar 166

Lambert, Paul 167
Lancashire CC 246–7
Lansdowne Road, Dublin
    49, 54, 73, 74, 102, 103,
    118, 245, 247, 253, 254
Latvia 73, 77
Laudrup, Michael 73
Law, Denis 191, 229
Lawrenson, Mark 75
Lazio 233
le Tissier, Matt 166, 218
Leeds United FC 55, 64, 91,
    116, 153–5, 159, 163,
    171–2, 176, 196, 216
Leicester City FC 166, 168,
    225
Lille 237, 239
Lineker, Gary 48
Linfield FC 102
Lippi, Marcello 215
Lithuania 73, 77
Littlewoods (League) Cup 24

Liverpool FC 5, 31, 32, 55,
    62, 77, 121, 144, 150,
    151, 153, 156, 167, 182,
    196, 206, 224, 230, 235,
    240, 246
Ljungberg, Freddy 240
LKS Łódź 182
Loughlan, Tony 83, 225,
    257
Luton Town FC 10
Lynch, Essie (RK's
    grandmother) 225
Lynch, Jack 3
Lynch, John (RK's cousin) viii
Lynch, Mick (RK's uncle) 2
Lynch, Pat (RK's godfather)
    2, 225

McAteer, Jason 124, 268
McCabe, Noel 20, 20, 34, 45
McCarthy, Mick 61, 246–53,
    256, 258–62, 264–71,
    274, 279, 281
McCarthy, Paul 6, 8, 10, 76,
    124
McClair, Brian 85, 151
McClaren, Steve 214, 231–2,
    234, 235
Macedonia 248, 249
McGrath, Paul 52, 53, 75,
    107, 122, 123–4, 126,
    199, 200, 245, 248–9,
    266
McLoughlin, Alan 102, 103
McMahon, Steve 32
McManaman, Steve 156
Maine Road, Manchester 95,
    96, 112, 136, 231
Maldini, Paolo 121, 124
Malone, Eddie 225
Manchester City FC 5, 95–8,
    136, 143, 231
Manchester Evening News 158,
    175
Manchester United FC 5, 18,
    46, 52, 53, 55, 64
    Shearer and 63
    Pearce and 71
    RK has talks with
        Ferguson 80–81
    offers for RK 82, 83–4
    RK's transfer fee 84, 85
    South African trip 85–9
    maturity and confidence
        of team 85–6
    Munich air crash 86, 94
    constant challenge of
        being a player 86, 191

Man. United FC – (*contd*)
  reasons for being
    champions 88
  drinking subculture 89,
    107, 169, 197, 199, 216
  RK scores his first goal for
    United 90
  wins the European Cup
    (1968) 94
  derby against City 95–8
  a young player's dream 98
  Busby's funeral 111
  achieves the double (1994)
    116–17, 129, 148
  second double 157, 246
  and Cantona's retirement
    160–61
  RK becomes captain
    168–9, 170
  the treble 185, 188, 190,
    191, 206–13, 224,
    229–31, 235
  community 194–5
  wins Champions League
    209–13
  decision not to enter FA
    Cup 218, 220
  and Club World
    Championship 218–20
  and Premiership success
    229
  Queiroz becomes the new
    coach 271
Maracanã stadium, Brazil
  219–20
Martin, Damien 6, 8–10
Match of the Day (television
  programme) 35, 150
Matherson, Stuart 175
Matthews, Stanley 3
May, David 157, 164–5
Mayfield junior club 4, 5, 8,
  15
Meade, John 21
Mercer, Joe 95
Merrett, Ken 226
Mexico 125, 219
Middlesbrough FC 58, 116,
  153, 156, 168, 179, 189,
  220, 221, 223, 234, 236
Midland League 21
Millwall FC 55, 246
Molde 180
Möller, Andreas 167
Moran, Kevin 199, 200
Morientes, Fernando 222
Munich air crash (1958) 86,
  94, 139

Murphy, Danny 240
Murphy, Timmy 5, 6, 12

National League (Ireland) 14,
  21
  Second Division 15, 17
National Under-18 Cup
  (Ireland) 18
Nationwide League 214
Naybet, Noureddine 239
Neville, Gary 93, 131, 137,
  138, 150, 151, 154, 168,
  182, 196, 202, 216, 220,
  239, 240
Neville, Phil 93, 131, 150,
  182, 196, 216
Newcastle United FC 39,
  137, 153–5, 161, 165,
  168, 188, 197, 205–6,
  222, 236
Necaxa 219
Nigeria 255, 276
Noble, Mr (orthopaedic
  surgeon) 173, 177
North End junior club, Cork
  2
Northern Ireland team
  72–3, 99–100, 102–3,
  199
Norway 119, 125, 126
Norwich City FC 40, 90,
  110–11, 114
Nottingham Forest FC 13,
  19, 87, 100, 136, 156,
  163, 183, 244
  RK's contract 22, 51,
    62–5, 69–70, 78, 79
  pre-season tour in Italy
    (1990) 26
  FA Cup 1991 38–40,
    44–9, 93
  Zenith Data Systems Cup-
    tie 40
  pass-and-move style 52
  major crisis (1993) 62
  relegation battle 69–70
  RK voted Player of the
    Year 72
  achievement in Europe
    206
Nou Camp, Barcelona 131,
  182, 188, 197, 208, 209,
  211, 212, 223

O'Kane, Liam 20, 21, 25, 57,
  58, 68, 71
Old Trafford, Manchester
  RK's love for 84, 216

previous Forest players at
  85
Munich memorial clock
  86
Cantona's love for 92
European nights 94
Ferguson struggles in his
  early years 99
players' lounge 105
and Busby's death 111
'Robbo' a legend 116
visiting teams 132, 164,
  192
and Cantona's retirement
  161
family atmosphere 195
Old Trafford cricket ground
  246
Oldham Athletic FC 113,
  114, 115
O'Leary, David 52, 63, 75,
  77, 84, 172, 246
Olympic Stadium, Rome 75
O'Neill, Martin 240
O'Rourke, Eddie 14–15,
  18
O'Rourke, John 19, 21, 22
O'Sullivan, Alan 6, 8–10
O'Sullivan, Gene 5, 6, 12,
  225
O'Sullivan, Kièran 225
Overmars, Marc 126, 184,
  216
Owen, Michael 182, 240

Pagliuca, Gianluca 123
Paisley, Bob 150, 209
Pallister, Gary 85, 88, 91, 96,
  98, 117, 140–41, 151,
  153, 167, 168, 179
Palmeiras 217
Panathinaikos 230
Parker, Gary 47–8
Parker, Paul 91, 117
Parma 179
Pearce, Stuart ('Psycho') 24,
  29, 30, 40, 45, 48, 55,
  58, 85, 199
  and Gazza 35
  inspires his team 39, 40
  and Clough 39, 57
  reputation 39
  determination 44
  professionalism 57
  RK's role model 59
  supports RK 64–5
  injury 66
  in Jersey 69

turns down a move to
Manchester United
71
and Forest's relegation
70–71
voted Player of the Year at
Forest 72
Italia '90 75
Petit, Emmanuel 184, 216
Peyton, Gerry 246
PFA *see* Professional
Footballers' Association
Phelan, Mickey 240
Phelan, Terry 126
Phoenix Park, Dublin 128
Pires, Robert 240
Pitcher, Darren 141–2
Poland 51–3
Poll, Graham 194
Porto 166
Portugal x, 246, 249, 252,
267
Poyet, Gus 227, 236
Poznań 53
Premier League
creation of 35, 56, 58
Forest fights for its life 62,
66, 69–70
money-driven 65, 133,
136
Manchester United wins
81, 91, 116, 156, 160,
161, 194–5, 197, 223,
230, 234
Cantona's view of 114
and the European game
132, 133
growth of 133, 136
United's success breeds
complacency 229
Stam's view of 233
Price, Maurice 16, 40
Professional Footballers'
Association (PFA) 78,
79, 81, 84
Footballer of the Year 227
PSV Eindhoven 26, 179, 233

Queen's Park Rangers FC 30
Queiroz, Carlos 271
Quinn, Jimmy 103
Quinn, Niall 52, 73, 252,
254–5, 266, 268–70,
273, 274, 282

Rangers FC 102
Rapid Vienna 164, 165, 166
Raul, Gonzalez 222, 223

Ray, Mr (orthopaedic
surgeon) 177
Real Madrid 19, 189, 191,
210, 216, 222–3, 224,
226
Redknapp, Jamie 156
Redondo, Fernando 222
Ricken, John 22, 37, 41, 50
Rijkaard, Frank 126
Ring, Christy 3
Robson, Bobby 75
Robson, Bryan 85, 90, 93,
97, 106, 109, 110, 165,
168, 169, 175, 191, 197,
199, 200, 216, 218,
231
RK's role model 18
in South Africa 88–9
injuries 91, 112
incident in Istanbul 94
respected 98–9, 116
as club captain 99, 105
and Ferguson 99, 116
and ticket allocation 105,
168
helps RK settle at United
106
important advice for RK
112–13, 117, 130
last game for United 116
influence on United 116
player-manager at
Middlesbrough 116
Bruce replaces as club
captain 133
Rockmount AFC, Cork
2–4, 6, 8, 9, 12, 14, 54,
100, 187, 225, 258
Rotherham United FC 30
Rumbelows (League) Cup
55
Rush, Ian 31, 32
Russia 247
Ryan, Jimmy 210, 211, 240

St James's Park, Newcastle
39, 154
St John's school, Cork 1–2
Saipan training ground 255,
256–7, 271, 272–3, 275,
276–7, 280, 284
Salako, John 38
Schmeichel, Peter 85, 91, 92,
98, 132, 141, 151, 153,
165, 168, 178, 184, 193,
202, 211, 217, 229
Scholes, Paul 93, 130, 131,
137, 138, 149–51, 175,

182, 185, 186, 189, 192,
196, 202, 206–10, 212,
216, 222, 235, 239, 240
Scholl, Mehmet 230
Selhurst Park, Wimbledon
139, 144, 162
Sergio, Paulo 230
Setters, Maurice 35–6, 41,
54, 74, 77, 101, 103,
119–22, 126, 266
Shankly, Bill 150
Sharpe, Lee 109, 115, 117,
151, 159, 176, 197, 200,
201
Shaw, Richard 138
Shearer, Alan 63, 79, 113,
236
Sheedy, Kevin 52
Sheffield Wednesday FC 12,
37, 69, 70, 90
Sheridan, John 124, 126
Sheringham, Teddy 55, 62,
66, 169, 180, 182, 185,
189, 192, 202, 205–6,
210–12, 220, 221, 228,
231
Simeone, Diego 190
Solskjaer, Ole Gunnar 166,
180, 182–3, 185, 210,
212, 235
South Melbourne 219, 220
Southampton FC 33, 35, 39,
40, 55, 63, 154, 162,
163, 165, 189, 218, 221,
223, 228, 236
Southgate, Gareth 142, 143
Spain 72–3, 99, 103
Speed, Gary 205
Sporting Lisbon 26
Springfield junior club 14
Stam, Jaap 166, 179, 180,
182, 221, 233
Stamford Bridge, London
136, 161, 217
Stapleton, Frank 75
Starbuck, Philip 25, 27, 30,
31
Staunton, Steve ('Stan')
60–61, 75, 122, 126,
252, 266, 267, 269,
270
Stein, Jock 209
Stone, Steve 25, 27
Storey-Moore, Ian 68
Sturm Graz 218, 230
Sullivan, Neil 162
Sunderland FC 162, 163,
166, 223, 254–5, 274

Sutton-in-Ashfield FC 27
Swindon Town FC 113, 114

Taibi, Massimo 217, 218
Taylor, Graham 66–7, 74, 75
Thatcher, Margaret,
    Baroness 58
Torquay United FC 109
Tottenham Hotspur FC 35,
    62, 154, 188, 192–4,
    218
  the centenary Cup final
    (1981) 5, 18
  FA Cup 1991 45, 47–9
  Rumbelows Cup 1992 55
Townsend, Andy 52, 102,
    120, 122–3, 126, 247,
    248
Tranmere Rovers FC 21
Tretschok, Ren, 167
Troubles, the 102
Turkey 35, 248

UEFA 132
University College Cork
    (UCC) 283
US Cup 244–6, 266
USA '94 *see* World Cup

Valencia 218
Van der Gouw, Marita 243
Van der Gouw, Raimond
    222, 243
Van Nistelrooy, Ruud 233,
    235, 239, 240, 242
Vasco da Gama 219, 220
Venables, Terry 47, 48

Venezia 217
Verón, Juan Sebastian 233–6,
    239, 243
Vieira, Patrick 184, 216, 240
Villa Park, Birmingham 44,
    140, 142, 143, 162, 184,
    185, 236
Villa, Ricardo 5

Walker, Des 24, 44, 45, 48,
    55, 198, 199
  nights out in Nottingham
    59, 67
  in Jersey 68–9
  and Forest's relegation 70
Walker, Ian 192
Walker, Jack 63, 65, 77, 79,
    214
Walsh, Martin 264
Watford FC 53, 74, 228
Watkins, Maurice 139, 214
Webb, Neil 85
Wembley 40, 44, 45, 47, 49,
    54–5, 62, 70, 116–17,
    156, 157, 188, 205, 206,
    219, 246
Wenger, Arsène 216
West Bromwich Albion FC
    28
West Germany 27, 75
West Ham United FC 44,
    45, 143–4, 151, 163,
    166, 168, 223, 234
Wetherall, David 171, 172,
    231
Whelan, Ronnie 31, 32, 53,
    75

White Hart Lane,
    Tottenham 45, 55, 154
Whiteside, Norman 107,
    199, 200
Wigan rugby league club 172
Wiley, Ann x, xi, 269
Wilkinson, Howard 91, 155
Wilson, Terry 30
Wimbledon FC 37, 53, 110,
    113, 114, 151, 162
Windsor Park, Belfast 102
Woan, Ian 25, 27
World Cup
  1966 244
  1970 120
  1982 199
  1990 24, 27, 35, 37, 47, 50,
    68, 75, 101, 118, 122
  1994 72–7, 99–103,
    117–28, 244–5, 252,
    257
  1998 185, 233, 248
  2002 ix, 249–71, 272–81
  2006 218
Wright, Ian 89

Yorke, Dwight 179, 180,
    182, 184–7, 189, 202,
    212, 218, 224, 242
Yorkshire CC 247
Youth Cup final teams (1992
    and 1993) 208

Zenith Data Systems Cup 40,
    54
Zidane, Zinedine 164, 183,
    187, 188, 206, 209